MODELLING AND SCULPTING THE FIGURE

TANYA RUSSELL

THE ART ACADEMY

First published in Great Britain in 2012
A & C Black Publishers Limited
50 Bedford Square
London WC1B 3DP
www.acblack.com

ISBN: 978-1-4081-4641-5

CIP Catalogue records for this book are available from the British Library.

Typeset in Futura Std
Book design by Evelin Kasikov
Cover design by Terry Woodley
Printed and bound in China

This book is produced using paper that is made from wood grown in managed, sustainable forests. It is natural, renewable and recyclable. The logging and manufacturing processes conform to the environmental regulations of the country of origin.

Cover image: George Triggs, *Broken*. Painted plaster, life-size. *Photo: Ben Wisely.*

Title page image: Tanya Russell, *Dancer (Rachel)*. Bronze, 40 x 12 cm (15¾ x 4¾ in.). *Photo: courtesy of the artist.*

Acknowledgements

In truth, I should acknowledge hundreds of sculptors that I have had the privilege of meeting and working with over the years – their accumulated knowledge, generously shared, fills these pages – but individual thanks are due to certain people without whom the book would not have been possible:

Mark Tattersall, the Art Academy's former Chief Executive and now a trustee, for his huge contribution in crystallising my ideas and wrestling with this text until it said what I wanted it to say.

My parents, Lorne McKean and Edwin Russell, for their guidance over the years.

Chloe Leaper, John O'Connor and Briony Marshall, former students at the Art Academy, now wonderful friends and talented sculptors, for their input to various sections of the book, and Jessica Wetherly for her practical assistance.

Shardae-Rose Angel, for modelling with such patience and elegance.

The students of the Art Academy, past and present, who I have had the joy of teaching and from whom I have learned so much.

The Art Academy's tutors and resident artists, for sharing their gifts, technical and creative, with unstinting generosity.

MODELLING AND SCULPTING THE FIGURE

TANYA RUSSELL

THE ART ACADEMY

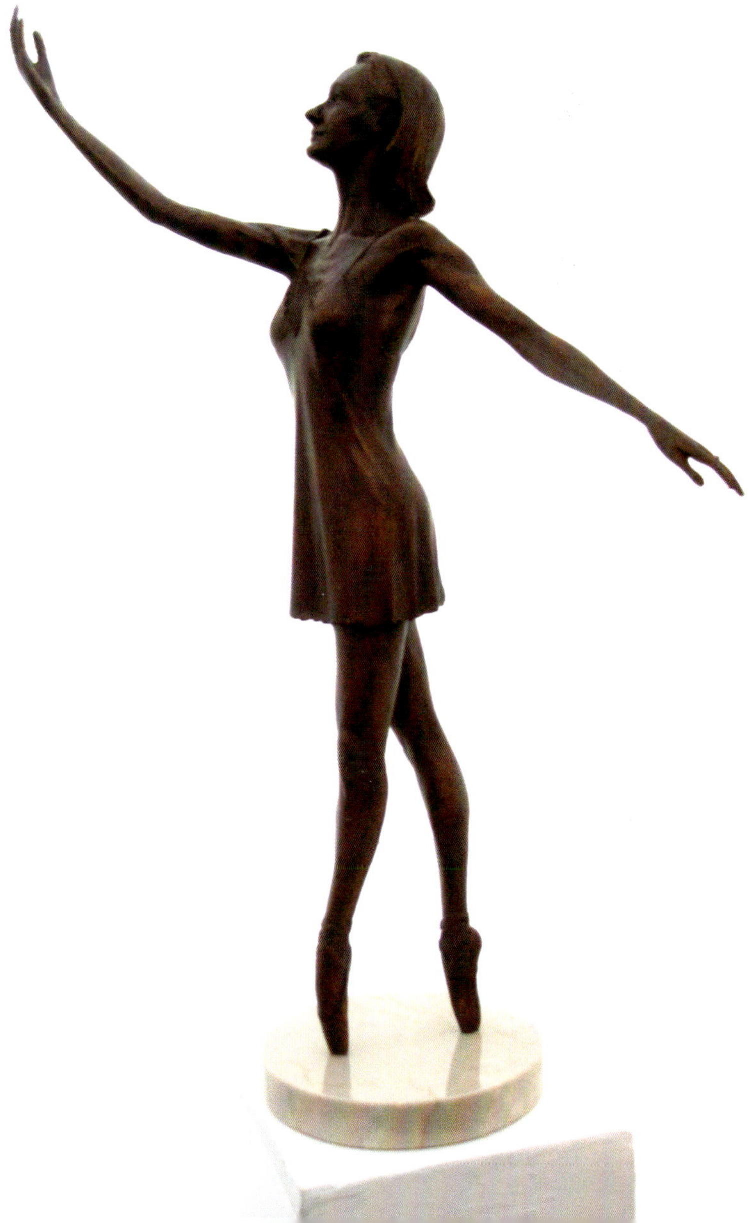

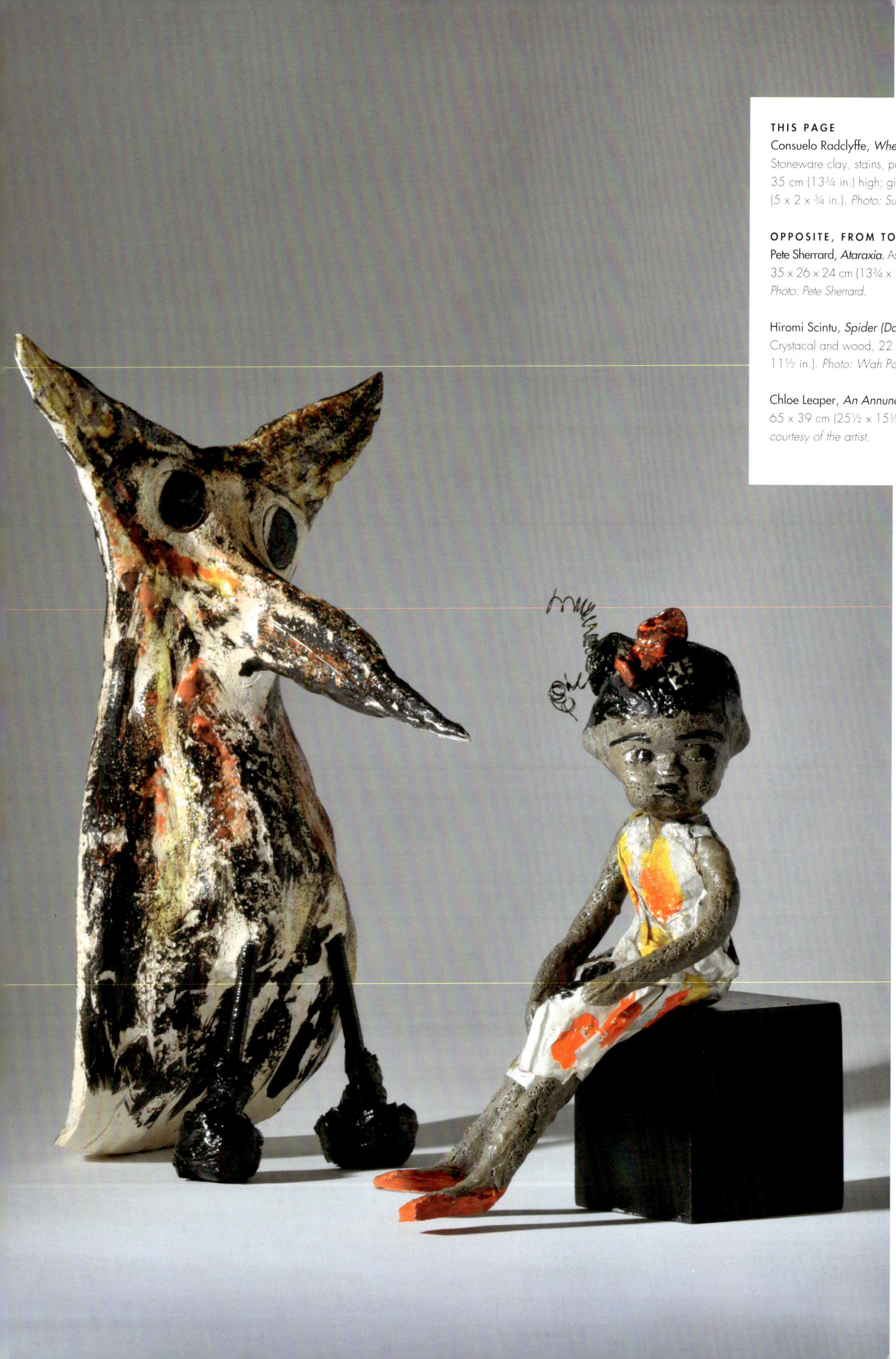

THIS PAGE
Consuelo Radclyffe, *When I was that big …* Stoneware clay, stains, paper. Big creature: 35 cm (13¾ in.) high; girl: 13 x 5 x 2 cm (5 x 2 x ¾ in.). *Photo: Sussie Ahlburg*

OPPOSITE, FROM TOP
Pete Sherrard, *Ataraxia.* Ash resin, stone base, 35 x 26 x 24 cm (13¾ x 10¼ x 9½ in.). *Photo: Pete Sherrard.*

Hiromi Scintu, *Spider (Dancing Figure).* Crystacal and wood, 22 x 29 cm (8½ x 11½ in.). *Photo: Wah Poon.*

Chloe Leaper, *An Annunciation.* Plaster, 65 x 39 cm (25½ x 15½ in.). *Photo: courtesy of the artist.*

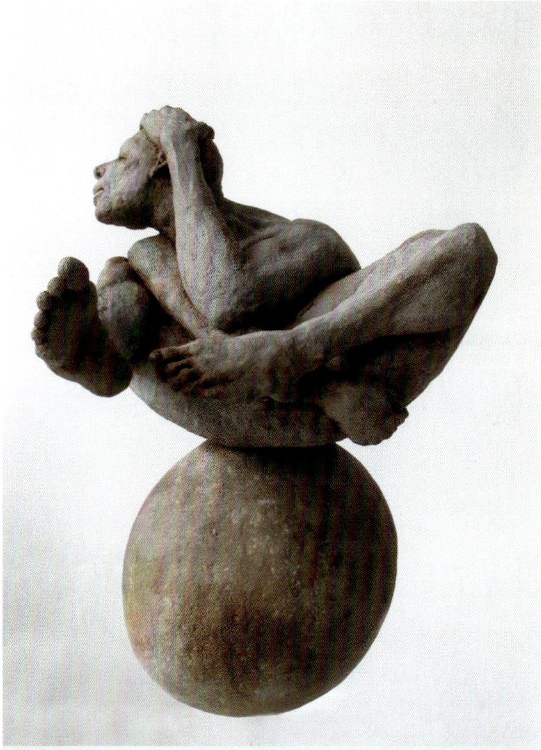

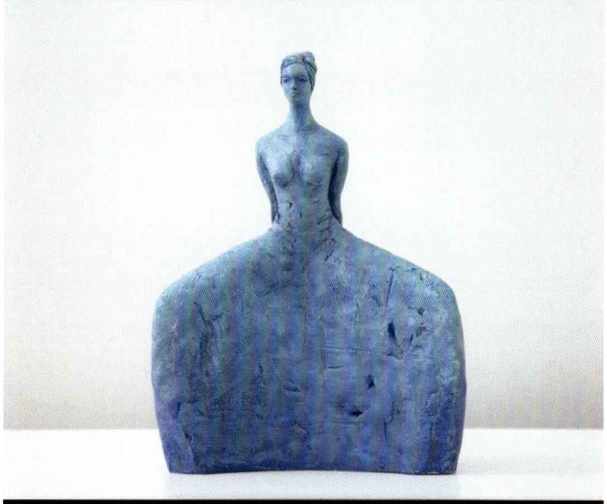

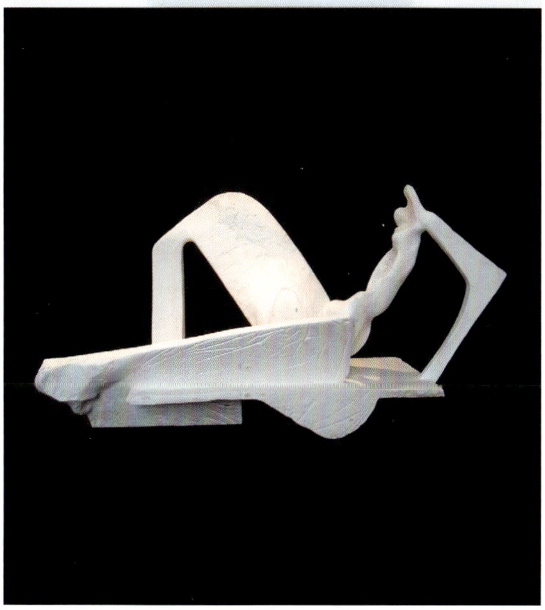

Contents

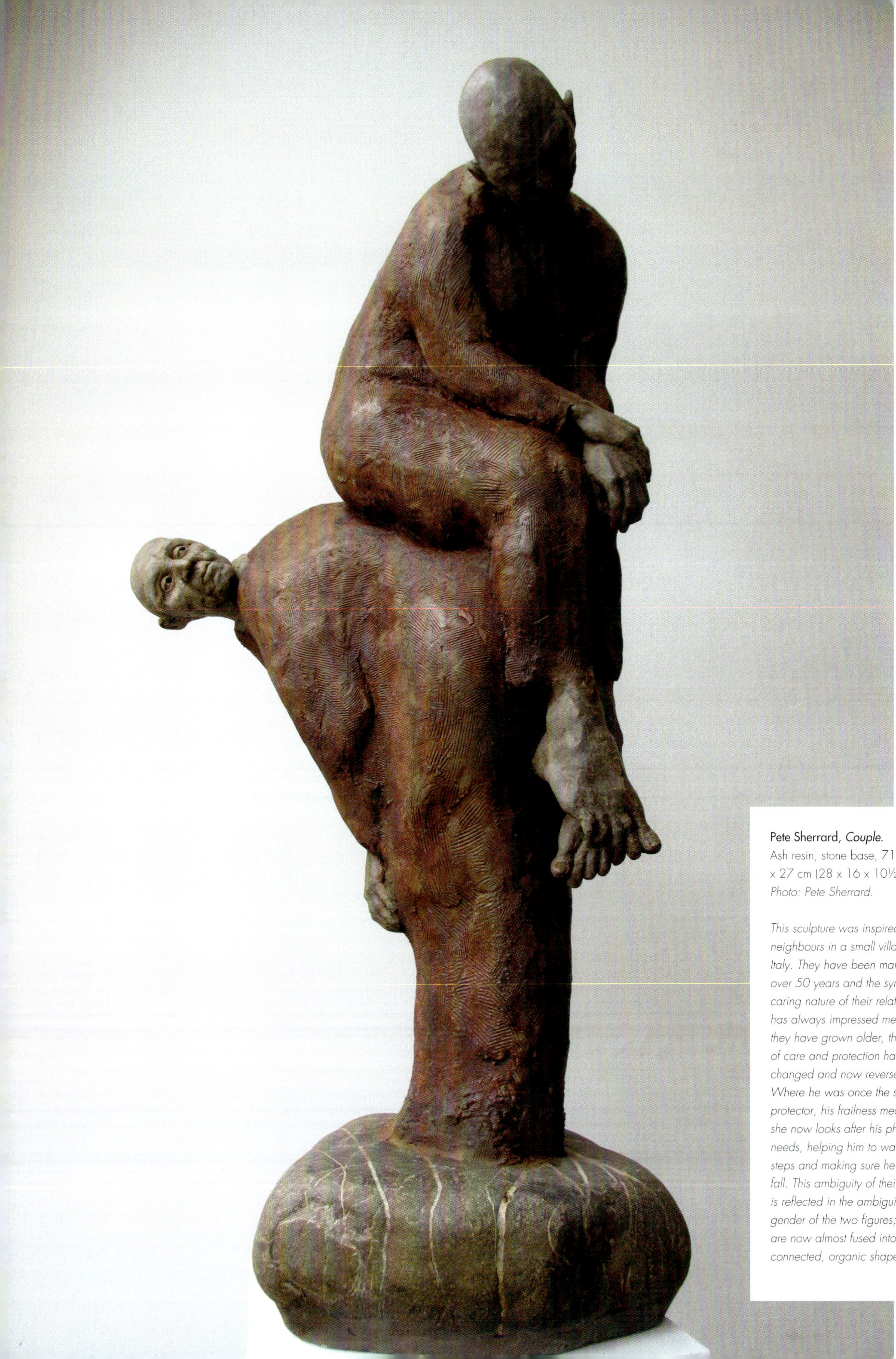

Pete Sherrard, *Couple*.
Ash resin, stone base, 71 x 41 x 27 cm (28 x 16 x 10½ in.).
Photo: Pete Sherrard.

This sculpture was inspired by my neighbours in a small village in Italy. They have been married for over 50 years and the symbiotic, caring nature of their relationship has always impressed me. As they have grown older, the roles of care and protection have changed and now reversed. Where he was once the strong protector, his frailness means that she now looks after his physical needs, helping him to walk down steps and making sure he doesn't fall. This ambiguity of their roles is reflected in the ambiguity of the gender of the two figures; they are now almost fused into one connected, organic shape.

INTRODUCTION

Sculptors are artists, and being an artist is about much more than just learning to use tools and materials so that you can apply your practical skills to the making of objects. In common with all creative people, artists are communicators.

I was born into a family of sculptors and learned about the power of creative practice from an early age. As I grew up watching my parents and their peers, it was clear that making things competently or beautifully was only part of the story – all the really successful sculptures seemed to have something more to them. They all conveyed different things, from a simple emotion or a subtle message to an awesome power or an overwhelming presence. Skill and creativity seemed to be in perfect balance and something of the artist was still present in all of them. I also sensed that artists have the massive privilege of being able to translate their experiences, their passions and the accumulated knowledge from their journey through life into physical form, but as with everything in life, with privilege comes responsibility, meaning that artists are faced with some very interesting questions.

My years of apprenticeship and artistic practice all reinforced these early realisations and the desire to help artists use their technical mastery to translate their inspiration into successful finished artworks has formed the basic ethos of the Art Academy, which I founded just over a decade ago. To this end, the students are taught by working artists who pass on their technical skills at the same time as nurturing each student's creative vision. No specific style is imposed – the aim is for each student to develop their own. Crucially, the students learn about life as a working artist, through observing (and sometimes assisting) the tutors and resident artists around them and taking the opportunity to exhibit, work on commissions and teach.

In turn I have tried to carry that ethos over into this book, which is as much about becoming an artist/sculptor as it is a technical manual on sculpting the human figure. It aims to provide guidance, inspiration and practical instruction for sculptors at many different levels, whether they are seeking to experience the personal joy and satisfaction of creativity or to make sculpture their life's work.

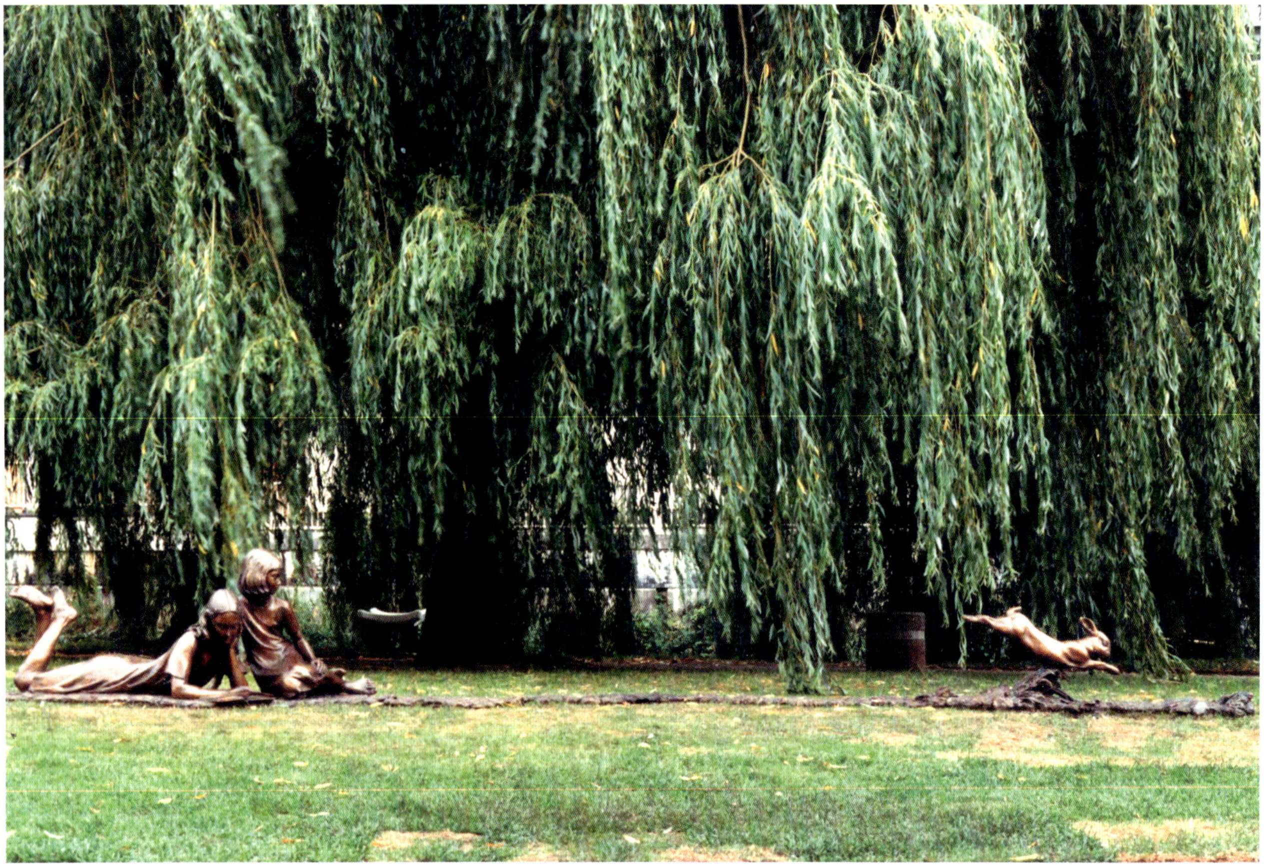

Edwin Russell, *Alice with her sister.* From the start of the book *Alice in Wonderland*, life-size bronze comissioned to be placed on the riverbank in Guildford, Surrey, 400 x 45 cm (157.5 x 17.7 in.). *Photo: courtesy of the artist.*

All the images used in the book are of work done by tutors, current students or alumni of the Academy.

How The Book Works

The early chapters of the book seek to prepare the reader for what lies ahead, firstly by looking at the language of art, then by covering the practical and conceptual steps needed to prepare for the creative process.

The second part of the book is divided into three sections:

- The Realistic Figure
- The Abstracted Figure
- The Expressive Figure

The realistic figure study is about learning visual vocabulary and grammar. The subsequent parts are about using these techniques to express thought, feeling, vision, emotion and meaning. These divisions are in fact artificial, as all artworks will include elements from all three of these sections. Virtually everything I suggest or discuss in one area is also relevant to the others, so each section covers what I feel is most relevant to that particular topic.

The Realistic Figure

Figurative or realistic sculpture is a wonderful art form, often full of emotion and conceptual depth. In the context of this book, however, the Realistic Figure chapter covers a technical figure study, an exercise in copying and understanding the purely physical form of the model. A finished figurative sculpture would of course require much more consideration in terms of its other aspects, whereas this study just looks at technical aspects such as anatomy, proportion and measurement. These are important and must be thoroughly understood, but are not the whole story when sculpting the figure.

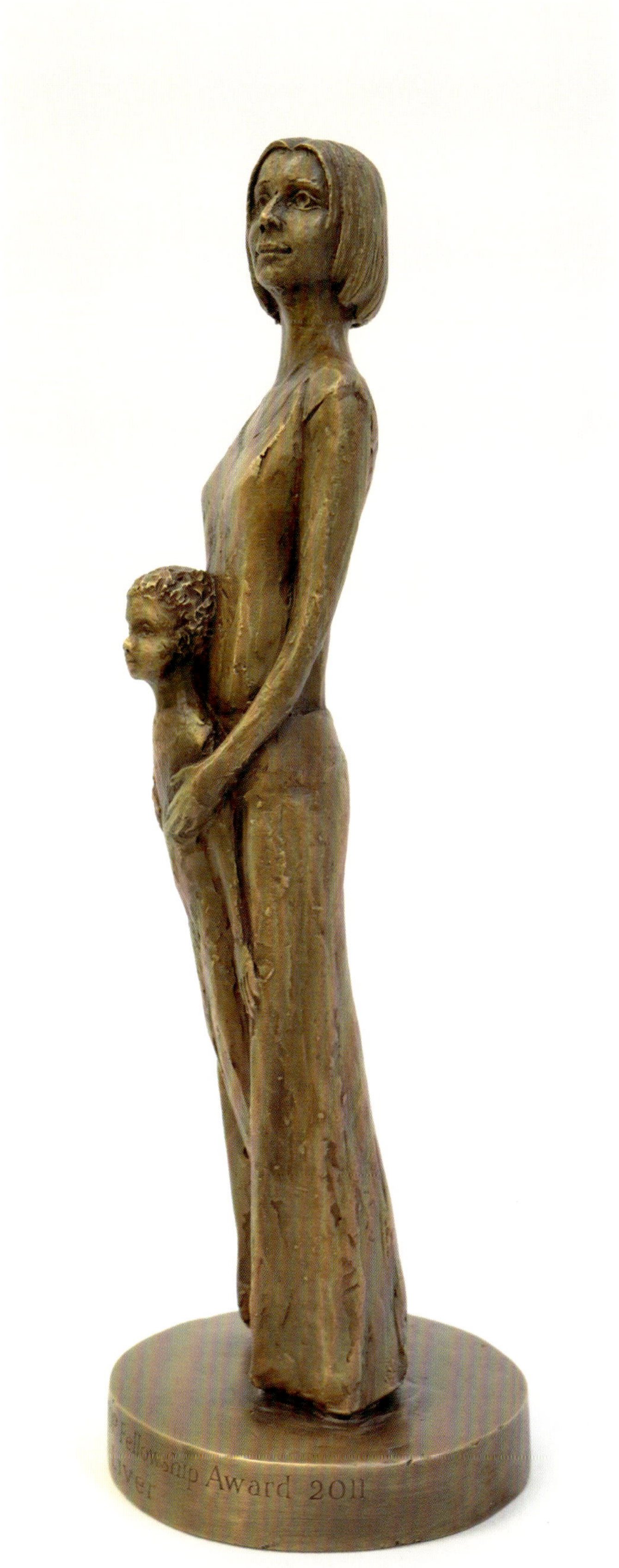

The Abstracted Figure

Considerable crossover exists between the abstracted figure and the expressive figure, but here we deal with the abstracted figure as a process of *formal* abstraction. Abstraction can range from complete abstraction (where no figurative form is apparent) through quite a high level of abstraction (where the form is still just discernable as a human figure, but much of the realism has been left out) to a small amount of abstraction (where the figure is clear, but certain aspects have been abstracted). I tend to look at abstraction as focusing on the absolute essence of something, distilling a form down to its most fundamental elements.

The Expressive Figure

The expressive figure is about working from an idea, concept or feeling, and using the human form to express it. For example, an artist might start with the concept of 'happiness' or 'suffering' and choose to express this feeling through sculpture, using the human form in more or less figurative ways to express it. This is a different process from simply creating a sculpture of a model smiling or holding a tortuous pose, for example.

Tanya Russell, *NSPCC Trophy*. Bronze, 25 x 9 cm (10 x 3½ in.).
Photo: courtesy of the artist.

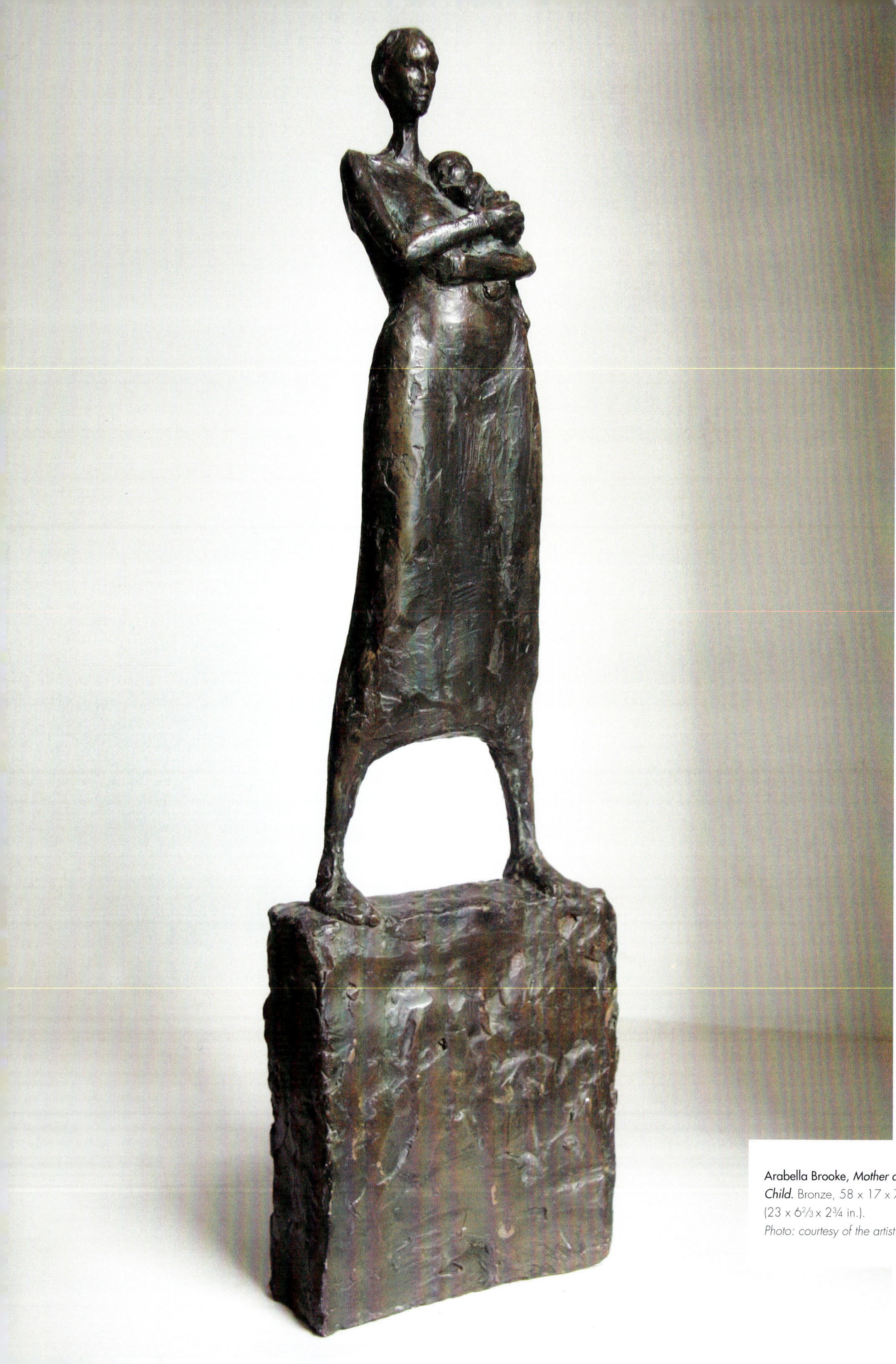

Arabella Brooke, *Mother and Child*. Bronze, 58 x 17 x 7 cm (23 x 6⅔ x 2¾ in.). *Photo: courtesy of the artist.*

1

THE LANGUAGE OF ART

Art and Language

Art can be many things: it is ephemeral and magical, almost impossible to pin down; it is the creative force that pulses through our nature, ultimately indefinable, as the creative impulse is the essence of innovation.

The comparison between verbal language and visual language is, I think, a very useful one. If we make a verbal sound with the express purpose of communicating something, we call it language. If we create something that we can see or experience for the purpose of communicating something, we call it art. It can be more or less successful in its intention, but it is still art. As soon as we create something, whether visual or verbal, we are *inevitably* communicating with those who see or hear it. In place of the tools of language – words, grammar, rhythm, intonation and so on – a visual artist uses form, line, colour, geometry, pattern, size and material to communicate, but the process of creating and responding in verbal and visual communication is much the same.

This leaves artists free to communicate whatever they wish, however they wish, using the materials, styles and techniques of their choice, and considerable skill is needed to make the best use of all that is available to them.

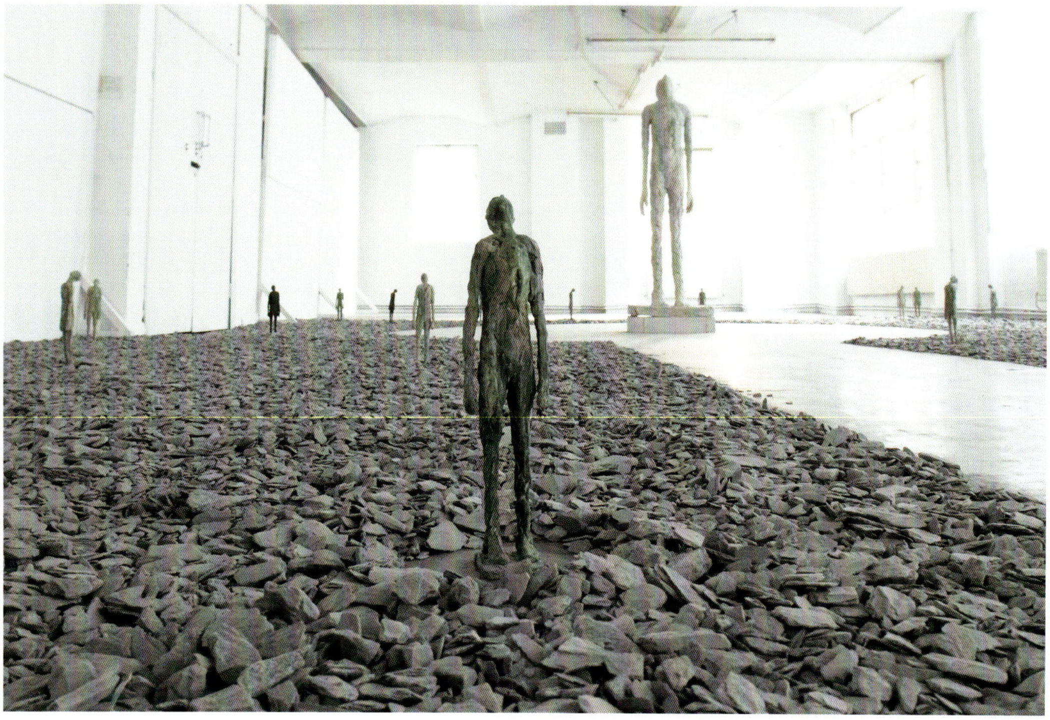

John O'Connor, *Stargazer Installation*. Cold cast slate and stone, 1.7 x 150 x 9 m (5½ x 490 x 29½ ft.). *Photo: courtesy of the artist.*

I believe that any kind of expression is valid, in whatever medium or style the artist considers to be best to express their intention: figurative, abstract, installation, performance, digital, temporary, site-specific, readymade, land art or anything in between or outside of these categories. They all have their place and most have existed across cultures since mankind first started making art. Artificial barriers have often been erected between them, with the supporters of various 'traditional' or 'contemporary' movements claiming superiority, but in truth one is essentially no better than any other: some simply have attributes that make them better suited to certain situations or forms of expression.

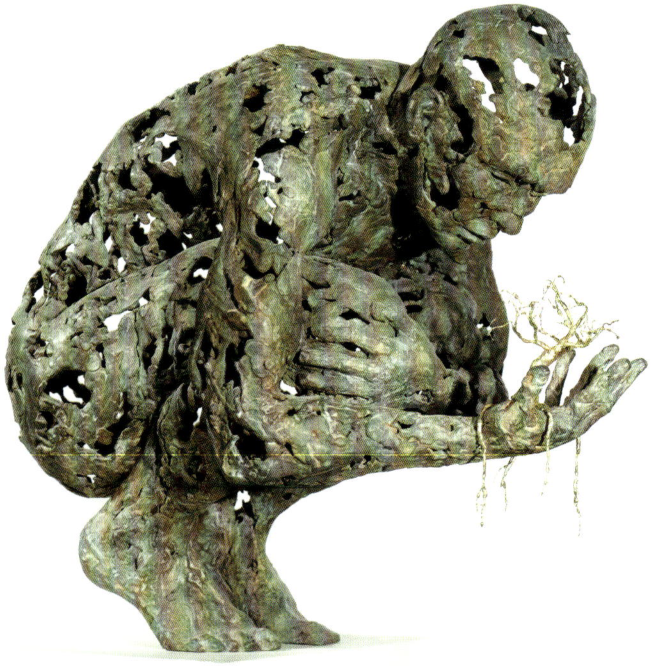

George Triggs, *Treeman*. Bronze figure and mixed media, 36 x 26 x 42 cm, (14 x 10 x 15½ in.). *Photo: Ben Wisely/Studio Seventeen.*

Treeman addresses the power of man, the fragility of nature itself; the childlike naivety of humankind and the beauty and permanence of our world; the vulnerability of nature aligned to the vulnerability of man; the wonder at nature, at the cost of its destruction; the inherent forms of the tree reflected in the figure; man's greed and desire for possession juxtaposed against his desire to nurture and care; how naive is his intention, how aware are we of the balance between us and nature, commenting on us being nature. This work allowed me to explore the limits of using bronze as a sculptural material. I am proud to have kept at it and produced a work that some people told me was technically impossible in bronze.

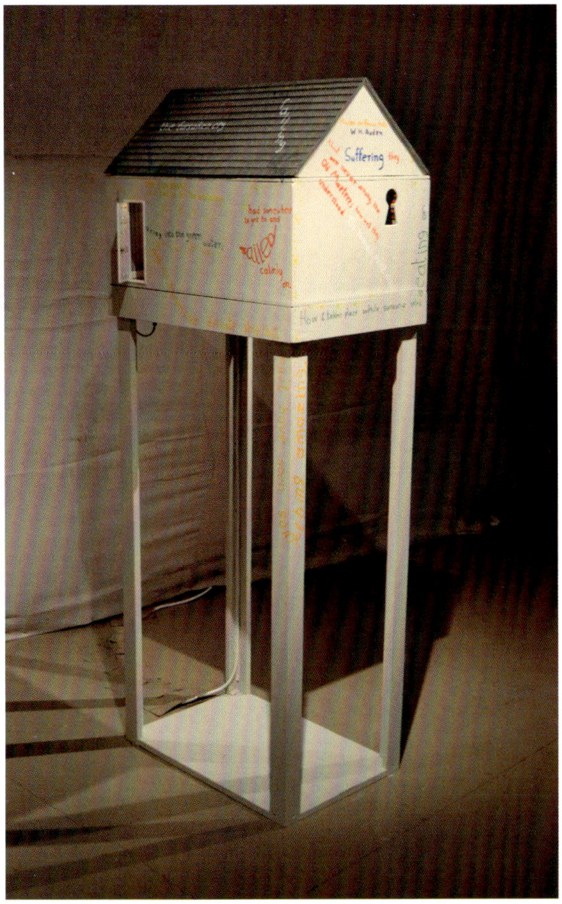

How Artists Communicate

> *'Art does not reproduce the visible, rather it makes visible.'*
>
> Paul Klee

Art is both created and appreciated by humans, who we can usefully think of as being broadly made up of four parts:

- A physical form
- A mental realm
- An emotional world
- A spiritual aspect

Artists can learn to communicate with their viewers and convey their intention through an understanding of these four basic types of human response.

TOP AND RIGHT Vivienne Wallace, *"One lump or two? Cane or Demerara?"* Mixed media, 155 x 58 x 41 cm (61 x 22¾ x 16 in.). *Photo: Meg Green.*

A paint/plywood fully furnished dolls' house recreation of a childhood event of chastisement and humiliation, set against the backdrop of a tea party, with visitors as witnesses. I have drawn an analogy with a child suffering as the world carries on its business through reference to Brueghel's painting Landscape with the Fall of Icarus *and W. H. Auden's poem about the painting.*

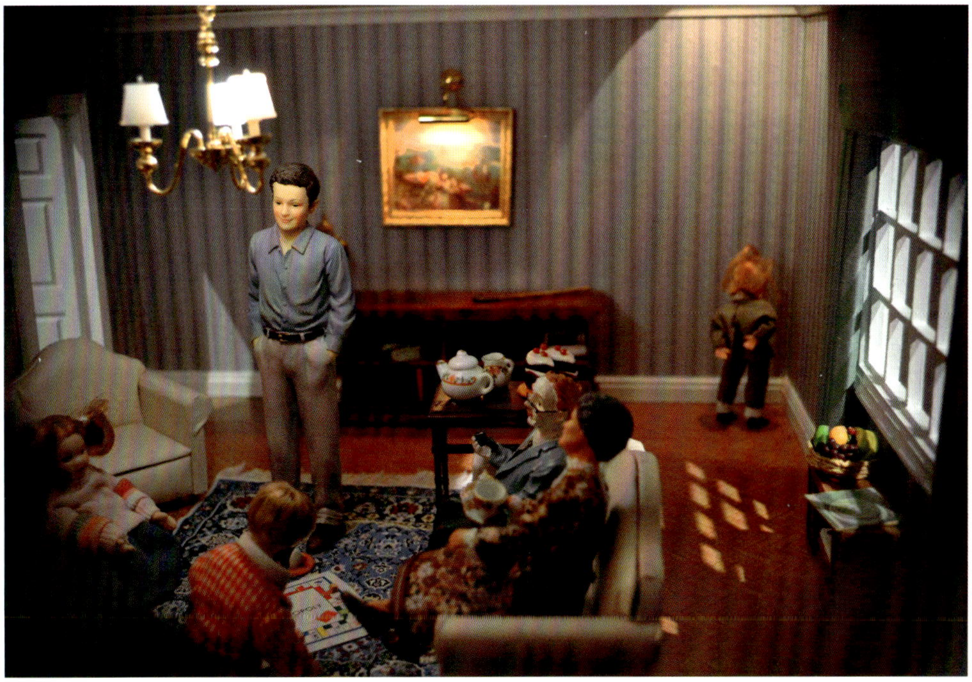

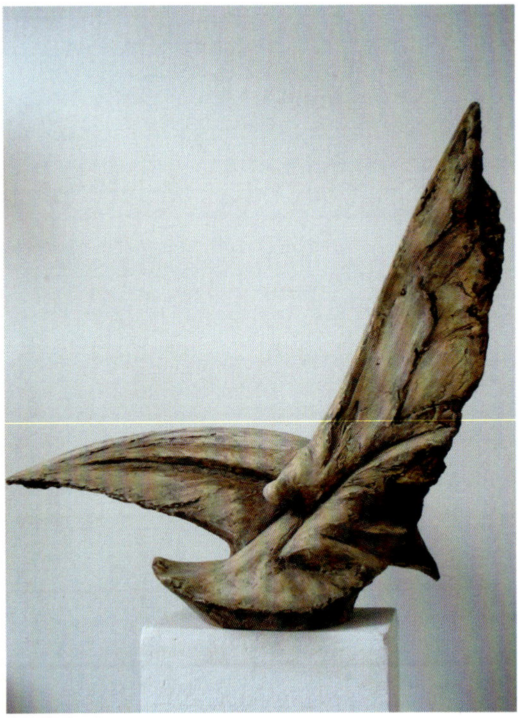

Chloe Leaper, *Psyche*. Plaster, 70 x 65 x 55 cm (27½ x 25½ x 21¾ in.). *Photo: courtesy of the artist.*

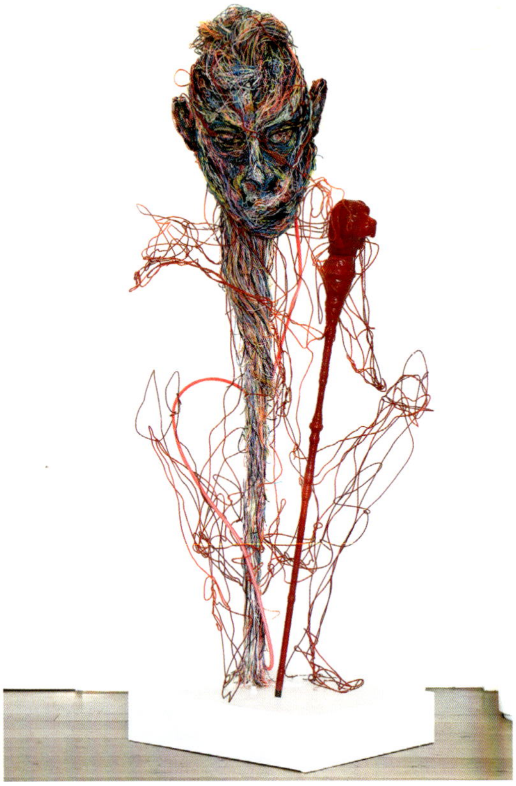

Jessica Nyssen, *John Doe*. Plastic tubing, wire, latex, resin, 222 x 100 cm (87½ x 39⅓ in.). *Photo: Artur Nizicki.*

Thoughts of immortality, interrupted by thoughts of dependence, interrupted by the final realisation of life's transience, carried on the tide of a calm acceptance of the end.

- **Physical or formal:** Humans undoubtedly share some common responses to colour, form and pattern. There is a wealth of interesting research on this topic* although mental, emotional or physical disturbances and cultural factors can, of course, influence these. An artist can therefore make a piece 'predominantly formal', the intention being to appeal to the viewer through a mutual appreciation of formal properties – line, form, colour, etc. These shared responses to formal properties can be observed through a simple exercise, which I have repeated many times in my teaching career (see Exercise 1 in Chapter 2, p. 28).

- **Emotional:** This is perhaps the simplest and most powerful level at which to communicate – indeed very few people will engage with something unless they feel an emotional connection with it. All people and even most animals fully understand emotions such as fear or contentment, and simple human emotion sweeps away barriers such as race, time, culture and religion. A 'predominantly emotional' artwork might typically examine something of almost universal emotional significance – for example, the bond between mother and child.

- **Mental:** This is the area where there is the most variety and therefore potentially the least automatic connection between artist and viewer, but when a mental connection is made it can be very powerful. Surprisingly often, we can relate to what other people are thinking, and a 'predominantly conceptual' work seeks to make that connection between the mind of the artist and the mind of the viewer above all else. Deep and fundamental concepts hold the greatest power and can connect with the greatest number of people; more superficial and frivolous concepts tend to be rather more individual

* General: Max Wertheimer, Manfred Davidmann, Leon Battista Alberti, Johann Wolfgang von Goethe, Immanuel Kant, Ernst Mach. On colour theory and memory: Karl R. Gegenfurtner, Felix A. Wichman and Lindsay T. Sharpe. On the Golden Proportion: Adolf Zeising, Volkmar Weiss and Harald Weiss.

and less accessible. Likewise, an artist who is deeply engaged in and passionate about a subject is much more likely to make this connection.

- **Spiritual:** In this context we are not using 'spiritual' in a specifically religious or formal sense. It refers to a deeply powerful personal experience, transcending our response to an artwork on a formal, emotional or mental level, and which we find hard to describe or understand. Many things can provide a 'doorway' to this type of response, but when and how it happens often surprises us and leaves us with a real sense of wonder.

These distinctions are not clear-cut – in fact almost every artwork contains elements of all four – and it is the harmony between them that is significant in determining whether the artist has successfully conveyed their intention to the viewer.

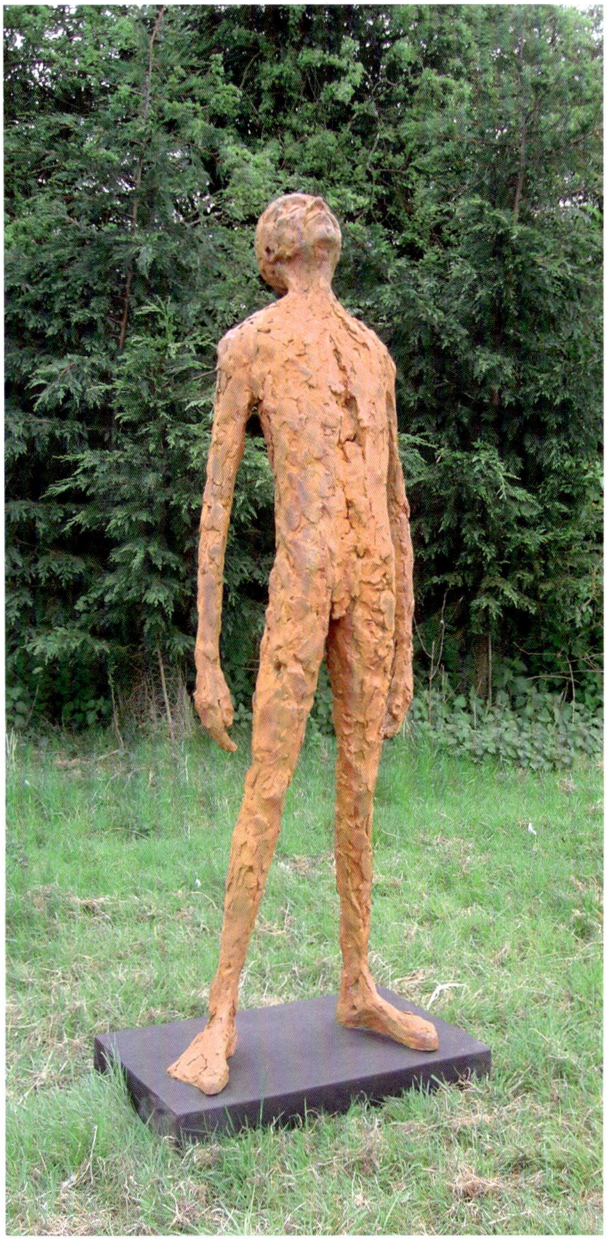

John O'Connor, *Spring*. Cold cast iron, 190 x 70 cm (75 x 27⅔ in.). *Photo: courtesy of the artist.*

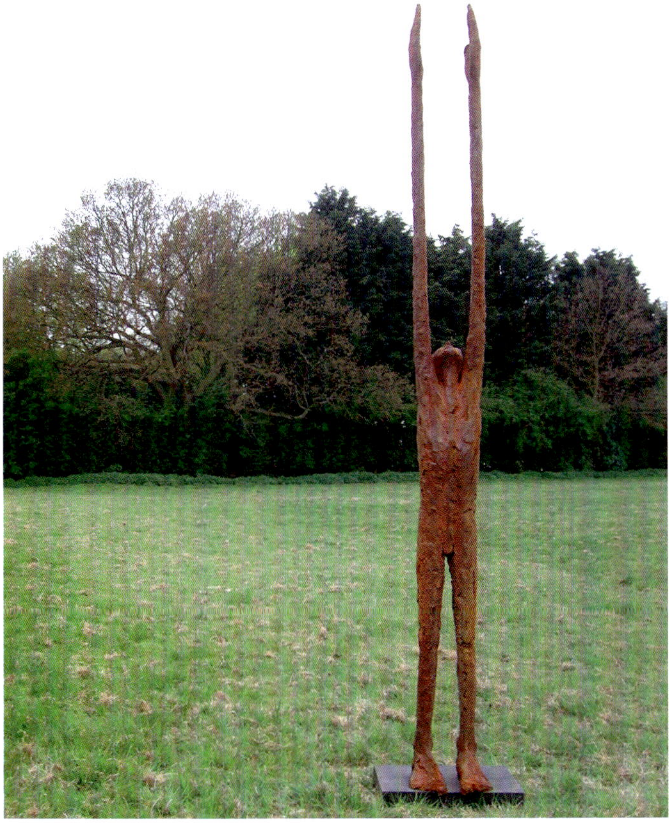

John O'Connor, *Beyond limitations.* Cold cast iron, 400 x 70 cm (157½ x 27⅔ in.). *Photo: courtesy of the artist.*

Critique

Critique is most definitely not criticism in a negative sense. Critique is an essential tool for discernment in all aspects of your creation and allows artists to compare their intentions with the response of the viewer. Artists are constantly critiquing themselves so as to move forward and develop their work, while critique from others provides a very useful objective response, which can be most informative. Often just looking at your work with someone else allows you to see it in a whole new light.

Critique can be a minute-by-minute process as you work, or might be a point at which you stop, stand back and look at the work objectively, seeing what is needed and making the appropriate changes.

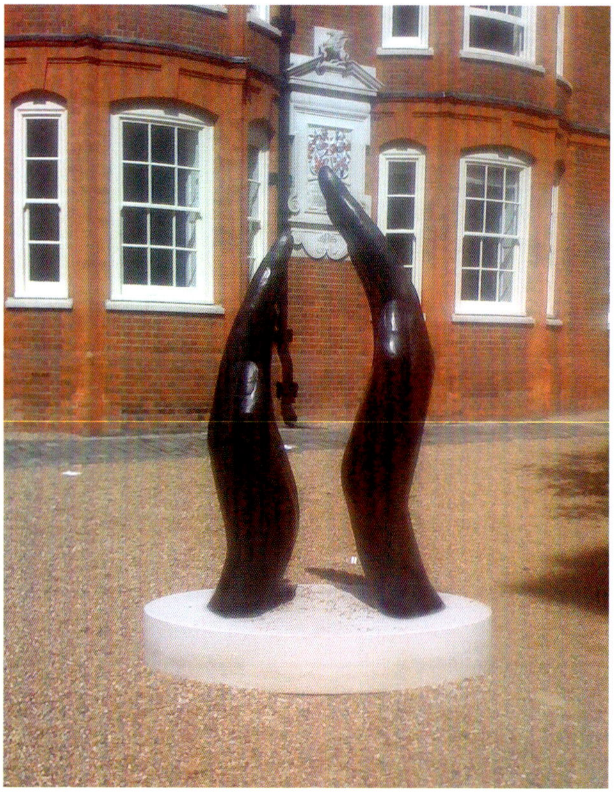

Tanya Russell, *The hands of justice.* Bronze commissioned for The Honourable Society of the Inner Temple, London, 200 x 120 cm (78¾ x 47¼ in.). *Photo: courtesy of the artist.*

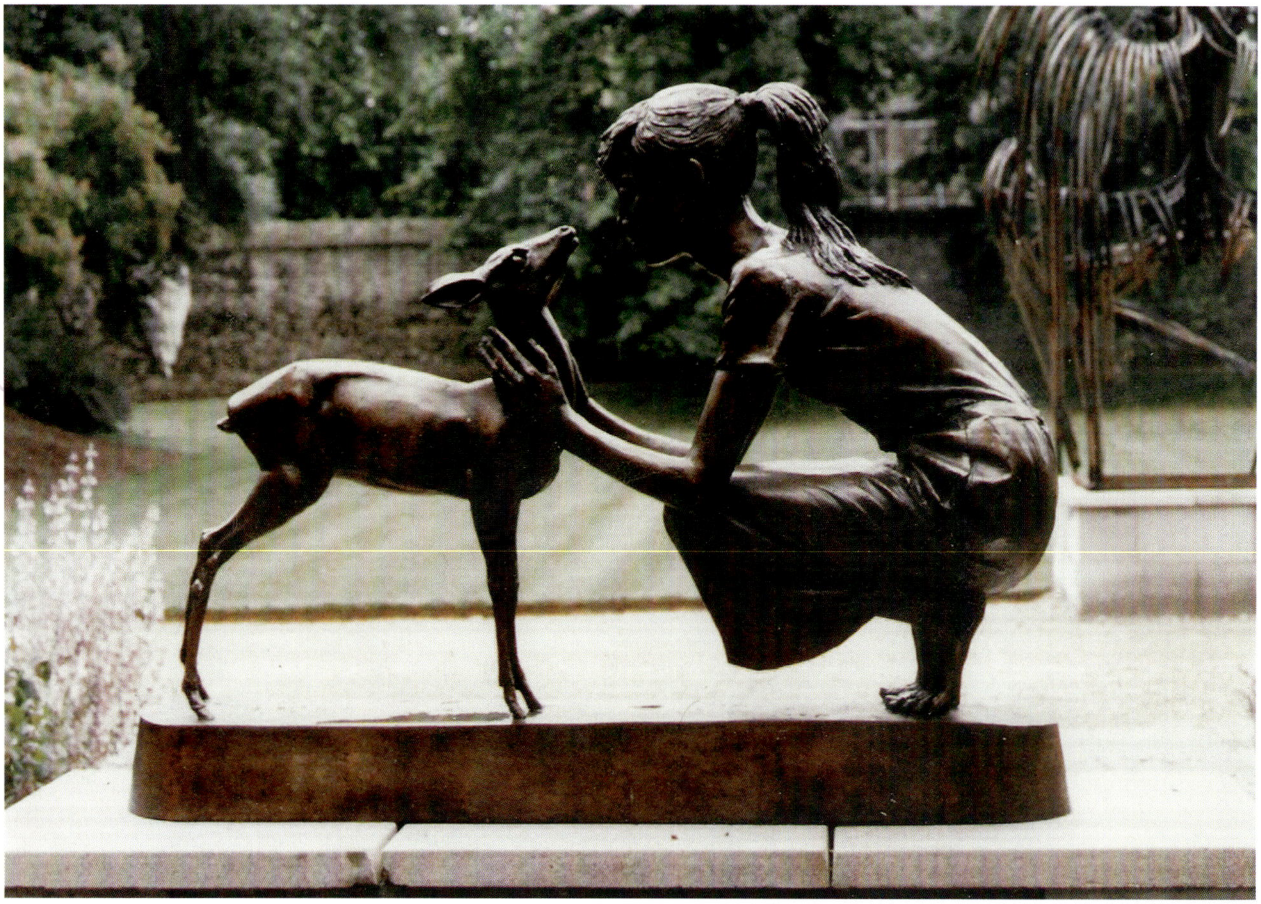

Edwin Russell, *Girl and Fawn.* Bronze, 77 x 109 cm (30⅓ x 43 in.). *Photo: courtesy of the artist.*

The Process of Critique

An understanding of the *process* of critique is very important in looking at your own work, and equally important when you are looking at that of other artists or someone else is looking at yours.

If you want the most honest appraisal of your work, let people look at it without colouring their judgment with any explanation. Once they have given a first response, you can explain your intention and a useful discussion can be had about their initial responses in light of this new information.

The ideas described on pp. 13–5 about the four basic ways of responding to art can be very helpful in the process of critique. When looking at an artwork, it is not particularly helpful to say simply whether you 'like' or 'don't like' something. A description of your physical, emotional, mental and spiritual responses will be much more valuable.

This is a simplified method of critique and many others have been developed over the years. A related but somewhat more developed method, used successfully over many years at the Art Academy, divides critique into six aspects:

- Concept
- Emotional depth
- Creative awareness
- Form and function
- Craftsmanship/aesthetic design
- Curation/presentation

These are the criteria by which you can evaluate your own or others' work. The full version of this critique methodology can be found on the Art Academy website, www.artacademy.org.uk.

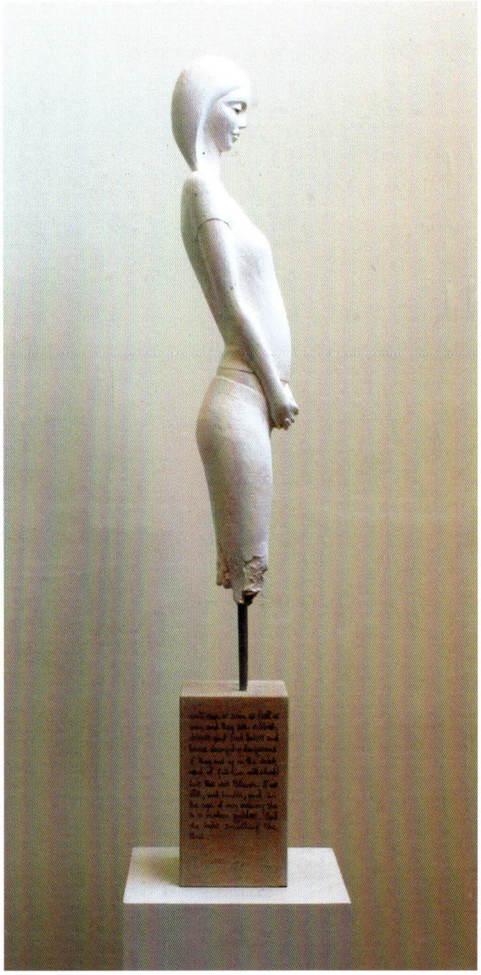

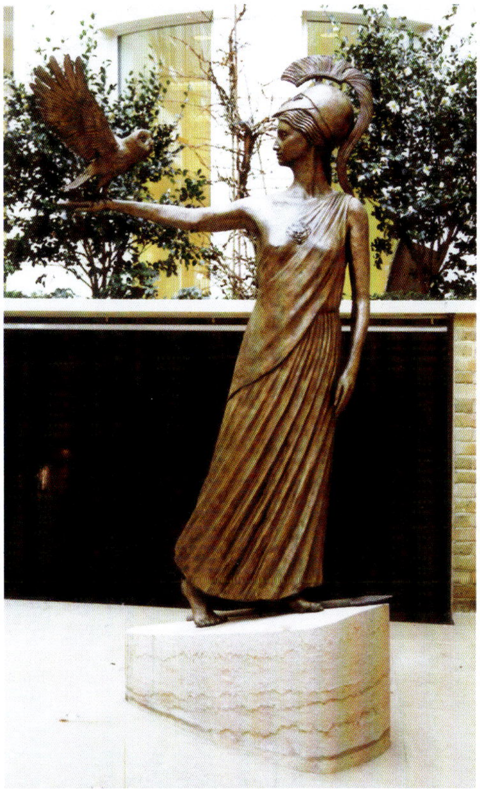

TOP Damian Fennell, *Woman III.* Crystacal Alpha K plaster, stainless steel, ancaster stone, permanent marker, 100 x 14 x 14 cm (39⅓ x 5½ x 5½ in.). *Photo: courtesy of the artist.*

BOTTOM Tanya Russell, *Minerva.* Bronze commissioned by Minerva Plc for their headquarters in Wigmore Street, London, 240 x 80 cm (94½ x 31½ in.). *Photo: courtesy of the artist.*

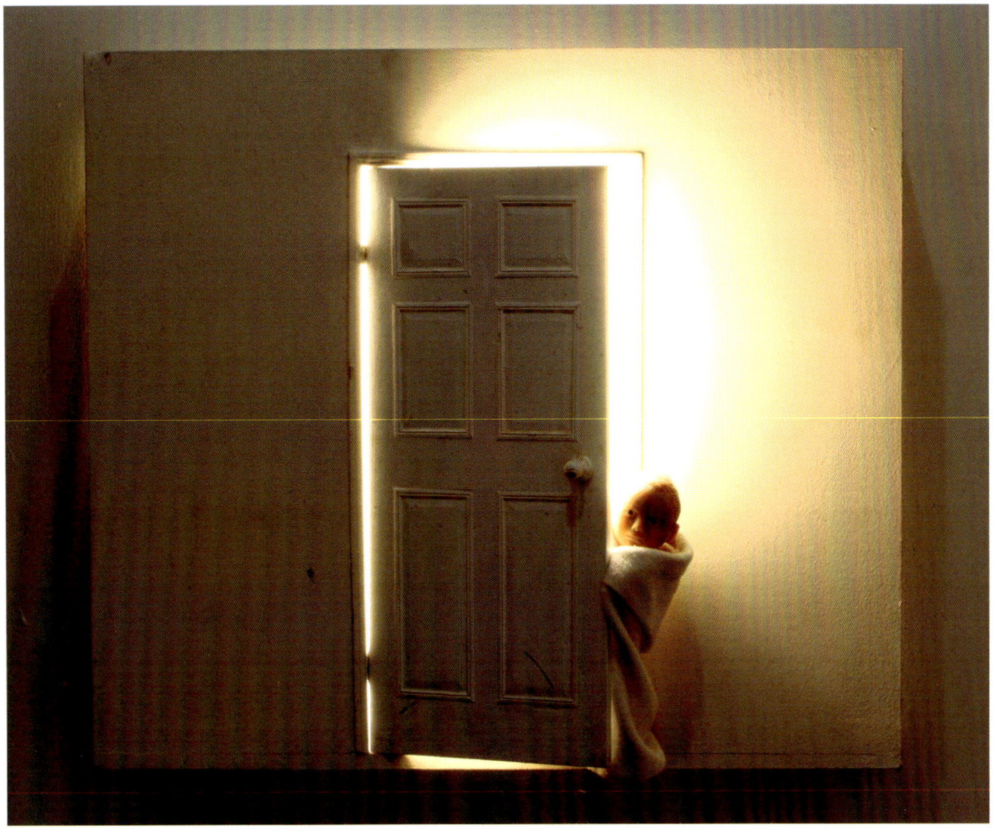

LEFT George Triggs, *Glimpse of sadness*. Mixed media, 30 x 40 x 14 cm (11¾ x 15¾ x 5½ in.). *Photo: Steve Clutton.*

BELOW Edwin Russell, *Centurion*. Bronze commission for St Albans, 300 x 200 cm (118 x 78¾ in.). *Photo: courtesy of the artist.*

Another useful method of critique can be the one-three-ten rule. The one person whose opinion is most important when looking at your own artwork is your own: you are the artist, the only one who really knows what you want to say. On the other hand, it can be very helpful to see your work through other people's eyes. If you were to get three people whose judgement you really trust to look at your work and their responses were broadly similar, you would definitely take note. It can also be useful to canvas the opinion of ten people you don't know. Once again, if all ten say approximately the same thing about the piece, you might very well want to listen to them.

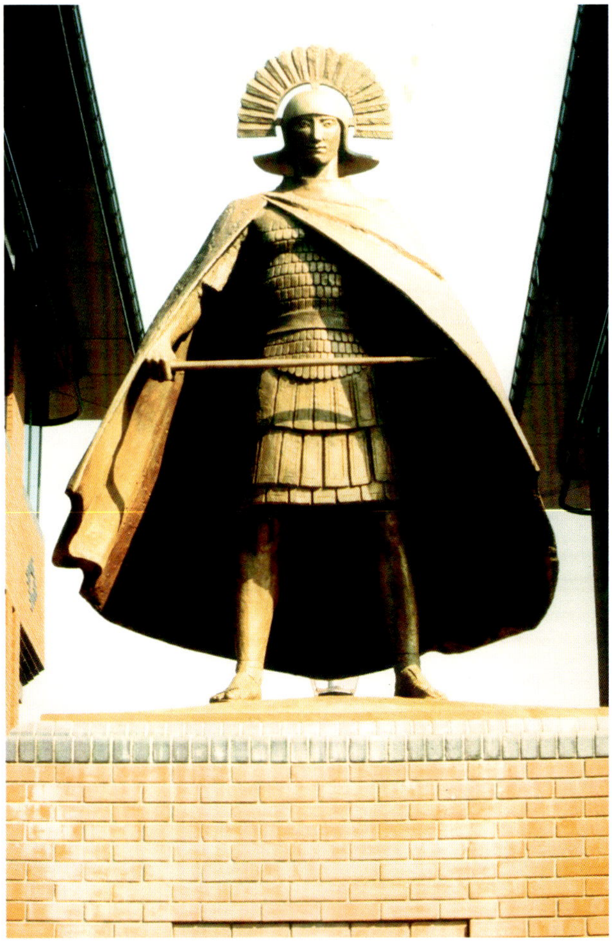

There are many reasons for creating art and therefore many ways of viewing it. Specific methods of critique have emerged to look not only at art addressing specific topics such as politics, gender or religion, but to look at all art from a particular perspective. It can be very interesting to critique an artwork in one way, and then to consciously adopt another method of critique to consider it afresh.

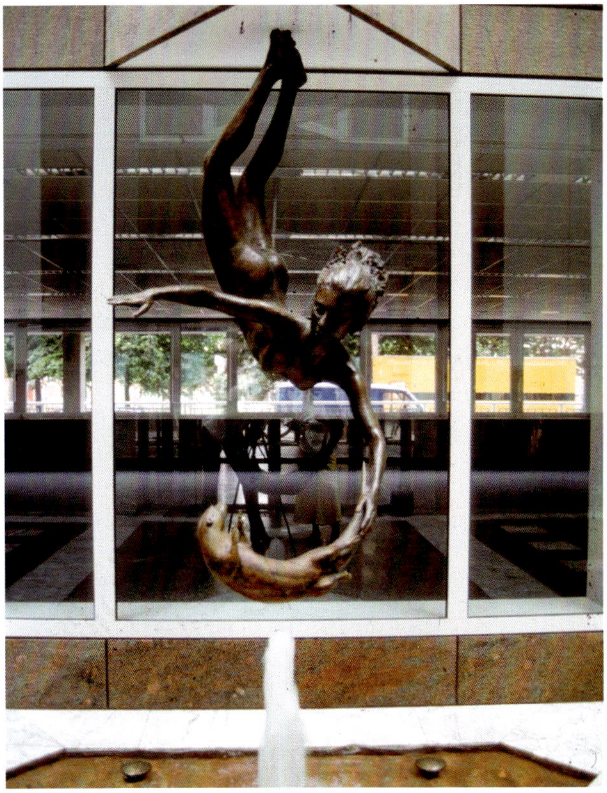

Lorne McKean, *Otter girl fountain.* Bronze commissioned for Mansell Court, Mansell Street, London E1, 450 x 95 cm (177¼ x 37½ in.). *Photo: courtesy of the artist.*

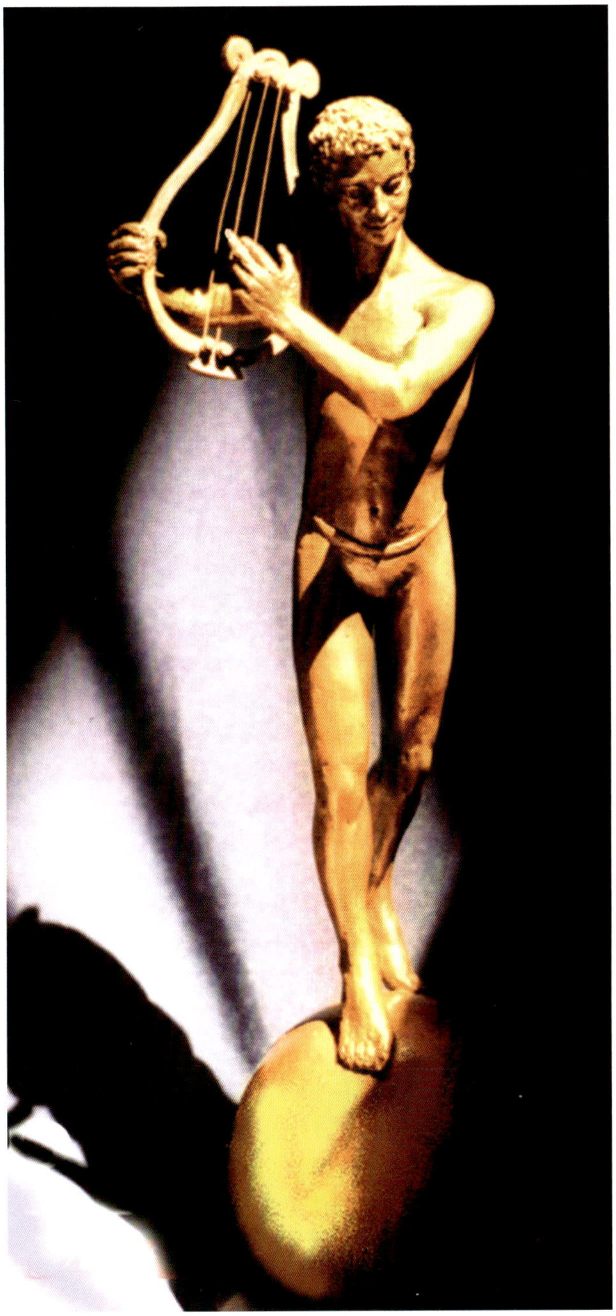

Tanya Russell, *Apollo.* Bronze, 26 x 10 cm (10¼ x 4 in.). *Photo: courtesy of the artist.*

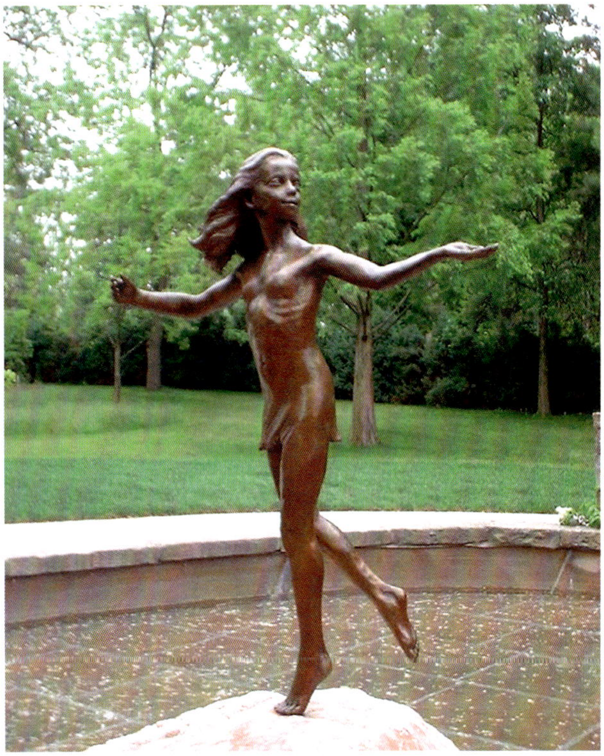

Tanya Russell, *Miranda.* Bronze life-size inspired by Miranda from *The Tempest*, for a pond in a school in Niagara, Canada, 150 x 110 cm (59 x 43⅓ in.). *Photo: courtesy of the artist.*

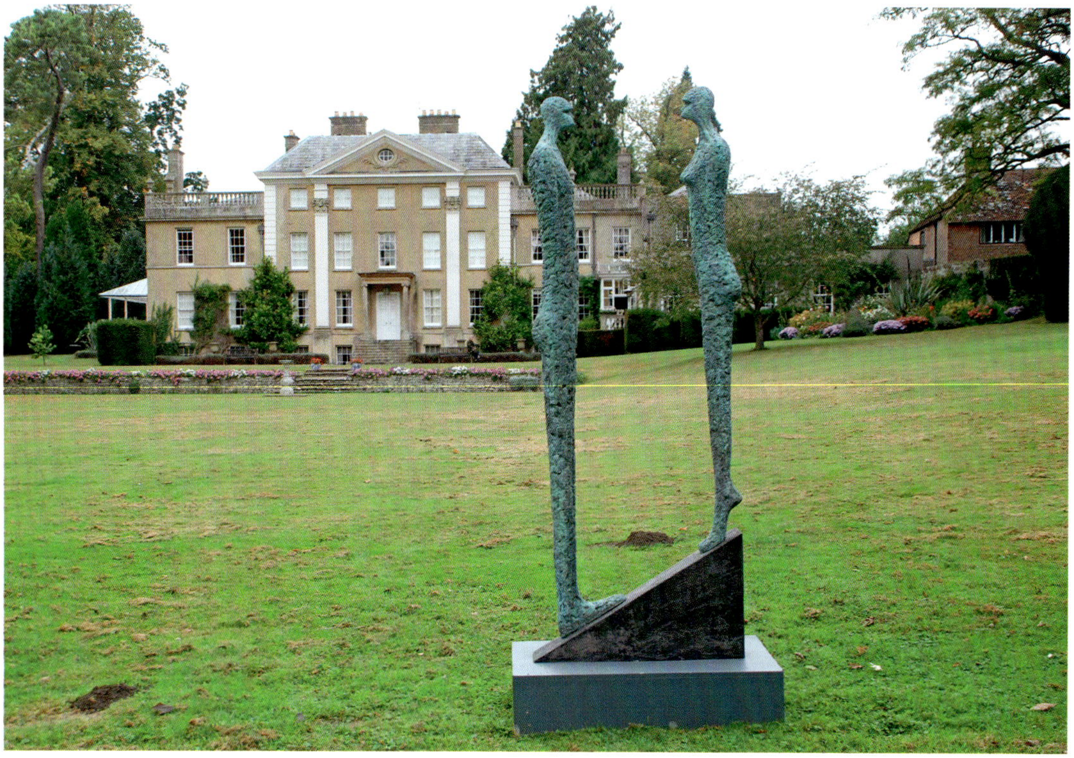

Michael Speller, *Equilibrium.* Bronze, 240 x 104 x 45 cm (94½ x 41 x 37 in.).
Photo: courtesy of the artist.

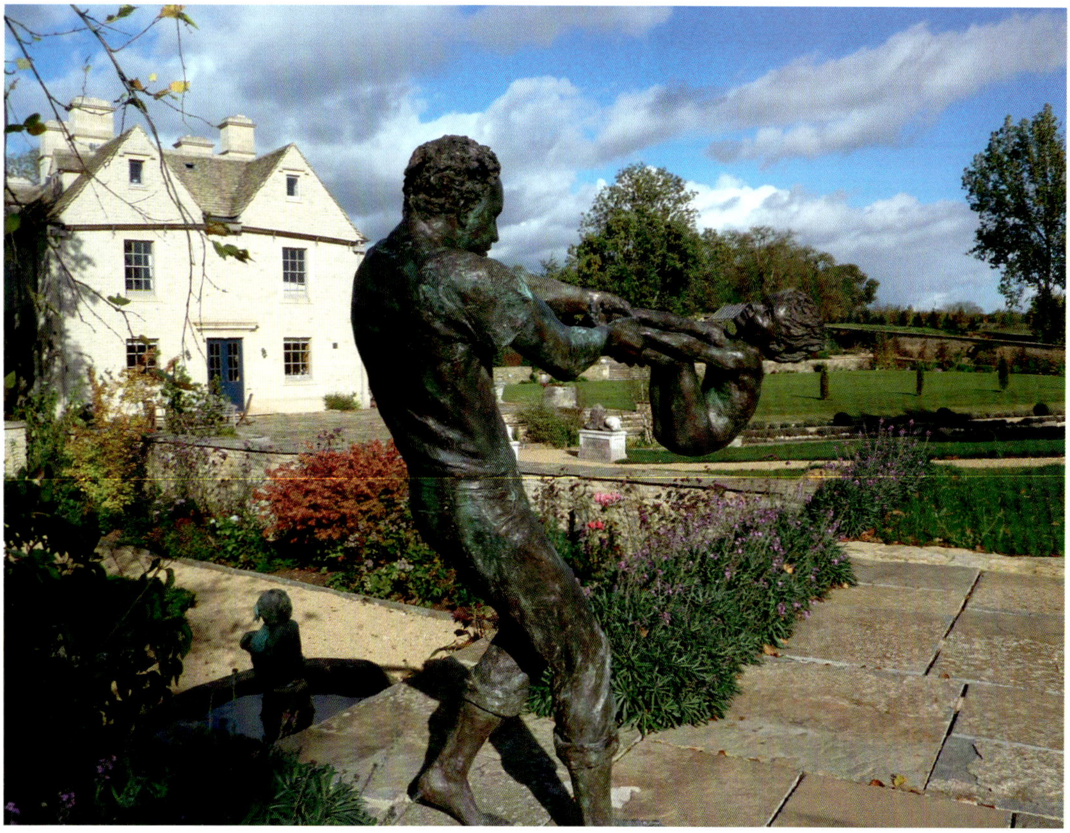

Lorne McKean, *Brothers.* Bronze life-size, 180 x 150 cm (71 x 59 in.).
Photo: courtesy of the artist.

The Artist's Process

Though every artist has their own way of working, the creative process can broadly be divided into four stages:

Stage 1: Mastery of Skills

The first stage involves learning about your tools and materials in detail. Through this you will gain confidence in what different materials can do and the effects they can create – for example, the nuances of mark-making through the use of different tools or the effects created by the subtlest changes of angle or pressure (the equivalent of vocabulary and grammar).

Stage 2: Inspiration

The second stage is to learn about yourself as a person; what inspires you, who you are, what your life and culture have taught you and what is important to you. Explore and enquire, become rounded, become inspired and passionate about the world (the equivalent of deciding what you are going to say).

Stage 3: Creative Journey

Go on a creative journey: research, study, bring together all of the knowledge you have acquired in Stages 1 and 2, try different art forms, play with materials, techniques and ways of expressing yourself, experiment, fail, try again. This is what is often called the 'design process' (the equivalent of outlining and developing a speech). More information about the design process can be found on the Art Academy website: www.artacademy.org.uk.

Stage 4: Creative Flow

Forget it all! Let creativity flow of itself, trusting that the magic will happen – this is the equivalent of working without a script, just speaking from the heart, not thinking about anything else. This way of working is subconscious but not unconscious or dreamy, because there is in fact a deep level of awareness operating, directing the precise nature of each mark made. It is way beyond our normal, more superficial and mechanical way of working, and all the knowledge you have previously gained works for you without you even thinking about it. This stage can often only occur when the other stages have been worked through. When people experience a spiritual response, it often seems to relate to or originate from artwork where the artist has been working at this level.

In some artistic traditions, these steps are followed in a linear progression, but I think it works better to be rather more flexible, developing and practising all four simultaneously. Initially the emphasis will be on the earlier stages, but if you have no taste of the latter stages, your work can become dry and boring, and you risk losing your inspiration and getting stuck at one stage. In addition, if you dwell too much on one step without trying the others, it can become very hard to move to the next one.

An artist should always be exploring and playing with new methods, materials and ideas, learning and discovering, until they hang up their modelling tools for the very last time!

> *'An artist never really finishes his work; he merely abandons it.'*
>
> Paul Ambroise Valéry

Originality

I would like to touch on originality in this section, as it is such an important and sought-after aspect of creative work. After much research, practice and observation, I have come to the conclusion that there is only one thing that can be truly original: the experience of an individual at a specific given moment. This experience, by this individual, at this exact time, has never been and can never be repeated. When a person has an amazing experience and they describe it truthfully, honestly and simply, the listener can connect fully with it; therefore it follows that if an artist honestly manifests their own personal experience in their work, then the work will communicate it in the same way. The closer the artist gets visually to their experience, the more powerful and original their work will be. If the artist is working at what we described on p. 21 as the Creative Flow stage then new forms and marks will naturally appear and express each original experience.

I find the theory of forms as explored by Plato and Socrates very interesting. In essence, they say that any object in the physical world is a copy of the idea or archetype of that form in the mental realm. Therefore, before someone can make a table there must be the idea of a table, and the form of the table is dictated by that idea and function. The physical object is just a copy of an idea, and what an artist then does when painting or sculpting it is to copy that copy. The viewer of an artwork is therefore actually seeing a copy of a copy.

This is the reason that an artist's experience is so important. When an artist sees something it is their experience of seeing that is important, whatever the object. Even if it is just a tree or a bird, what the artist seeks to express is what they experience in that moment of observation – otherwise they are merely creating a copy of a copy.

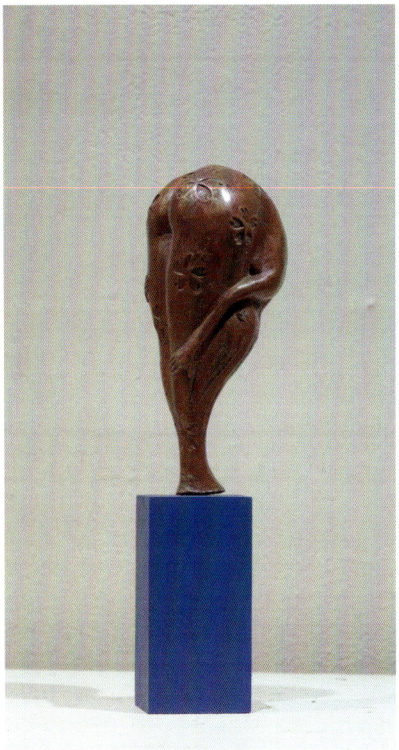

Hiromi Scintu, *Sakura.* Cold cast copper on wood base, 25 x 7 cm (10 x 2¾ in.). *Photo: Wah Poon.*

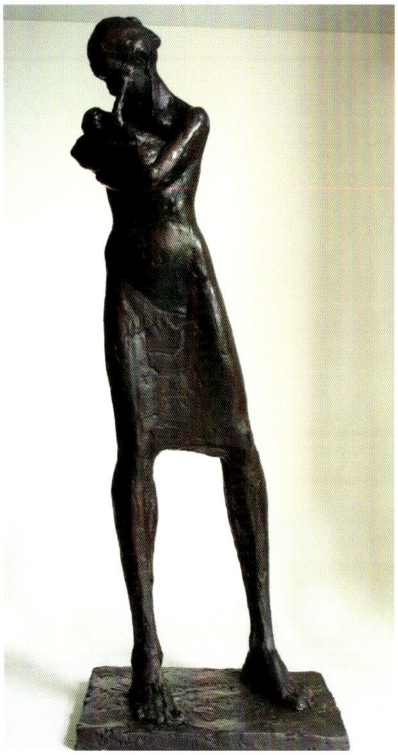

Arabella Brooke, *Shifting Focus.* Bronze, 80 x 25 cm (31½ x 9¾ in.). *Photo: courtesy of the artist.*

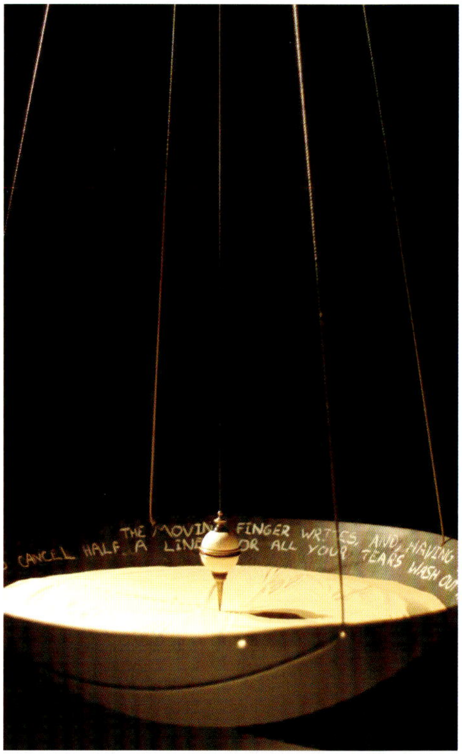

Kerr Gemmell, *Sands of Time.* Interaction sculpture, play sand, ivory plumb-bob, steel bowl, hanging wire, height 250 cm (98½ in.), bowl diameter 75 cm (29½ in.). *Photo: courtesy of the artist.*

Thousands of elephants and rhinoceros have been butchered merely for their ivory. Trying to replace or recoup their numbers will only serve to add further strain to the already stressed ecosystem. Like the lines drawn into this dish of sand, mankind's influence can only ever cover up these scars with more.

Beauty

Beauty is not 'prettiness'. This is a common misunderstanding and is partly responsible for people making the statements that beauty is not valid in contemporary art. Artists can often show people the beauty of the most unlikely and sometimes insignificant things – a found object can suddenly be given a new value when taken in a new context; a chance mark seen on a wall, or something normally considered ugly, can be seen in a completely new light through the artist's vision. Beauty works at all the different levels described previously – physical, emotional, mental and spiritual.

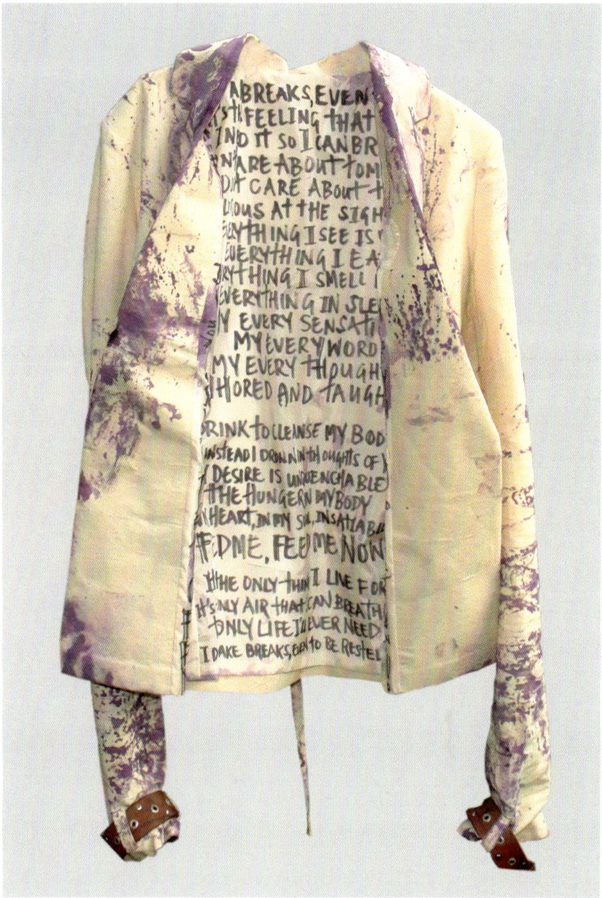

Karin Jolly, *Obsession of Paint IV.* Handmade jacket of artists' canvas, silk, leather and paint, 90 x 60 cm (35½ x 23⅔ in.). *Photo: courtesy of the artist.*

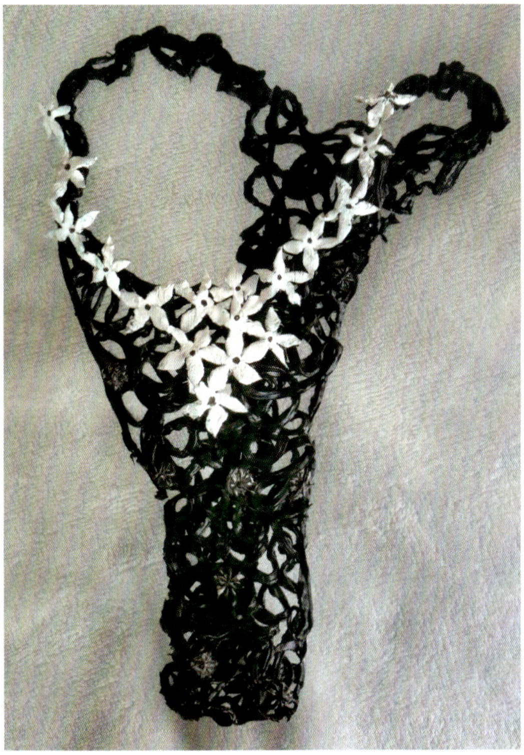

Karin Jolly, *Obsession of Paint II.* Winner of Art Academy, Mixed Media Prize 2009, recycled baked oil paint, 20 x 14 cm (8 x 5½ in.). *Photo: courtesy of the artist.*

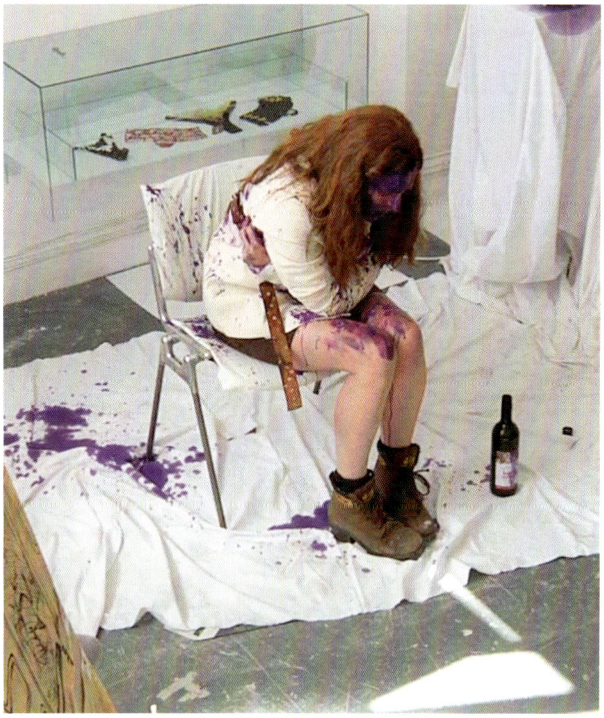

Karin Jolly, *Obsession of Paint IV.* Performance piece. *Photo: courtesy of the artist.*

Physical beauty: The best expression of formal beauty I have come across is summed up in a quotation from the fifteenth-century architect Leon Battista Alberti:

'In order to be as brief as possible, I shall define beauty to be a harmony of all parts, in which whatsoever subject it appears, fitted together with such proportion and connection, that nothing could be added, diminished or altered, but for the worse.'

Alberti, *Ten Books on Architecture, Book VI*

Mental or conceptual beauty: A solution to a puzzle, an inspiring idea, a great revelation or a point clearly and elegantly made, can all be beautiful.

Emotional beauty: Emotional beauty in this sense is very much in the eye of the beholder, and love is so close to beauty that when one is experienced, the other is automatically there – the very act of loving something renders it beautiful. Things or people do not need to be conventionally or physically beautiful to be regarded as such, and it is the underlying rather than superficial that is being appreciated.

Spiritual beauty: Everyone has experienced moments in their lives when they have seen the world in a brighter light. This is an internal experience, although it can be triggered by a physical experience. It is not restricted to positive, uplifting experiences; there are many recorded moments of people having their most sublime, beautiful, spiritual experiences at the worst physical moments.

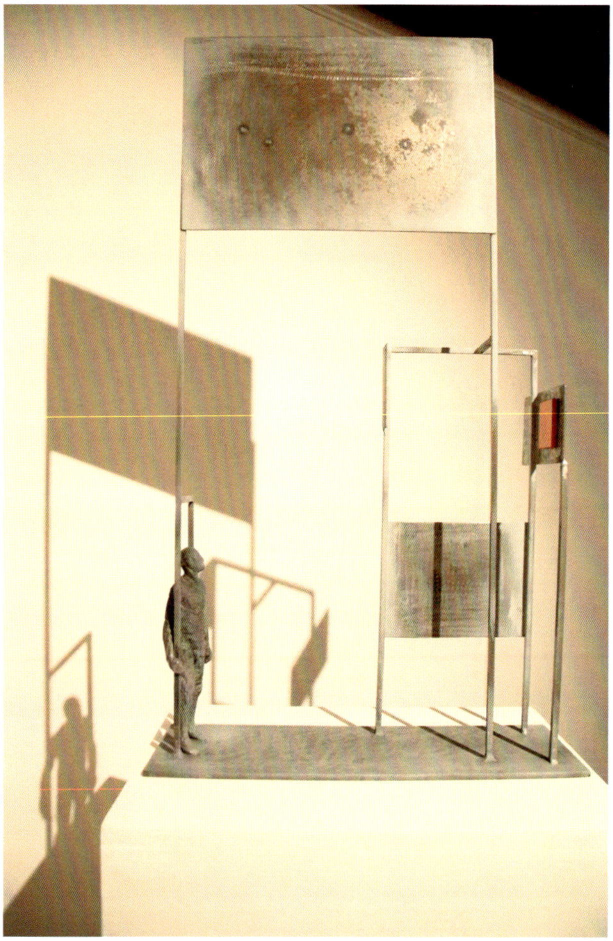

Edward Murray, *Space Voyager, Concept 2.* Newclay, steel, 70 x 50 cm (27⅔ x 19¾ in.). *Photo: courtesy of the artist.*

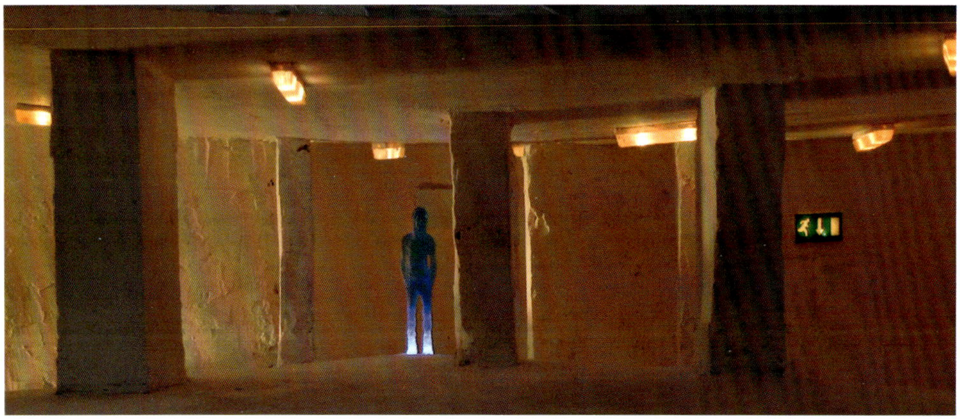

George Triggs, *Blue Youth*. Plaster, glass, fairy lights, 30 x 90 x 90 cm (11¾ x 35½ x 35½ in.). *Photo: courtesy of the artist.*

In Blue Youth, *the blue glass figure glows and flickers, emanating a power that is both seductive and concerning. It beckons you into a world that has no reassurance of safety. You are left with the fear of confrontation; a youth's repressed rage. You are challenged to reject or nurture him, see him as beautiful or ominous.*

Intention

Intention is a recurring theme in this chapter because it is absolutely key to the outcome and effect of an artwork. The first studio practice project for students at the Art Academy focuses on emotional depth. In this, we ask students to research the artist who, for them, most powerfully conveys emotion. Part of their research involves finding an artist who has commented on his or her own work – in every instance the effect of the artwork is found to be very closely linked to the intention of the artist.

The range of intention can be very broad, from the simple desire to depict something you have seen, to conveying a particular message or feeling or evoking a specific response from the viewer. The intention may even be to provoke questions or create confusion. The deeper and clearer the intention of the artist, the more powerful and durable the effect on the viewer. This is not to say that every artwork must aim to change the world – the intention may be simply to entertain or decorate – but the more motivated the artist is to convey their intention and the more skilfully they manifest it, the more successful they will be in transmitting it to the viewer.

Intention is closely linked with vision: if you want to create great art you need to have great vision.

'It is very important for the artist to gauge his position aright, to realise that he has a duty to his art as well as to himself, that he is not king of his own castle, but rather servant of a noble cause. He must search deeply in his own soul, and develop and tend it, so that his art has something to clothe, and does not remain a glove without a hand.'

Wassily Kandinsky

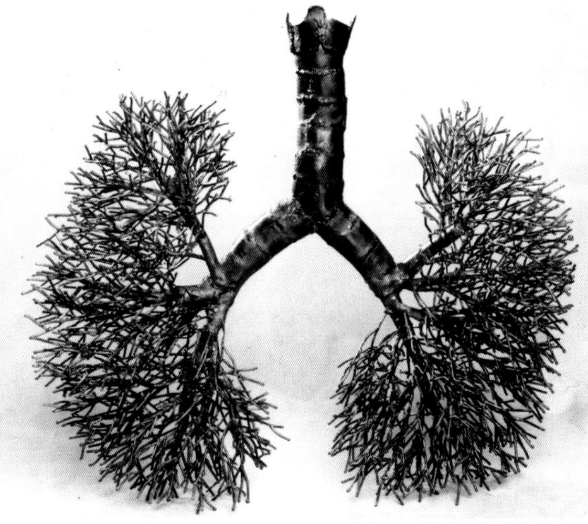

Jill Simpson, ***Steel Lungs***. Welded mild steel, 26 x 26 x 13 (10 x 10 x 5 in.). *Photo: Philip Kitchen.*

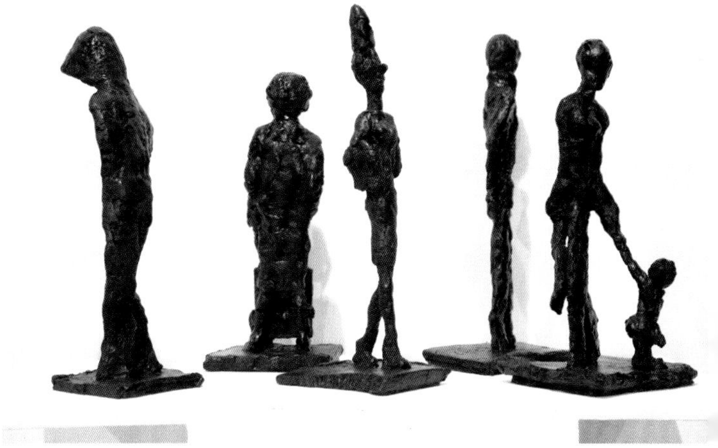

Lynn Todd, ***The Holloway Road***. Jesmonite and epoxy resin, 25 x 40 x 15 cm (9¾ x 15¾ x 6 in.). *Photo: courtesy of the artist.*

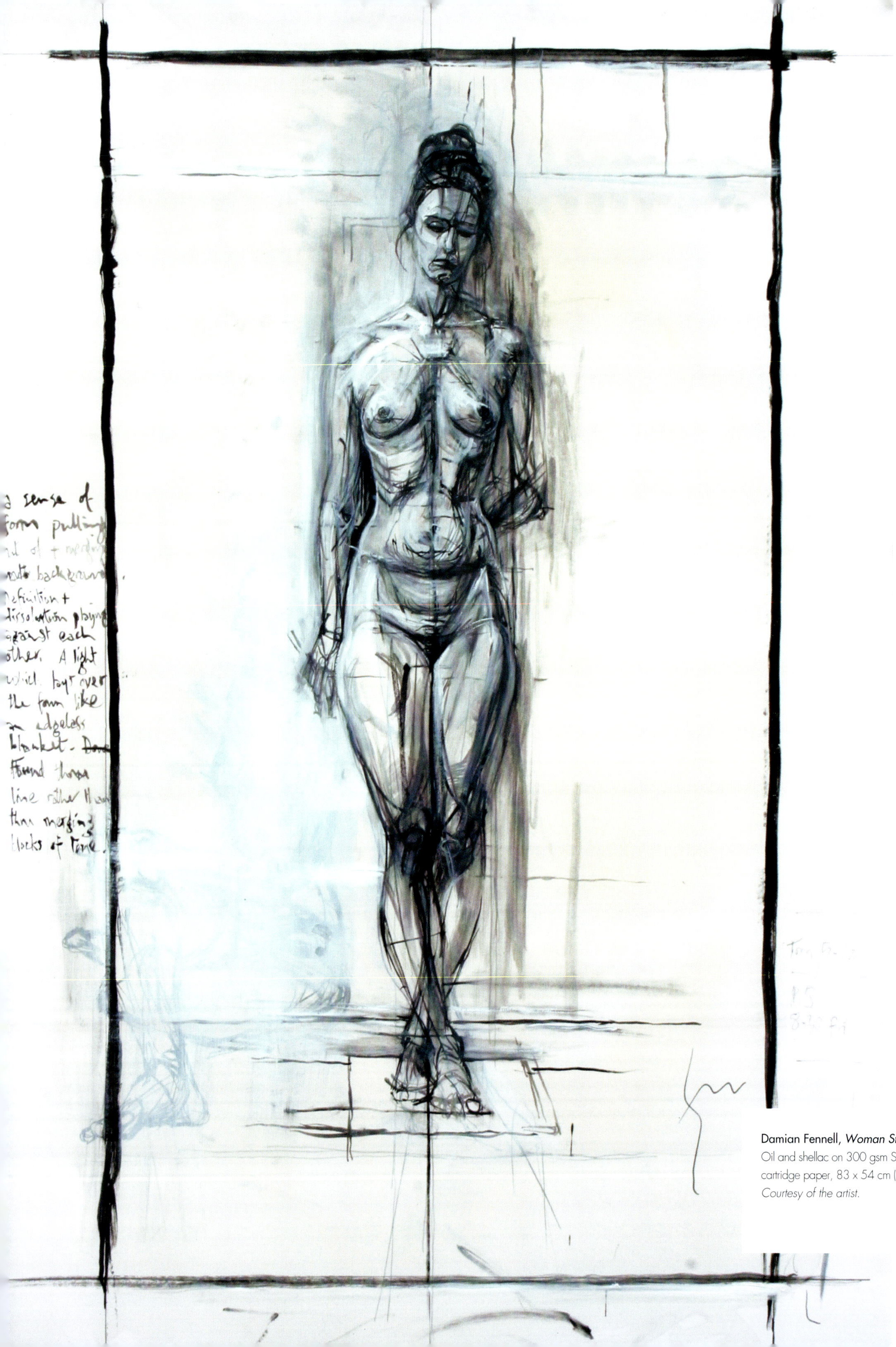

Damian Fennell, *Woman Standing (Helen)*.
Oil and shellac on 300 gsm Snowdon cartridge paper, 83 x 54 cm (32¾ x 21⅓ in.).
Courtesy of the artist.

2

GETTING STARTED

Preparing To Be Creative
Things to Consider Before You Start Sculpting
Modelling Materials
Tools and Set-Up for a Half Life-Size Figure in Clay

Preparing To Be Creative

In this chapter we will look at getting started in practical terms – preparing your tools, materials, workspace and so on – but first, we have some enjoyable and valuable exercises to get you thinking creatively.

Warm-Up Exercises

Sculpture is about creativity and life, awareness and dynamism, so it is very important that you are in the right frame of mind from the start. Sculpture also has quite a lot of technical and practical issues to deal with, so it is useful to get yourself into a creative and vibrant state before dealing with these. These warm-up exercises will help to get you looking, loosening up and tuning in to the power of form and materials to convey meaning and feeling.

☛ EXERCISE 1

This is a simple exercise that shows how we, as humans, share common responses to colour, shape, texture and proportion. It is best done with a group of people, but you can do it on your own, too.

You need to say what feeling you get from the colour or shape – feelings like happy, angry, passionate, calm, expansive, infinite. Avoid mental associations, like 'My grandmother's teapot was that colour, so it reminds me of that.' We are looking for innate, instinctive, automatic responses, so there is no need to try and be 'creative' or 'clever'.

1. Have a piece of paper and a pen or pencil to hand. One by one, look at the three colours to the right, and write down how they make you feel – when looking at each colour, cover up the other two.

2. Now look at the three shapes on the right and write down the different feelings they evoke. If you are struggling, think to yourself: does the circle feel just like the square, or is it different? Then try and describe the difference.

3. Look at the different materials around you (paper, metal, textile, wood, etc.). Look at them, touch them and see how you respond differently to each one and associate different qualities with them.

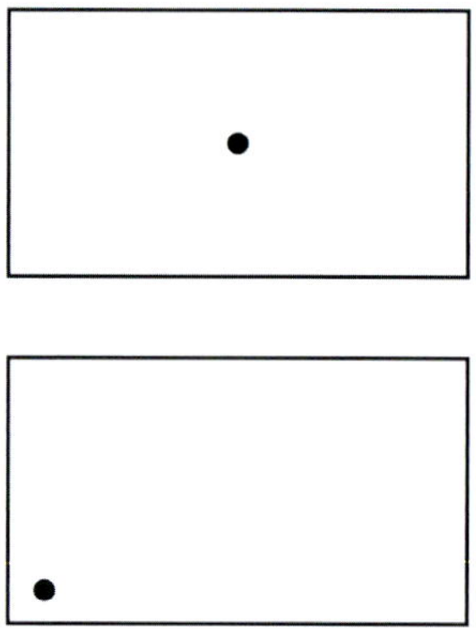

4. Finally look at the pictures on the right and see how placing the dot in different positions in the box creates a completely different feeling. Again, jot down your response to the different placements.

You can continue to explore your visual language and carry this exercise on to other things – shades, proportions, 3D shapes and so on.

EXERCISE 2

Purpose

There are several valuable lessons in this exercise:

- Letting go! You are going to create forms really quickly – in less than a minute. The forms will be abstract and very loose, so you cannot worry too much about *what* you create, but more about *how* you do it.
- Understanding the importance of emotion in an artwork.
- Appreciating how much feeling and meaning you can convey through simple choices of material, shape and texture, putting into practice what you have learned from the previous exercise.

MATERIALS AND EQUIPMENT

- A few handfuls of good clay (see p. 32 for suitable types of modelling clay)
- Thin-gauge aluminium wire
- A few pieces of white A4 paper
- Adhesive tape
- A table
- Wire snips
- Scissors

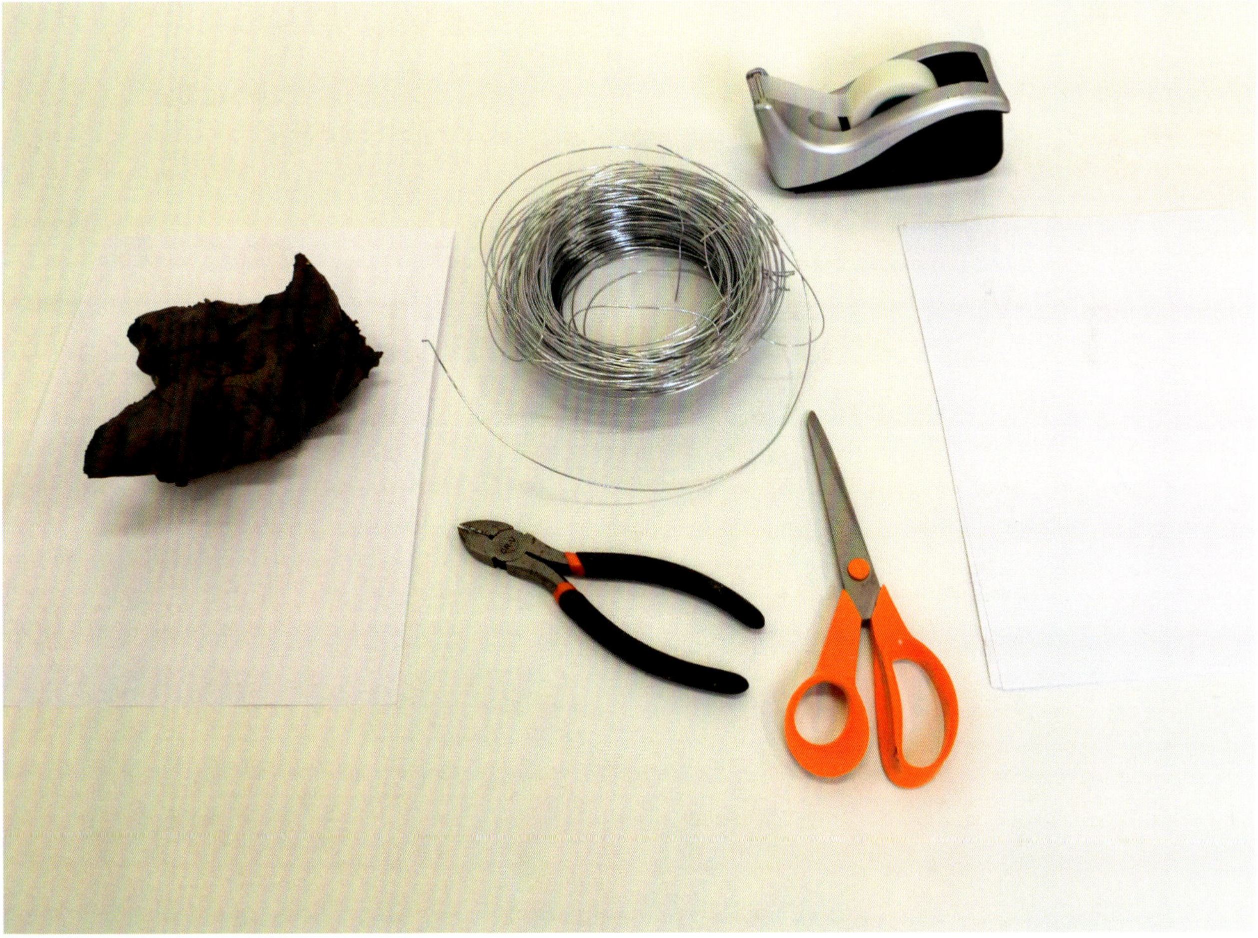

Materials and equipment for Exercise 2.

Preparation

Cut four lengths of wire about 20 cm (8 in.) long. Put all the materials and equipment on your table.

The Exercise

Take a piece of wire and in only one minute twist it to express each of the emotions listed below, in order, one at a time. Be spontaneous!

1. Anger
2. Peace
3. Focus

Now try the same thing, but this time using clay, paper, wire or a combination of these. Note in the photo, right, how a twisted piece of wire can be stood up in a small ball of clay. You could fold, cut, tear or crumple the paper, and the clay can be modelled in any way that you wish. Once again, spend no more than a minute on each one.

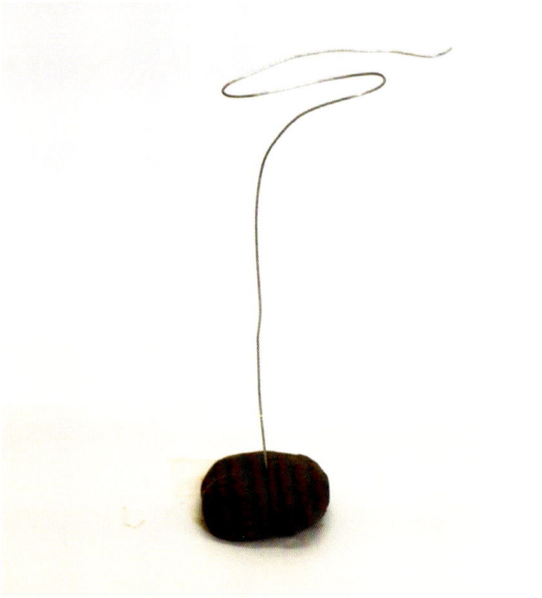

Twisted wire stood up in a small ball of clay.

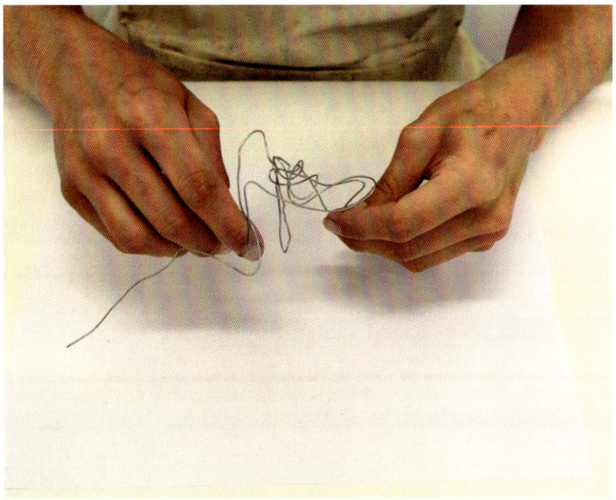

Using wire to express anger.

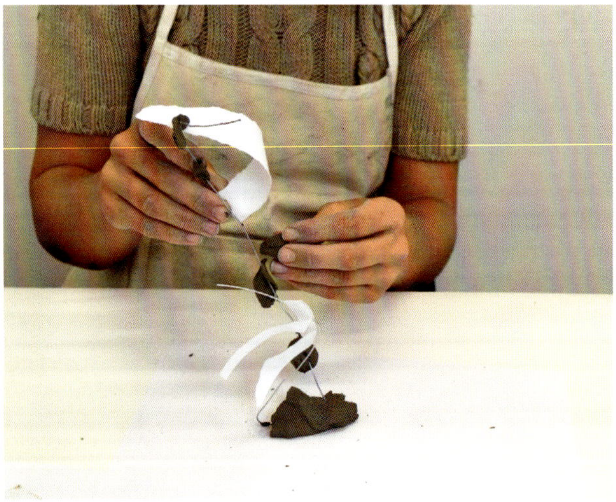

Combining materials in Exercise 2.

Relax for a few minutes, then try the next part of the exercise.

Consider the simple scenarios listed below. See how they make you feel, try to connect with the experience and then when you 'feel it' just pick up whichever materials you like and quickly create something that shows that feeling.

1. You are sitting by a beautifully calm pond on a still day, all by yourself. It is totally silent and you are just looking into the pond.

2. Think of something you find exciting, which really gets the adrenaline pumping, such as an extreme sport or an imminent long-awaited meeting with someone you care about.

3. You are sitting on top of a high mountain, there are eagles soaring overhead and you can see the landscape spread out before you for miles.

4. You can repeat this exercise with other stimuli, such as sound, smell, touch and taste.

Things to Consider Before You Start Sculpting

Sculpture by its very nature is quite technical, sometimes involving time-consuming processes and complex mediums. Whatever you are going to do, it is well worth your while thinking about it carefully before you start. A failure to think through the materials and processes can turn sculpting from a joy into a bit of a nightmare! Preparation of the workspace is equally important – avoid clutter and ensure that you have enough space to move around and are working at a suitable height.

Make sure that you are in a great frame of mind. The ideal state is different for each artist, but a useful guide is to allow yourself to be like a still pool of water. When a pool of water is stirred up, it gets choppy on the surface and the silt makes it all muddy – it is then hard to see clearly and things look distorted. When the pool is still, the water becomes clear, and is fully responsive to everything around and in it. A stone landing causes ripples, but just the right amount, not too many and not too few. This state of awareness and responsiveness can be a very useful state to work in. Artists often naturally fall into a state like this, but if you are feeling frustrated, agitated, sleepy or bored, it can have a huge impact on the effectiveness of your work. Each person needs to find their own way to reach the best state of mind for their work.

It is not possible to go through all the permutations for practical preparation here (assuming that the emotional and conceptual preparation has been done already). Some useful practical considerations could be:

1. **What is the purpose of the artwork?** Is it a study, a creative exercise, a specific concept, a commission? (

   Artworks generally fall into one of three categories:

- A study that we are doing for our own learning or development.
- A piece commissioned by another person/company/organisation.
- An artwork that we are doing for exhibition and sale in a gallery or show.

How you proceed (money spent on materials, the size, the durability and so on) might well depend on which category the artwork falls into.

2. **What material or materials do you want to sculpt in?** This will depend on the size of the piece, the texture, the form, your preference, the feeling you are trying to produce, etc. Materials are explored in more detail later in this chapter.

3. **What will happen to it next?** Where will it be placed: inside or outside; in a light or dark place; is it seen from above or below? Are you sculpting in the final medium or will the finished piece be in another medium? How will it be mounted? Is it a unique piece or an edition?

4. **Consider your model, if using one.** How long can they sit for? Are they young or old? What pose will you choose and why?

5. **Are you going to work predominantly from photographs or will you have plenty of sittings with the model?** Photographs can be useful, but you will be able to work from them much more proficiently if you have a good knowledge and experience of sculpting from life. It is important to have as many sittings as you possibly can with the model, for two reasons: firstly, as we are working in three dimensions, it is almost impossible for a photograph to capture all angles of the form, so there is a tendency to produce flattened and generic forms; secondly, it is much harder to capture the character and expressiveness of the model without them being there. This seems to happen almost by osmosis when you are in front of the model and working on your piece.

Modelling Materials

Materials for modelling can broadly be split into two groups:

- **Soft modelling materials**: clay (water-based), Plasticine/ Plastiline (oil-/wax-based), wax (oil-/wax-based), self-hardening clay.
- **Other materials**: textiles, wire, plaster, masking tape, found objects.

Other materials for creating sculptures are covered in later chapters (see pp. 92–9).

Clay (water-based material)

Description

Clay is a naturally occurring fine-grained mineral composite, and as it is a water-based medium, it dries out if left unwrapped.

There are all kinds of specialist clays (crank, porcelain, paperclay, etc.) that you might use if you were doing a sculpture for a ceramic firing process, but for a standard figure-modelling process, a basic stoneware or earthenware clay can be used. The clay you decide to use will depend on your preferences for texture, colour and firing temperature. Note that any sculpture constructed with an armature cannot be fired. It will have to be moulded and cast. This is discussed in more detail in Chapters 3 and 7.

To be a finished medium in its own right, clay must be fired in a kiln. If just left to dry it will crack and disintegrate. Artists have had some success in letting clay dry a little and then painting it with PVA (polyvinyl alcohol – a water-soluble synthetic polymer). This can preserve it for a while, but does not make it a finished material. Often an artist will take a mould from a clay sculpture and cast it in a more permanent material, such as bronze.

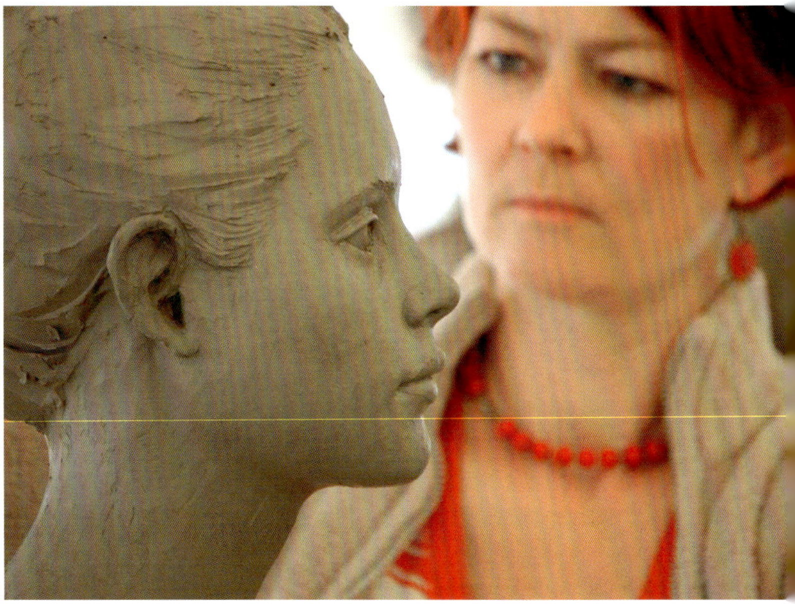

Tanya modelling a portrait in clay.

Good for:
Large figures, relief work or things that are relatively solid. Clay can generally hang for only a couple of inches without some sort of support from wood or wire, although it depends on the type of clay and method of modelling used. It is great for getting natural, organic-looking textures and fluid marks. You can apply and manipulate it quickly and easily, it naturally creates dark and light shades, and with large tools you can get strong planes and contours.

Not so good for:
Small, thin or fragile sculptures, especially if they have an armature inside them. Clay quickly becomes unworkable if left to dry too much, and will crack up and disintegrate. Even on a half life-size figure, I would suggest making delicate parts, like the hands, in a wax-based material to avoid this happening.

Care and storage:
Clay can be kept either in airtight bags or in plastic or metal bins and must be maintained at a perfect consistency to preserve its qualities for modelling.

Used clay can be recycled. Get a bin (a normal household bin with a lid will do), put the clay into it and, depending on how dry it is, sprinkle in some water, cover it with wet rags and then put plastic on the top. If it has dried out completely, crumble it up into very small pieces first.

When working on a clay sculpture, spray it fairly frequently with water, although too much might make it collapse. If you won't be working on it for a while, ensure the piece is wrapped in damp rags and covered completely in thin plastic – clothes pegs are good for ensuring that it is airtight.

Plasticine/Plastiline/Chavant/wax (oil-/wax-based material)

Description

These materials are oil- or wax-based rather than water-based, so they do not dry out in the same way as clay. They are mostly commercialised and known by their brand names (such as Plasticine, Plastiline and Chavant).

Plasticine and some other brands have a base of oil or petroleum jelly, and although they are softer, they are not as malleable and 'stretchy' as wax-based mediums such as Plastiline, and most fine artists prefer the latter. The type you use is really up to you and much depends on the sculpture you are creating. Each medium comes in a range of textures from hard to soft.

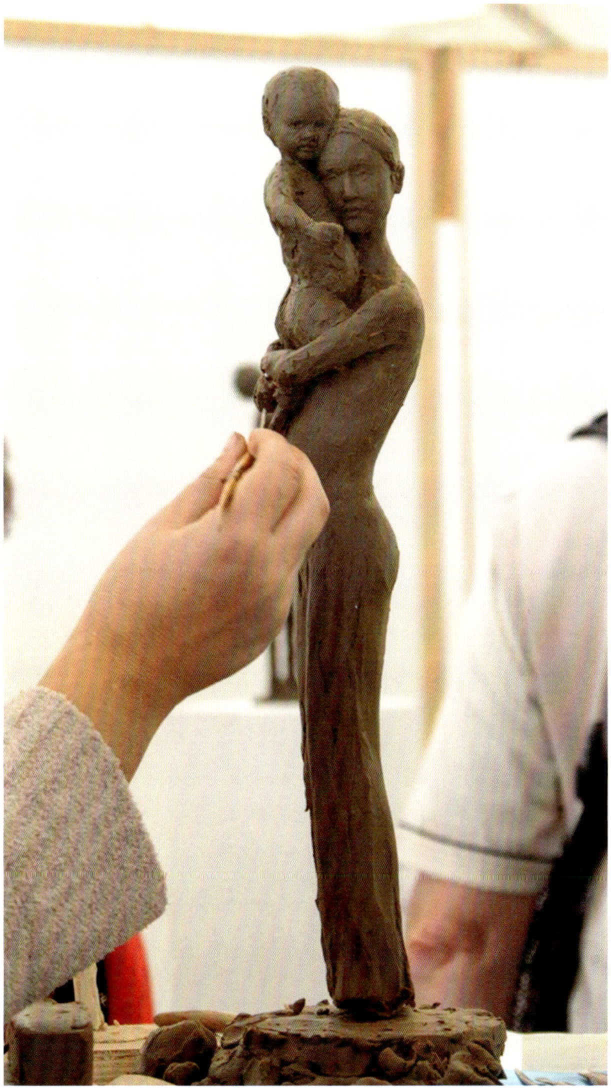

Good for:

Smaller, detailed sculptures. Use harder-textured mediums when fine detail is required; the softer ones behave more like clay and can be applied more easily and quickly. The very hard ones, although difficult to use, can create some very interesting and unusual effects.

These materials are also good for maquettes for larger sculptures (see Chapter 6, p. 106). Although not finished mediums, they can be quite durable if well cared for.

Not so good for:

Large sculptures, as the materials are expensive and much slower to apply than clay, or for working in very hot weather, as they have a tendency to melt.

Care and storage:

Keep these mediums at an even temperature and free from dust. If they are too hard to model with comfortably they can be warmed gently to get them to the correct consistency.

If you are taking a wax sculpture somewhere warm and you are concerned it will get too hot, cover it with a damp, light cloth. Never leave a sculpture made from an oil- or wax-based medium in a hot car, in a window in direct sunlight, or near a heater. It will melt!

Tanya modelling in a wax-based material.
Photo: Ronald Nydegger.

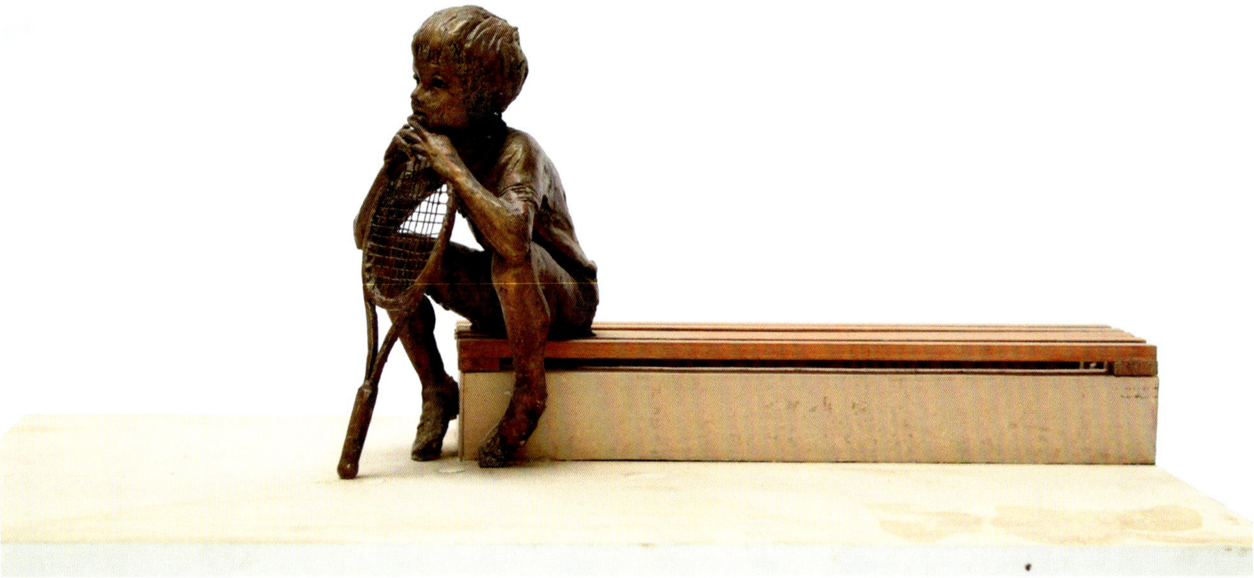

Lorne McKean, *Boy resting after tennis*. Maquette in Milliput, figure finished with clear varnish and fine bronze powder, H: 14 cm (5½ in.). *Photo: courtesy of the artist.*

Other Modelling Materials

There are many other modelling mediums, such as air-drying clay or Milliput, an epoxy containing additives that make it harden. Milliput is good for small models or maquettes that need to be kept for some time or transported, and can be coloured with paints or sprinkled with bronze dust and varnished to give a bronze look.

Explore the range of other materials available, as new ones come on the market all the time.

A half life-size figure in clay is an ideal starting point for exploring figure sculpture, and this is covered in detail in the following section.

Tools and Set-Up for a Half Life-Size Figure in Clay

It is worth taking trouble with your set-up – although it is true that a bad workman blames his tools, I would also suggest that a good workman greatly values his tools and chooses the best!

Make sure you have the right range of tools. Sculpting with just one tool is like trying to trim a hedge with a spade – you probably could do it but it would take a very long time.

As we go through the book, you will need various different items of equipment. The variety of tools you can use is almost limitless, but the following is a list of the sculptor's essentials (there are ways of being inventive with what you use if budget or other factors are a constraint – I will suggest a few of these as we go along).

Sketchbook and Pencils

It is very useful for a sculptor to sketch their model before they start. The purpose of drawing is really to get you to look more carefully and fully. It tunes in your attention and your eye, so that you actually see what is in front of you. It is an easy way of studying the form, without having to deal with the material issues involved in sculpture, and it is also a great way of exploring ideas. Drawing can also put you more in touch with the character of the model.

Through drawing, you can see the flow and geometry of the model's pose – as we will come to see later, the underlining structure of the pose is essential for a good sculpture.

If you carry around a sketchbook, you start thinking like an artist. Use your sketchbook to capture the wonders that you see around you, to note down ideas that come to you, and to start your design process.

Draw whenever you can: do in-depth studies, quick sketches, and play and experiment with your forms and ideas.

Remember that drawing for a sculptor is a tool – you are not necessarily aiming to draw a finished artwork, so don't worry about the result in terms of its appearance, just about what it teaches you.

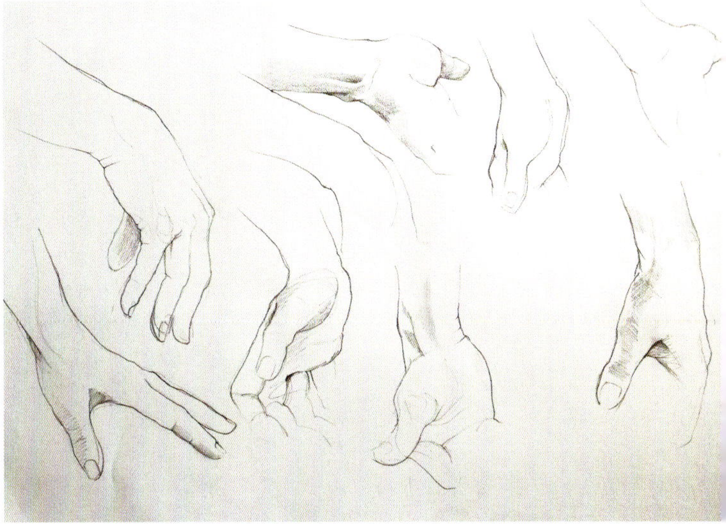

Hand studies by Melodie Cook. *Courtesy of the artist.*

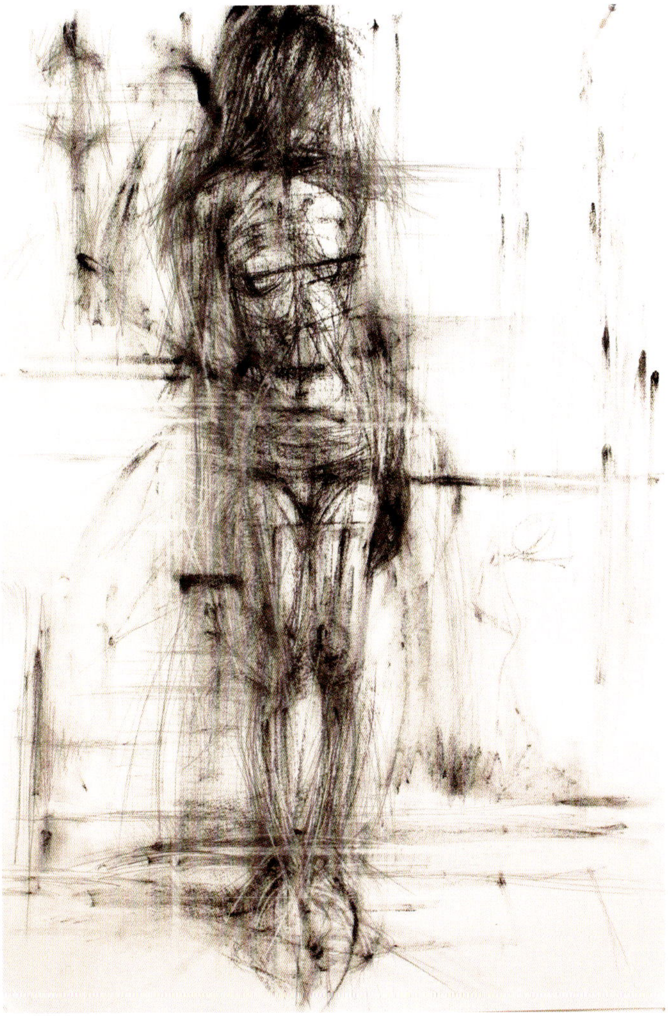

Damian Fennell, *Woman Standing (Lucy)*. Charcoal on 400 gsm stockwell watercolour paper, 119 x 84 cm (47 x 33 in.). *Courtesy of the artist.*

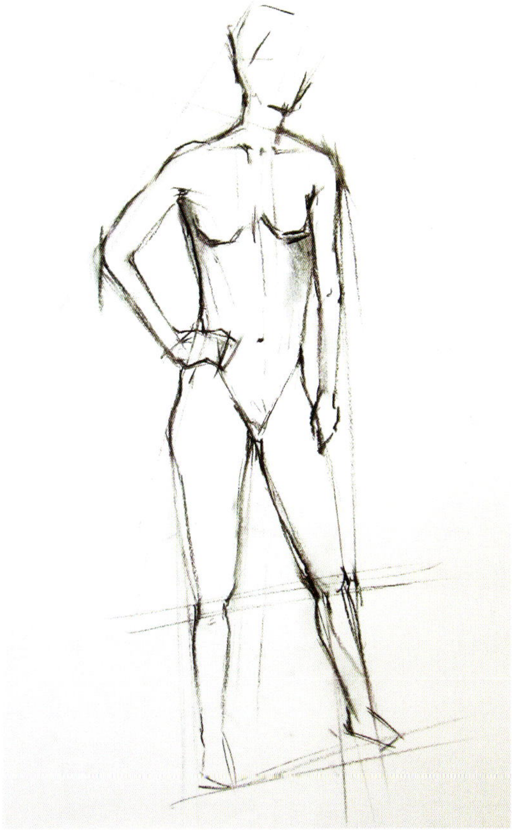

Five-minute figure drawing by Francesca Corra. *Courtesy of the artist.*

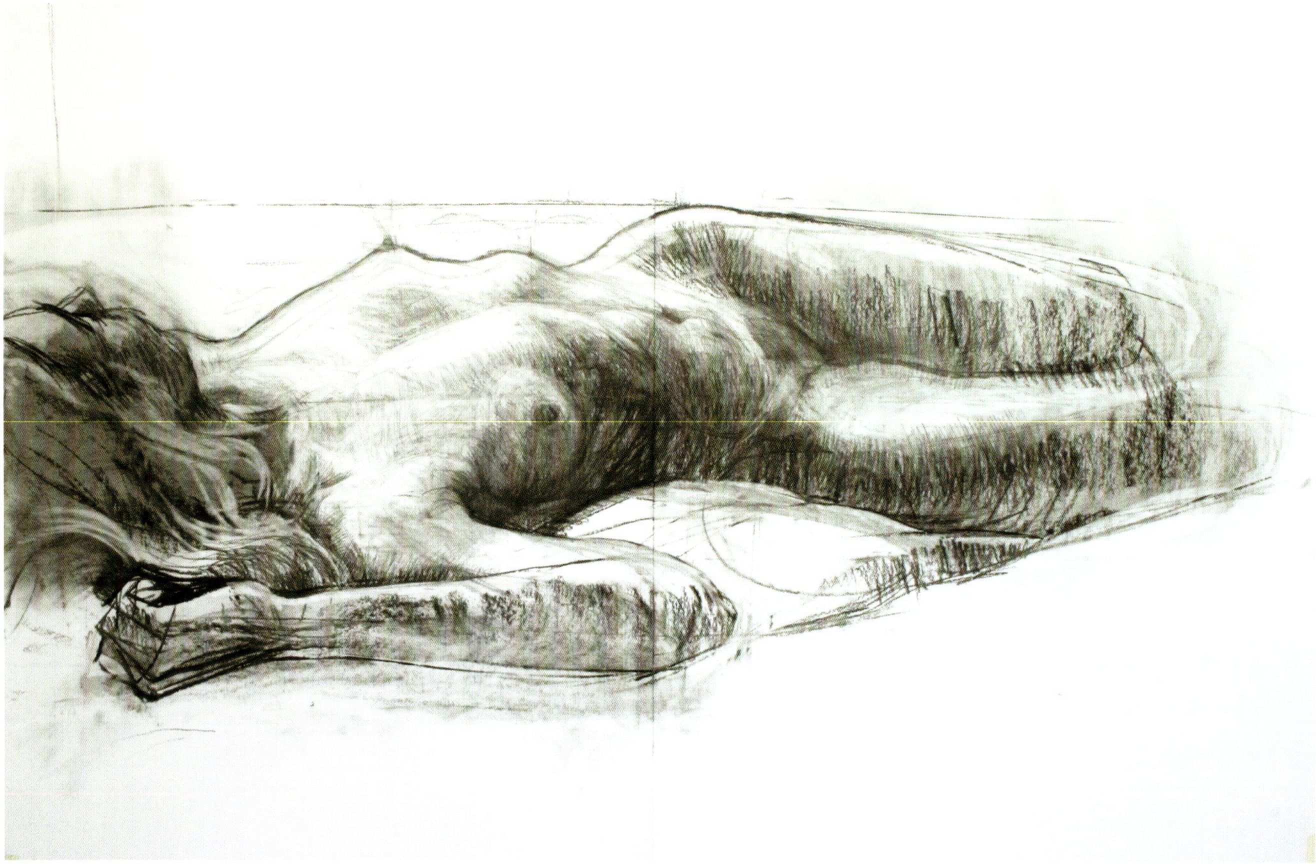

Damian Fennell, *Reclining Torso (Valeria)*. Charcoal and pencil on standard cartridge paper, 100 x 130 cm (39½ x 51¼ in.). *Courtesy of the artist.*

Modelling Tools

Getting good modelling tools is very tricky these days. If you ever get the chance to obtain good-quality old tools from a sculptor, leap at the opportunity. Otherwise buy the best ones you can and modify them as required, make your own, or have them made for you.

Modelling tools are a very personal thing and the range of tools you use will depend on your style of working and the marks that you wish to make. Below is a description of the standard range that suits most people – beyond that, you might need to find or make the exact tool you need, even for just one mark, to get it right.

For clarity, the tools are divided into four sections:

- 'B' tools
- Larger character tools
- Metal tools
- Other tools

'B' Tools

The main British sculpture tools supplier, Alec Tiranti Ltd, has a range of useful, wooden, general modelling tools in their 'B' series. It can help to sand these down once purchased to make them thinner and suppler. The 'B' tools need to be flexible but strong, with a flat edge on one side but no sharp edges. This can really make all the difference to the sensitivity and depth of your modelling, as you need to be able to roll around forms and create rich curves.

You will generally use the full range of tools on a half life-size figure: B5, B6, B7, B8, B9, B10 (the number denotes the length in inches – the company used to offer a B12, which is very useful, but no longer makes it, so if you ever come across one, buy it!). You can make your own B-type tools from scratch using box, holly, applewood or similar woods, which have a certain suppleness or spring to them.

There are of course other wooden tools available and other shapes that can be made, some of which you may occasionally find useful, but the 'B' series provides all the basic tools for figure modelling.

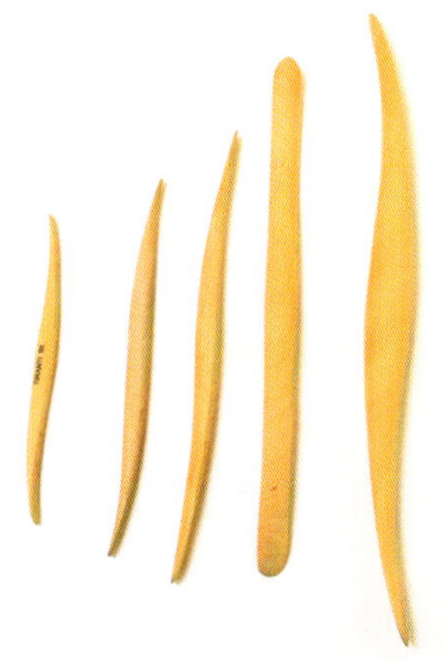

A range of my other favourite wooden modelling tools is shown here – some can be purchased, some are handmade.

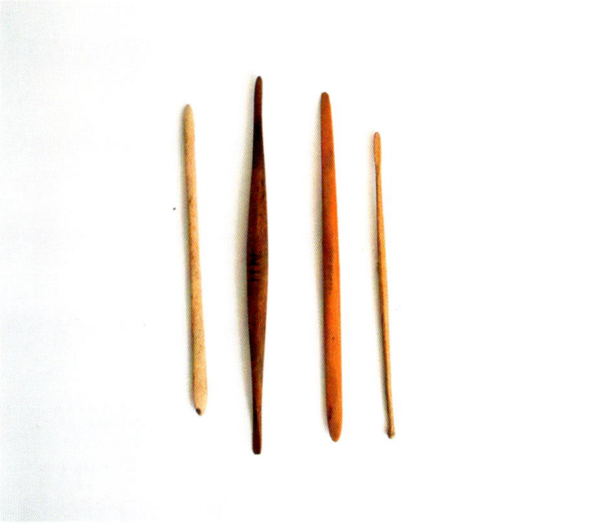

'B' range of wooden modelling tools available from Alec Tiranti Ltd.

Larger Character Tools

These are fairly vital for larger modelling. They might also be used for portraits or other work where bold modelling (with the creation of large planes and strong texture) is needed – unfortunately these normally have to be made, as suppliers tend not to stock them. The image at top right shows some of the tools that I have that I find most useful.

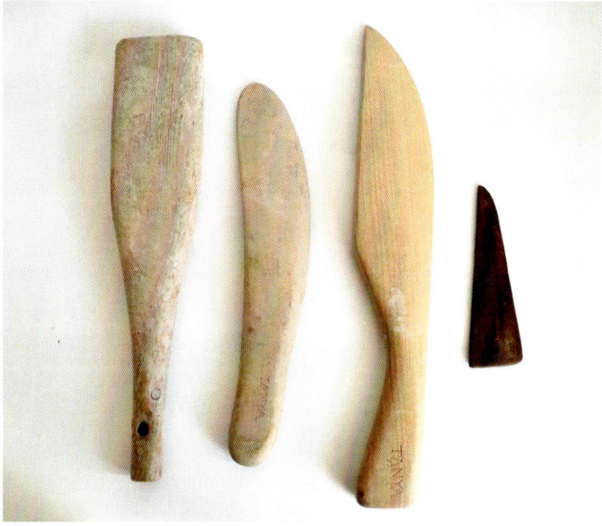

Large character tools, the largest being around 40 cm (16 in.) long.

Metal Tools

These tend to be used for smaller, more detailed modelling and follow very similar principles to the wooden tools. The ends I use the most are the rounded ones, as they allow detail while retaining rich, rounded forms. Occasionally a slightly sharper end is useful.

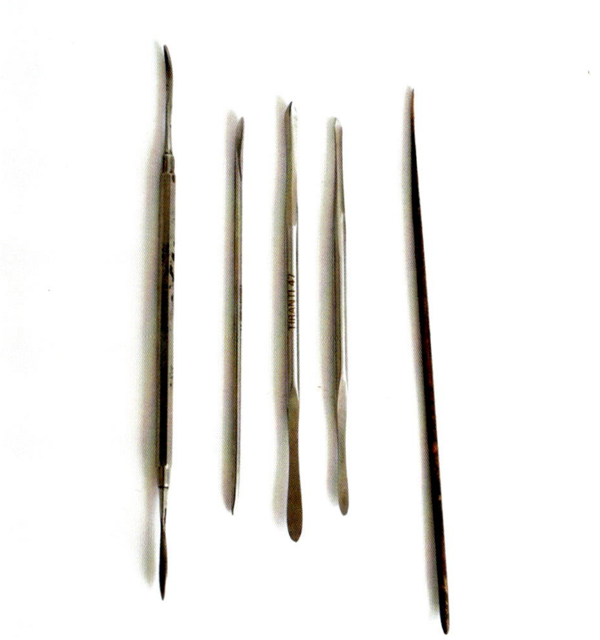

Metal modelling tools.

Other Tools

- **Timber** – a good piece of wood measuring 5 x 2.5 cm (2 x 1 in.) is very handy for larger modelling.
- **Wire scraper ends** – in various sizes, depending on the size of your sculpture, are very useful to remove areas of clay or to create specific textures.

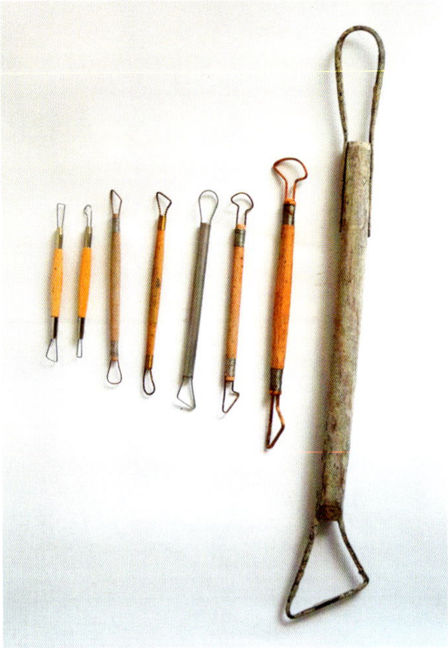

Wire modelling tools.

- **Kidneys, rubber or metal** – you tend to use these to flatten the clay, only when you are doing a larger figure and want quite a smooth surface (a credit card does the same job as a hard kidney – an out-of-date one would probably be best!).
- **Callipers** – spend some money on your callipers, as they are a lifetime investment. Do not buy cheap floppy plastic ones that come undone at the first twitch. The best ones are aluminium, quite strong and do not have too much of a curve on the end, as this limits their use. Size-wise you need a large pair (around 50 cm/20 in.) for the model and a smaller pair (around 30 cm/12 in.) for your sculpture.
- **Proportional callipers** – these can be useful, as you can set your scale on them so that you do not need to keep calculating the difference, but need careful use as they can be very inaccurate if not properly used. I have so far found large proportional callipers (around 60 cm/24 in.) only in the USA, not in Britain.
- **Calculator** – this is used to calculate your dimensions when working to a scale.
- **Armature** – this is a subject all of its own, and will be covered in a lot more detail in Chapter 3.
- **Revolving modelling stand** – this is an important item. It is very hard to model anything, even little sketches, without being able to stand back and see your piece at eye level. You also need to be able to keep turning the sculpture so that you work on all parts of it together. This stand for your sculpture should be sturdy and robust and the feet should not be too close together, otherwise it is in constant danger of toppling over. Depending on your general use, you can get lighter-weight portable stands, or heavier, more robust ones that can take a lot more weight. If you cannot get a modelling stand, there are table stands or whirlers you can buy from art shops and pottery suppliers – you could even use a revolving cheese board. If using these, make sure that you get your sculpture up to eye level.

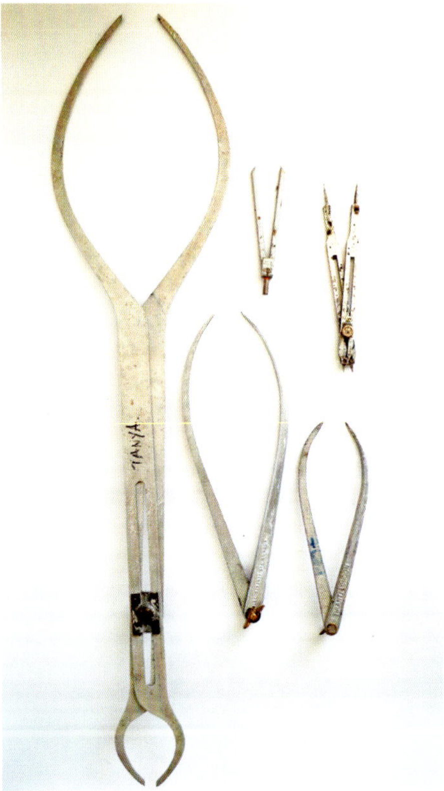

A range of callipers and dividers.

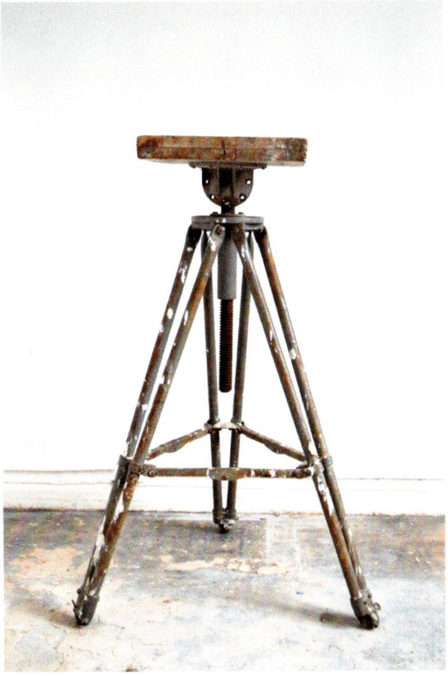

Revolving modelling stand for sculptures, heavyweight.

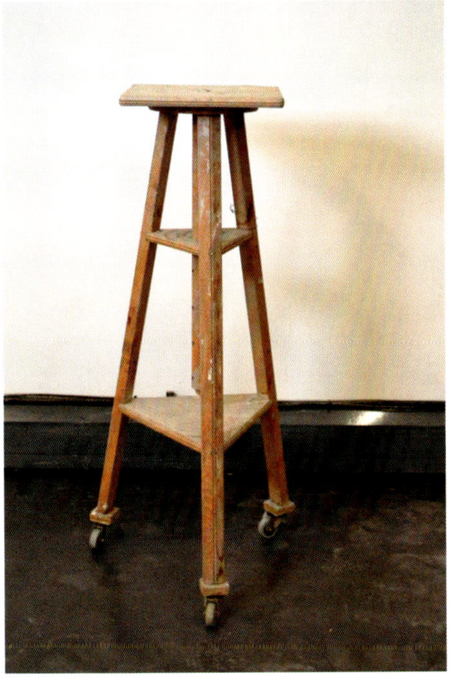

Revolving modelling stand for sculptures, lightweight (wheels have been added to the basic wooden stand to allow it to be moved around the studio).

- **Clamps** – use clamps to keep your piece secure when you are turning it round on the stand or in case someone accidentally bumps it. You need to use two clamps, one on each side, to ensure that it is secure.

- **Plastic bag** – a bin liner, light laundry plastic, or any light strong plastic for completely wrapping your sculpture, keeping it airtight and stopping it from drying out when you are not working on it.

- **Water spray** – for spraying the clay and keeping it wet. You can use a household spray bottle (the type used for ironing) or a professional spray bottle. The professional ones are obviously a better choice for larger works.

- **Model furniture** – the ideal is to have your model posing on a turntable, as then you can turn them without them having to come out of the pose. You can also use a revolving chair for portraits, but make sure that it is high enough for the model's head to be at your eye level. If you do not have a model turntable, you will have to be enterprising and either move yourself around the model or get the model to turn regularly, being careful to stay in pose.

- **Cloths/poles** – placing cloths or blankets on the surface where the model is standing or lying can make the model more comfortable. Make sure the model is warm enough if they are lightly clothed or naked. If their arm is raised, a pole can be useful, otherwise they will not be able to hold the pose for long.

- **Lighting** – daylight is by far the best where possible. If not, then good downlighting (not too focused) is best, so strip lights are preferable to spotlights, as the latter may produce strange shadows that distort your work. If your lighting is not good, you will find your modelling will change dramatically and you may be rather surprised when your piece is seen in a better light – not always in a good way!

- **Clay and wax-based material** – for a half life-size figure you will mainly be using clay, with some Plastiline possibly used for the hands, as fingers are so thin that the clay dries out too quickly to model them properly.

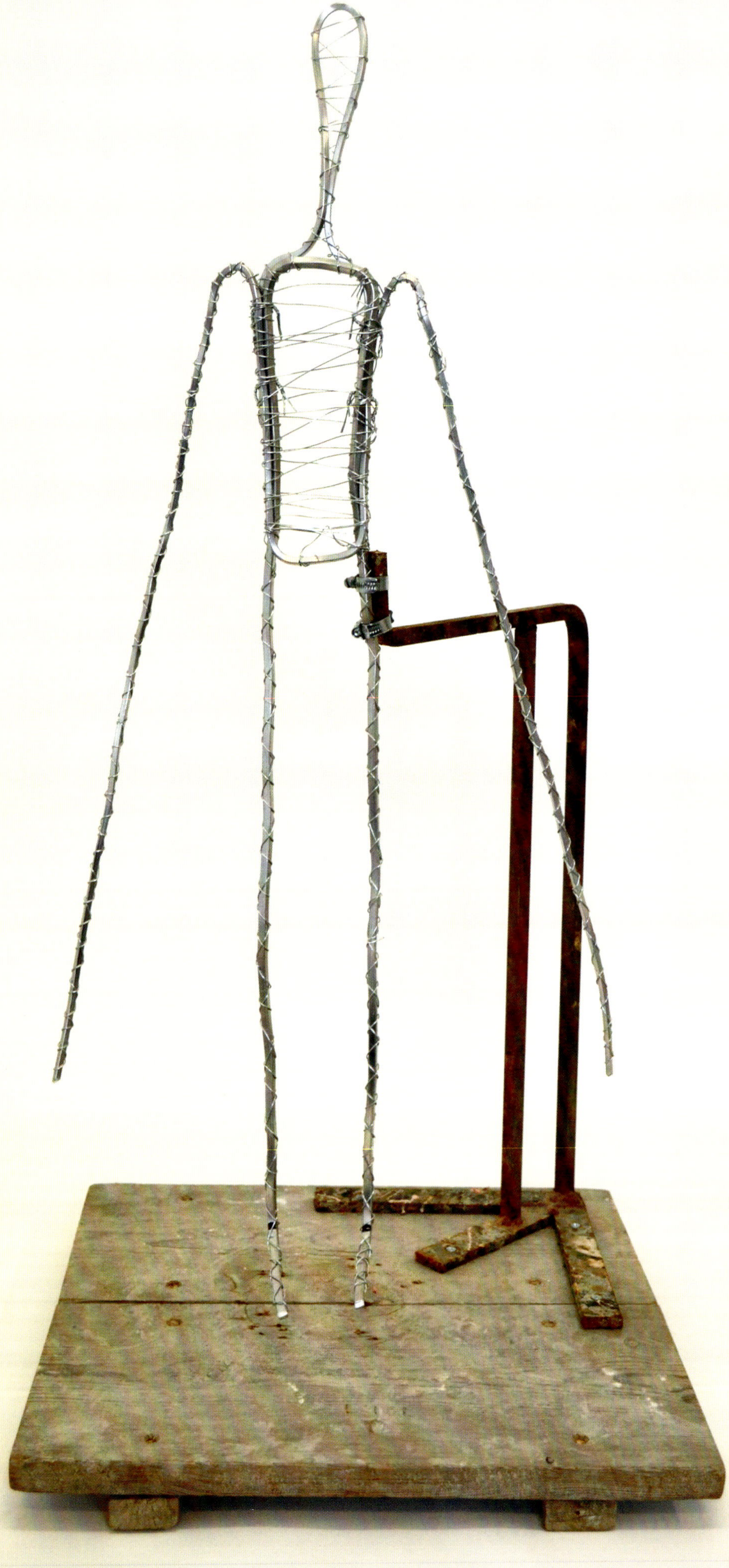

Half life-size armature.

3

ARMATURES

Using Armatures

Constructing a Standing Half Life-Size Armature

Making Hand Armatures

Making a Bust Peg for Modelling a Head

Using Armatures

An armature is an internal structure that supports a modelled sculpture, rather as our skeleton supports our body. Sometimes additional external supports are added, too, rather as a walking stick might be used to support a weak body. Like flesh, modelling materials provide very little structural support of their own, so many sculptures need to be built on armatures. Armatures are as variable as the sculptures we make, so in this chapter we go through the basic types, which you can adapt to your own needs.

Armatures are very important for sculptors – every armature is different and great care should be taken to get them right. When constructing an armature you are constantly balancing strength and flexibility. Unless you are sculpting at a very large scale you will want your armature to be strong enough to support your modelling, but flexible enough to bend or move as you sculpt. Most armatures up to three-quarter life-size should be constructed on a fixed steel figure iron, with flexible aluminum used for the limbs. Wooden armatures can be used, but these are not ideal as they are bulky and inflexible. They are far from ideal for a normal figure as limbs are very thin – wire is much more suitable. Wooden armatures could be used for something like a torso, where bulk is more important than flexibility. Armatures are also used for making maquettes (see p. 106–10).

When you progress to making a life-size figure armature, it is not always possible to make it flexible, as strength is paramount. At this advanced stage, you will be making armatures in steel, which will need welding and bending with a propane or oxy-acetylene torch. Unless you are fully qualified in the use of these tools you should seek professional help to construct an armature at life size.

Constructing a Standing Half Life-Size Armature

We are going to look first at how to make an armature for a standing half life-size figure, using aluminium wire.

MATERIALS

- Figure iron (this is an external metal support, which can either be purchased readymade at different sizes, or can be made if you have the required metalworking skills)
- Wooden board
- Screws
- Aluminium wire, medium (4.76 mm) and thick (6.35 mm). Ideally it should be square in section, but round can be used if that it all that can be obtained)
- Galvanised steel binding wire
- 16–25 mm jubilee clips. These work for most armatures, but adjust as necessary if your figure iron is of an unusual size.
- Copper wire for the hands, 20-gauge and 25-gauge (or fuse wire)

EQUIPMENT

- Electric drill
- Drill bits
- Vice or two pairs of mole grips
- Pliers
- Wire snips
- Large wire cutters
- Tape measure
- Calculator
- Dividers
- Callipers
- Sketchbook and pencil

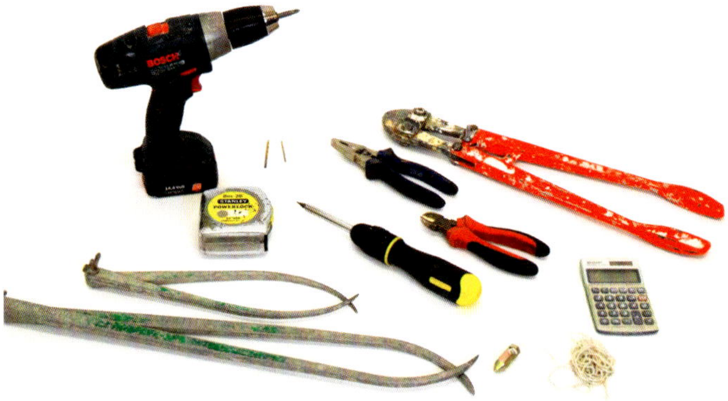

Tools needed to make a half life-size armature.

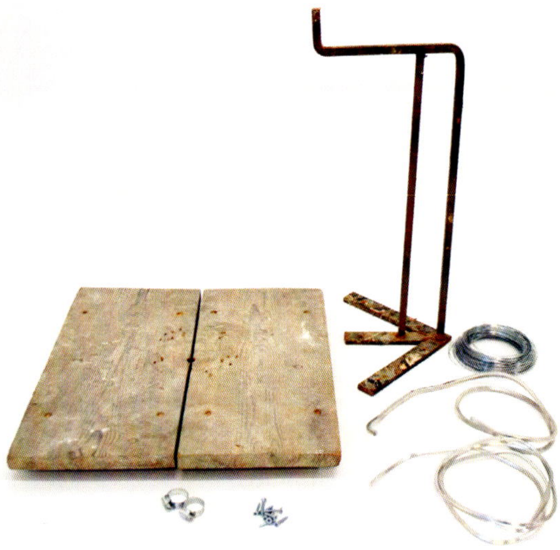

Materials needed to make a half life-size armature.

Preparation

Place your model in pose on a large enough board, card or piece of paper, on the turntable or on the floor, so that when you drop a plumb line down from any point on the figure it can be marked on this base (a plumb line is used to take vertical references and measurements from your model and sculpture, as shown in the photo on the opposite page). Draw around the model's feet and any other supports (e.g. the pole, shown opposite) to ensure the model can go back into exactly the same position each time they have a break.

A reference point is essential to ensure accuracy in your sculpting. Ensure that the model is facing a straight edge on the model turntable, card or board, and that when you fix your armature on the board it is facing a similar straight edge on its base. It is much easier to get the twists in the body correct when it is lined up with a straight edge. Keep to this all the way through. When doing any plumb lining, you can make sure that you are standing in the right place in relation to both straight edges.

Look at the model from all angles and absorb the flow of lines. See the central line and notice where the narrow points are. Spend a little bit of time drawing the model in the pose, so that you are familiar with the form.

It can be useful to do a quick drawing of the model and then draw the armature inside. This can give you a very good feel for what the armature should look like before you start.

Making the Structure

The next stage is to make the aluminium structure for the armature. This is suitable for any standing pose and can be bent into the shape of your particular pose once it is finished and fixed onto the figure iron. The figure iron will be fixed onto the wooden board and your armature will be attached to it once completed.

At this scale you can make your armature straight and put it into the pose once it is constructed. For larger-scale works you need to make parts of the armature out of welded steel for strength and construct the armature to match the pose.

The general principles of armature making are to maximise the armature's malleability while retaining sufficient strength to support the finished clay piece. This allows the sculptor to move the armature if necessary during the process.

Square-section aluminium normally comes in four thicknesses:

- Thin – 3.17 mm
- Medium – 4.76 mm
- Thick – 6.35 mm
- Extra thick – 9.53 mm

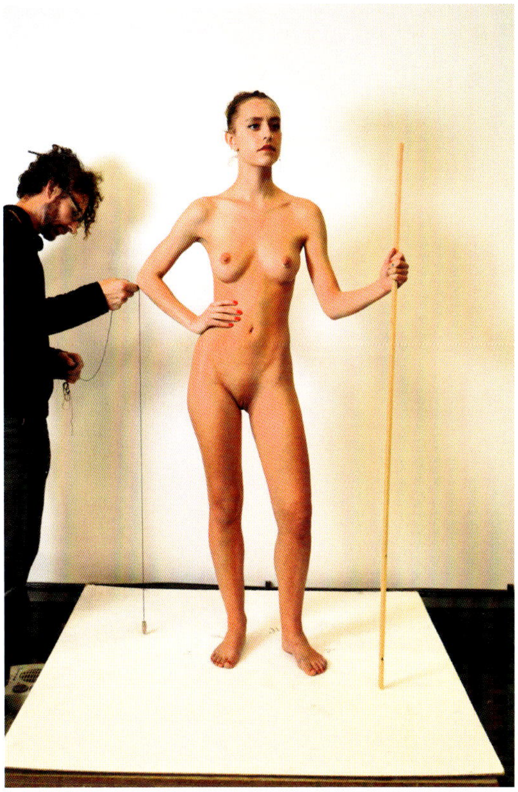

The model is set up on a turntable and white board.

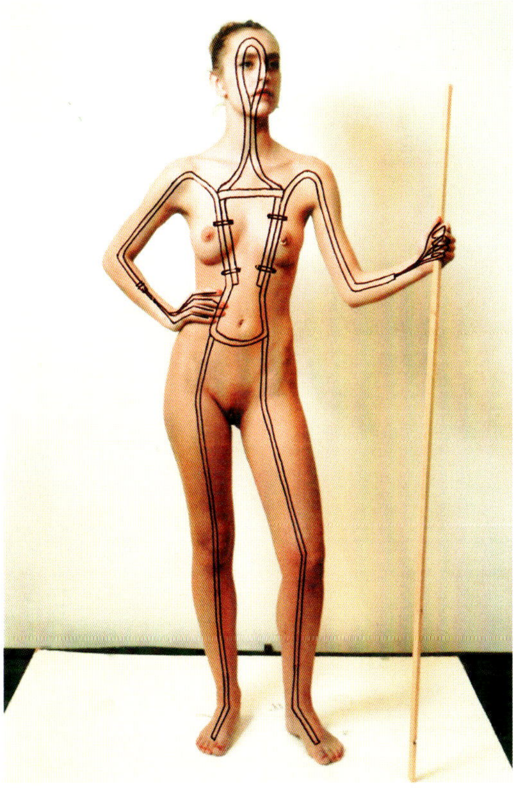

This shows the relationship between the armature and the pose.

For this armature we are only using two of these thicknesses. For the half life-size figure we use thick wire for the leg section, medium for the arms, and medium for the head (depending on the pose). If one of the arms is sticking out and not supported in your particular pose, you may need to use thick wire for the arms too, but it is best avoided if possible, as it can make the torso hard to manipulate.

The basic template for the figure armature, which I have used for many years at the Art Academy, starts with one section of aluminium wire going up the legs and across just below the shoulders. A second piece goes up the arm, down the torso, across the waist, then up the other side of the torso to the shoulder and down the other arm. The arms are not solely attached across the shoulders, to avoid both arms moving when you try to adjust just one of them. The head is then formed of a loop of wire that also attaches on the top of the torso. See the illustration below.

The armature wire needs to sit in the centre of the limbs of the sculpture and well within the mass of the torso – a common mistake amongst beginners is to make the width of their armature close to the width of the shoulders. In the image below right, you will see that the armature sits well inside the body.

Measurements

The following method explains the measurements you need to take from your model to ensure that your armature is correct in terms of size and proportion. It is a method developed by Briony Marshall for the measured figure class at the Art Academy.

Leg section

A. Floor to hip (vertical), hip being the head of the femur.
B. Hip to hip width.
C. Hip to about 7.6 cm (3 in.) below the shoulder (vertical). This doesn't correspond to an anatomical point as it is inside the ribcage and below the clavicle.
D. Width of torso 7.6 cm (3 in.) below the shoulders, with 5 cm (2 in.) removed on each side.
E. Additional wire is required for the bends at the hip, and an allowance at the end of each leg (20 cm/8 in., as shown in the table on p. 45).

Length of thick wire needed for leg section = (A x 2) + (C x 2) + D + E. Note: B is a measurement used when bending the armature into shape, not for determining the length of wire required.

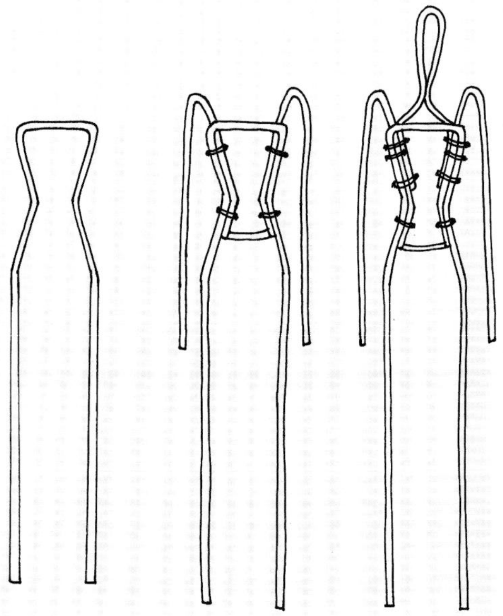

Sections of the armature.

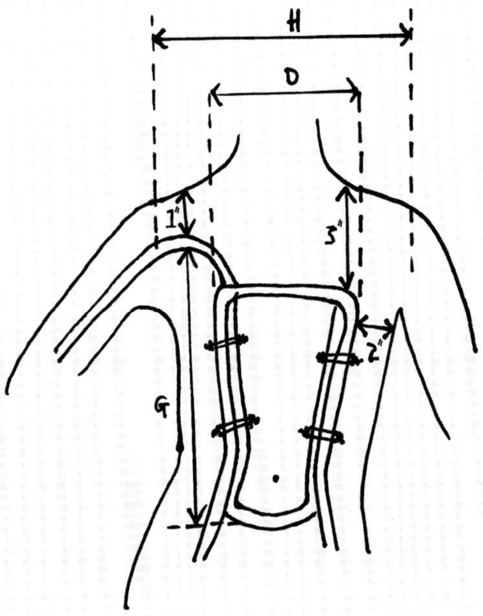

Measurements to be taken for the top half of the armature.

Arm section

F. Tip of middle finger to shoulder (approx. the head of the humerus).
G. Vertical height from 2.5 cm (1 in.) below shoulder to 5 cm (2 in.) above bottom of rib cage approximately.
H. Shoulder to shoulder distance (again, the head of the humerus).
I. Additional wire for errors on the arm length (10 cm/4 in., as shown in table below).

Length of medium wire needed for arm section = (F x 2) + (G x 2) + D + I. Note: H is not used to calculate the length of wire – it is just used to determine the point at which to bend the armature for the shoulders. The width of the cross bar at the base of the rib cage will be slightly less than D.

Head section

J. Distance from top of head to navel.
K. Distance from 5 cm (2 in.) below top of head to 7.6 cm (3 in.) below shoulder.

Length of medium wire needed for head section = J x 2. Note: K is just used in order to determine at what point to join the head to the leg and chest section.

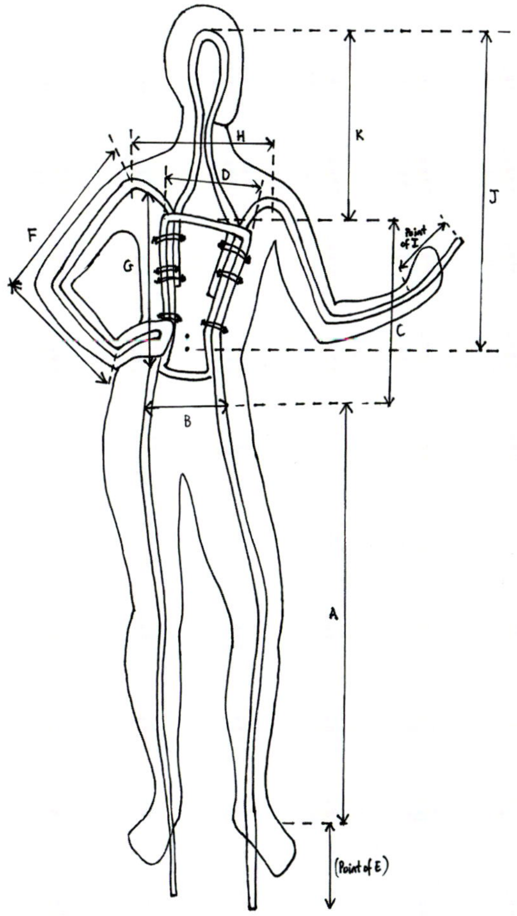

Measurements to be taken for the whole armature.

Table for recording your measurements

divide by 2

	Description	Life-Size (On Model)	Half Life-Size (On Clay)
A	Floor to hip		
B	Hip to hip		
C	Hip to 7.6 cm (3 in.) below shoulder		
D	Width of top of armature		
E	Extra		20 cm (8 in.)
	Leg wire: (A x 2) + (C x 2) + D + E =		
F	Tip of finger to shoulder		
G	Height of armature 'ribcage'		
H	Shoulder to shoulder		
I	Extra		10 cm (4 in.)
	Arm wire: (F x 2) + (G x 2) + D + I =		
J	Top of head to navel		
K	Height of armature head		
	Head wire: J x 2 =		

Construction Tips

I suggest you cut your lengths of wire to the correct length, then work from the centre of each piece, measuring and bending as you go. You can use marker pen on the aluminium wire to mark where the bends need to be. Use the vice or two pairs of mole grips for nice clean bends. Remember to hold the wire a bit back from where you want the bend to be.

Attach the wires together with butterfly ties – these can be made of galvanised steel wire or copper wire (see opposite page). Add two butterfly ties to each side of the torso and more if necessary. Double wrap the whole armature with galvanised binding wire, as shown on p. 48. This helps the clay grip to the wire.

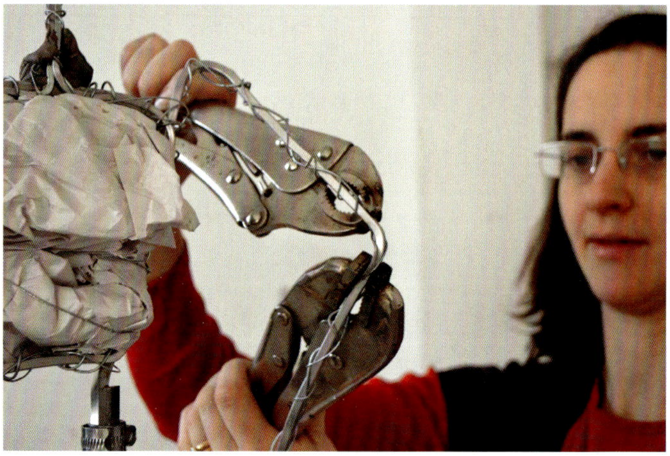

Mole grips are useful for getting an accurate bend.

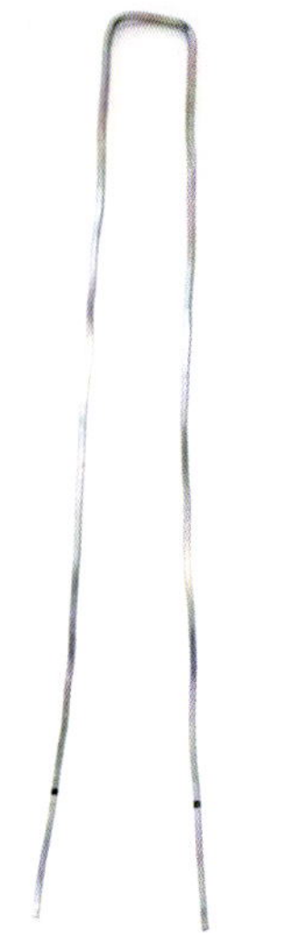

Armature section – torso and legs.

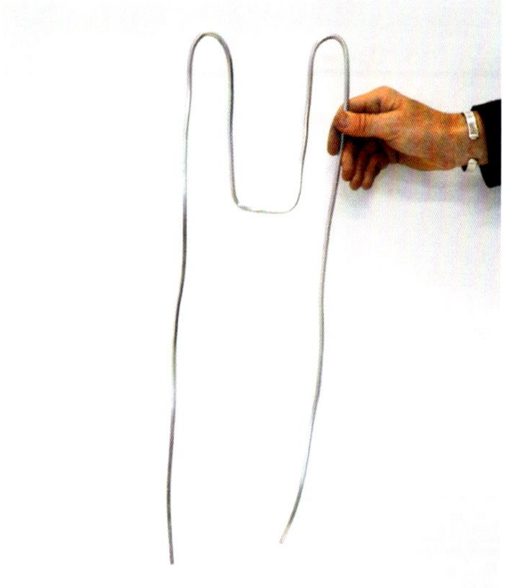

Torso – shoulders and arms.

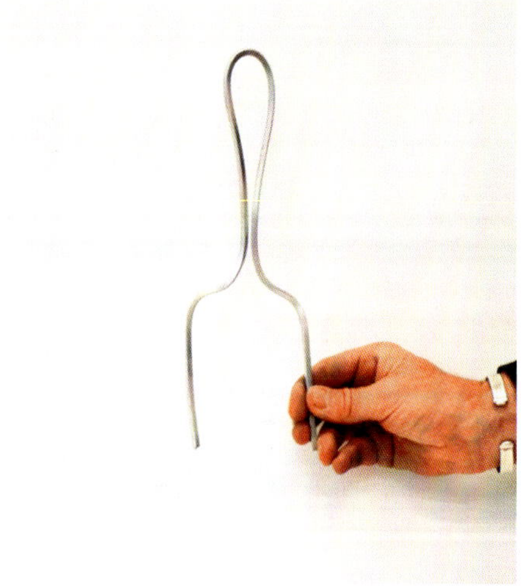

Neck, head and some extra torso for attachment.

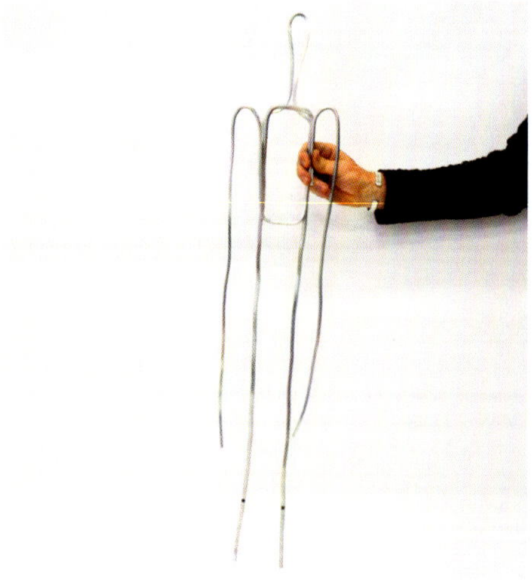

All three pieces of armature are ready to be tied.

Making Butterfly Ties

Follow the steps below to bend and twist the wire correctly.

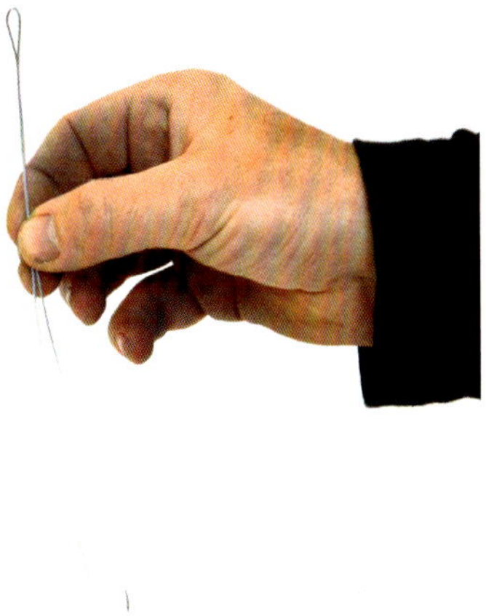

Step 1 Bend the wire in half.

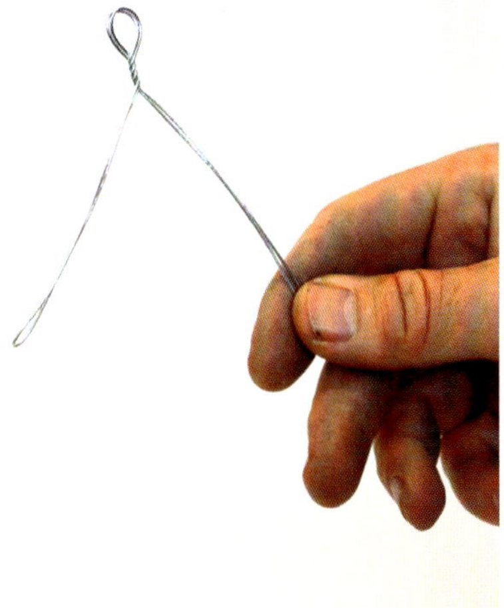

Step 2 Bend the wire in half again and twist the end with pliers.

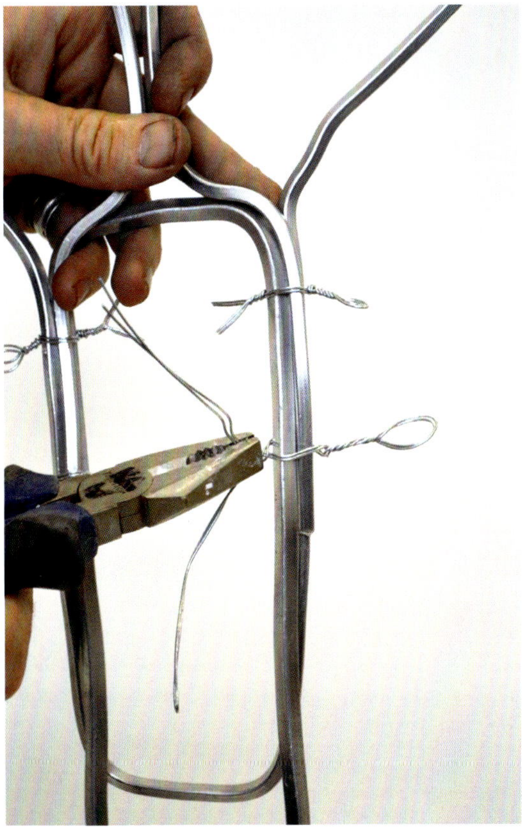

Step 3 Twist the butterfly tie on both sides around the armature wire until the tie is very tight.

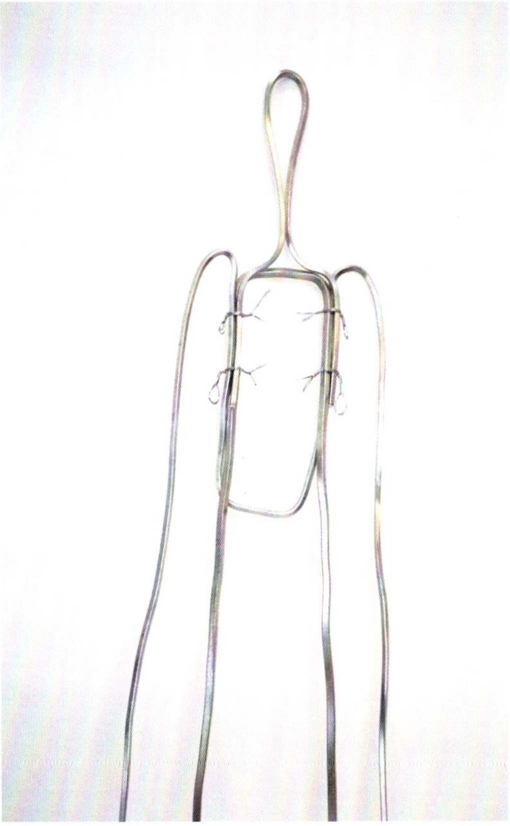

The torso section of the armature is fully tied.

Next, fix the figure iron onto your board, in such a position that you are sure the feet of your sculpture will fit fairly centrally on the board.

Attach the armature to the figure iron, so that the figure iron exits the body at the level of the hip and at an angle of around 45 degrees in relation to the orientation of the figure. This is to ensure that it exits at a position that will not have much surface detail (in the flesh of the buttock as opposed to the cleft). This leaves the whole front and back of the figure free for modelling. Do not attach it at a lower point than this otherwise there will be too much unsupported weight above the figure iron. Use two jubilee clips to attach.

Measure the height of the waist on the model from the ground and the top of the head, adjust for scale (in this case, divide by two) and squeeze in the armature at that point to get the narrowness in the waist.

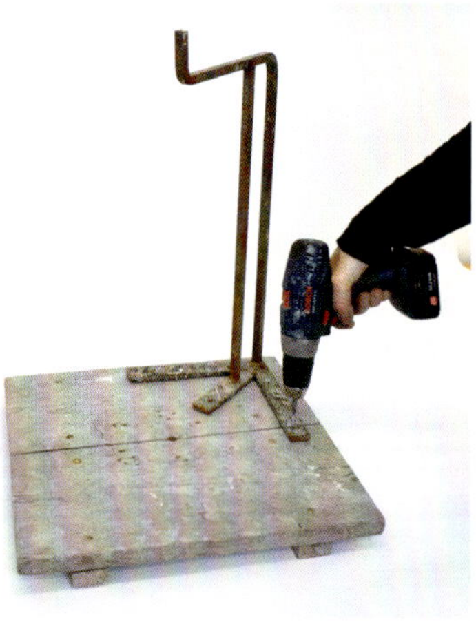

Screw the figure iron onto the board.

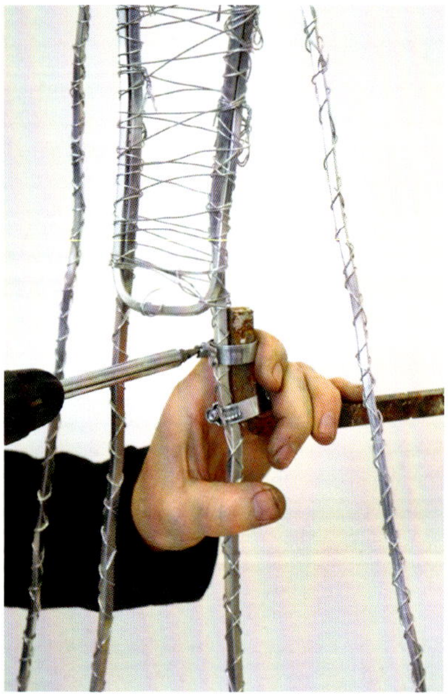

Using two jubilee clips, attach the armature in the correct position onto the figure iron.

Using a Clay Base

If you will be using a clay base under the figure, the height at which the armature sits off the ground is not as important as fixing it in the right place in relation to the figure iron. Your clay base can be anything from 2 to 15 cm (¾–6 in.). The base is helpful in anchoring the feet and in allowing some adjustment to the length if needed at a later stage. You must ensure that this base is flat and level otherwise it can throw out the accuracy of your measuring. The height of the base can be adjusted again during the casting process as you wish.

It is also very important to ensure that the front of the armature, and therefore the figure, is directly facing the front edge of your clay base. This equates to the front edge of the stand on which your model is posing and which, as explained on pp. 42–3, allows you to ensure that you are standing at the correct angle in relation to both the model and the sculpture. If the pose involves the body being turned to one side, the front of the base can be aligned at 90 degrees to the weight-bearing foot.

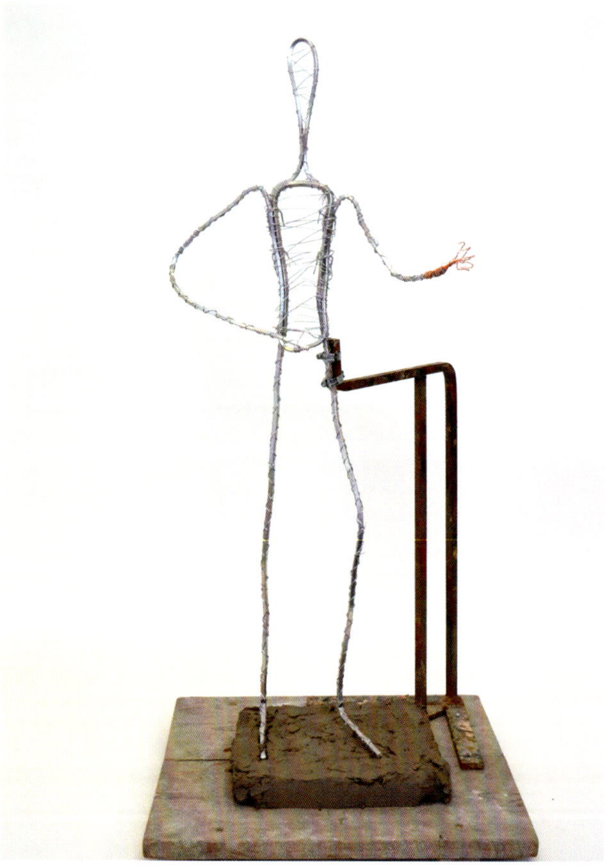

Build a flat clay base to the required height for the armature and the figure iron, orientated correctly to the front.

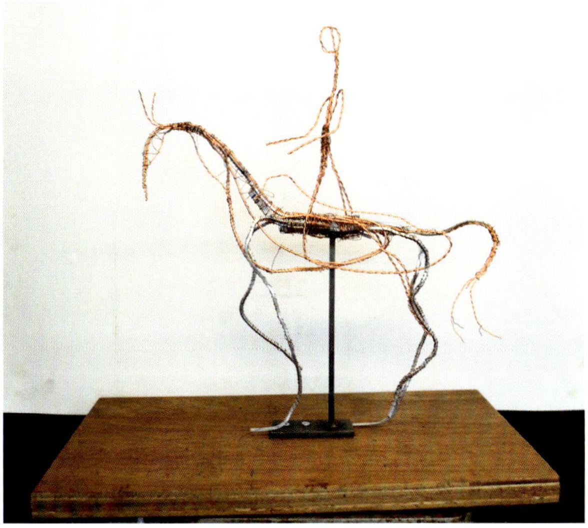

Armature made with steel figure iron, aluminium and copper wire for sculpture of European Dressage Champion Carl Hester performing 'Piaffe' on the stallion Utopia, by Lorne McKean.

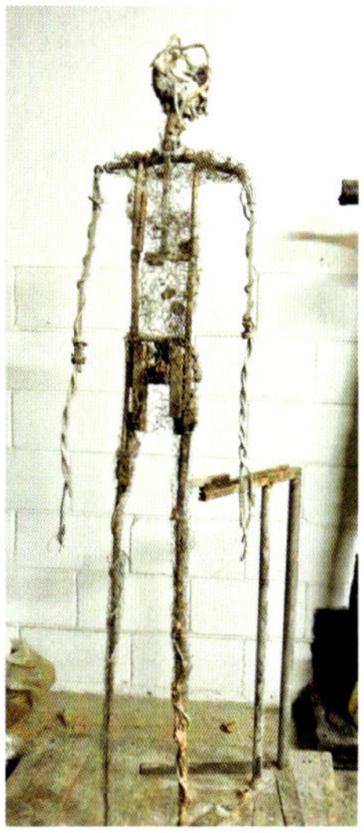

Life-size armature from welded steel, aluminium and chicken wire, by John O'Connor.

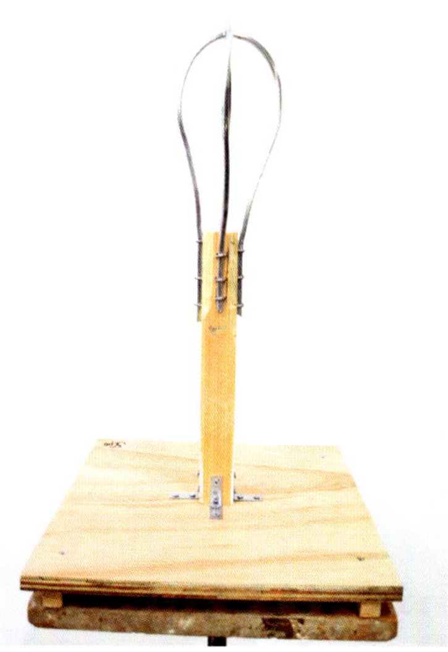

An example of a bust peg.

Making a Bust Peg for Modelling a Head

The type of armature you use for a portrait head that is built separately from the figure is called a bust peg. A bust peg is easily constructed with a piece of reasonably thick board, brackets and screws, a length of 5 x 5 cm (2 x 2 in.) wood, some aluminum wire and staples. There are many ways of doing it, but the simplest version is shown here.

1. Cut a board around 2 cm (¾ in.) thick and 45 cm (17¾ in.) square. Use wood that does not warp or bend.
2. Cut a piece of 5 x 5 cm (2 x 2 in.) wood and attach vertically to the centre of the board using four brackets.
3. Cut two 75 cm (29½ in.) lengths of medium thickness square aluminum wire and staple to the sides of the vertical post as shown in the photo above. The bust peg is now ready to use.

If you are intending to hollow and fire the head, you can either wedge crumpled newspaper inside the aluminum circle of the bust peg in order to make the head easier to slide off, or you can dispense with the aluminum altogether and firmly tape a small lump of newspaper to the top of the post. This will hold the clay relatively well and makes it much easier to slide the head off the post, but you will often need to support the portrait from underneath with clay, in order to stop it sliding down the peg while you are modelling.

Making Hand Armatures

It is useful to make separate hands to attach to your armature so that you have a wire support for each finger. In the pose we have used in this chapter (see p. 43), I have used only one hand armature – the hand resting on her hip does not need separate support as it is supported by the main structure, but the hand holding the stick needs wire in the fingers in order to hold its shape.

Making a hand armature is very simple. Start by cutting five lengths of 20-gauge copper wire long enough not only for the fingers, but also for each length to come at least halfway up the forearm (you want to tie the wires to the arm in the fleshy part of the arm, not in the wrist). Tie the five pieces of wire together below the hand with 25-gauge copper wire or fuse wire. Wrap each finger with the thin wire (this will help to hold the modelling material when you apply it), then attach all the tied wires firmly to the arm, wrapping more wire around like a bandage. Cut the fingers to the required length later on, when you have progressed further with the modelling.

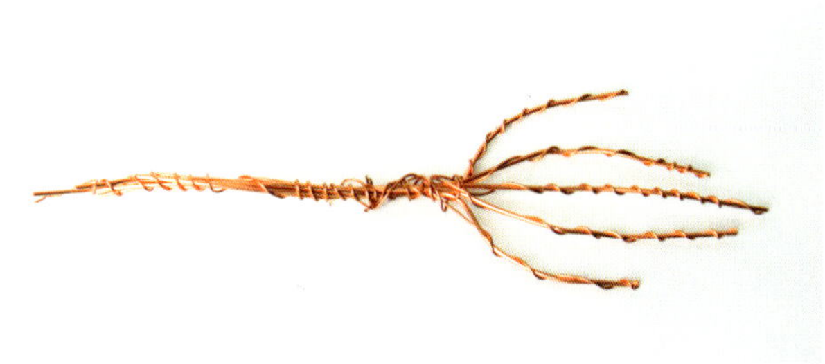

A hand armature made from wire.

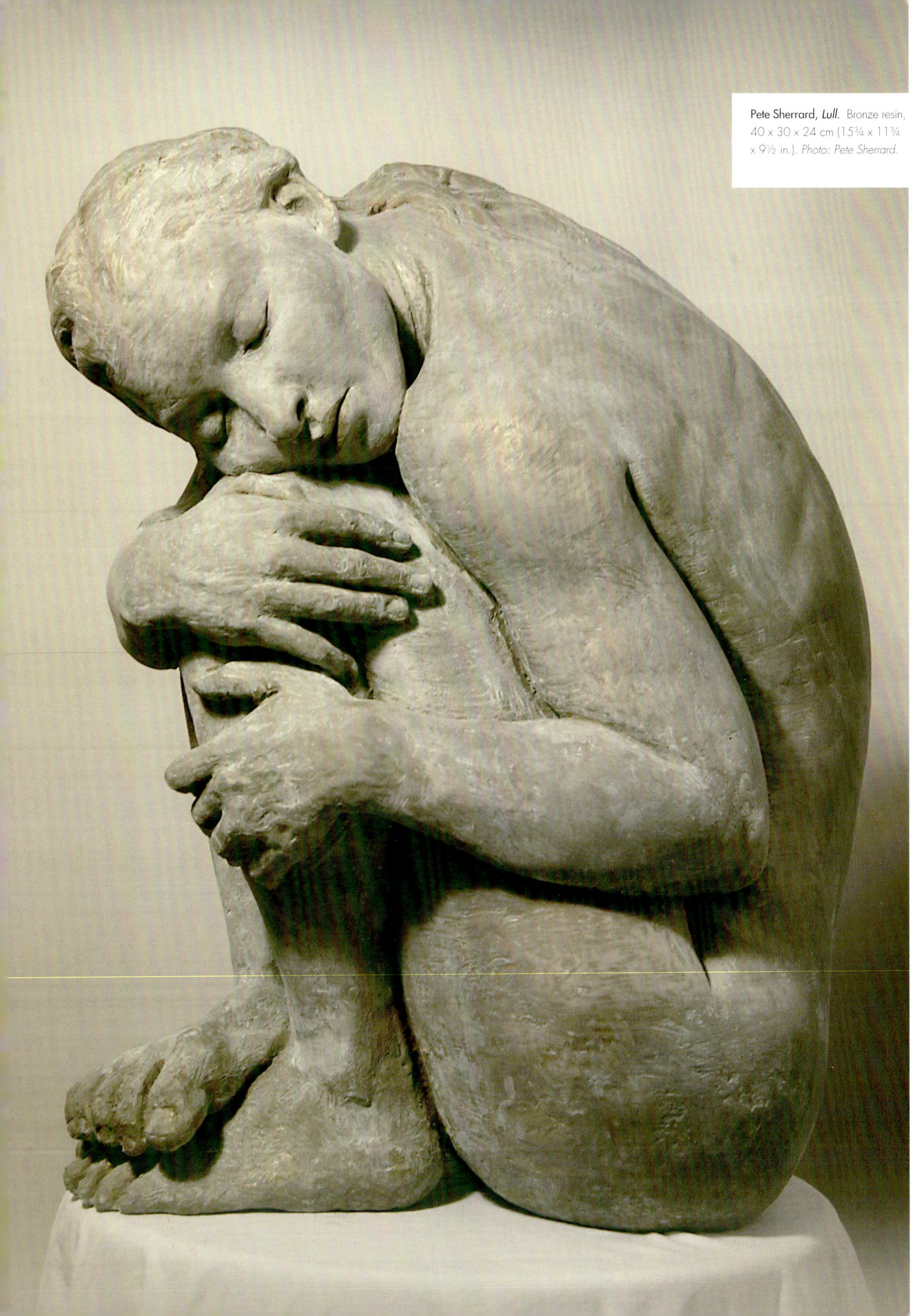

Pete Sherrard, *Lull*. Bronze resin, 40 x 30 x 24 cm (15¾ x 11¾ x 9½ in.). *Photo: Pete Sherrard.*

4

THE REALISTIC FIGURE

Purpose, Size and Choosing the Pose

This chapter is about studying techniques, learning fluency in your sculptural language, and expanding your skills.

Purpose

The realistic figure in the context of this chapter is very much a figure study, the aim being to look at the process of modelling a figure rather than producing a sculpture for sale or exhibition. This is the equivalent of learning the grammar and vocabulary that allow you to express yourself. The human form is so beautiful in its own right that studies can ultimately be very satisfying to the artist and the viewer.

Normally when starting a sculpture your first considerations would relate to your intention: what you have seen or experienced that you want to convey to your audience. These aspects are less important in a figure study, but you should still feel inspired by the process of studying and learning about the form.

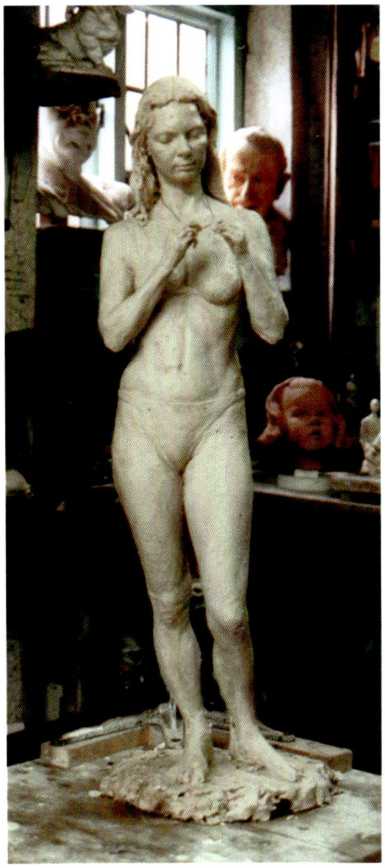

Tanya Russsell, *Rebecca.* Plastiline study at half life-size, 65 x 25 cm (25½ x 10 in.). *Photo: courtesy of the artist.*

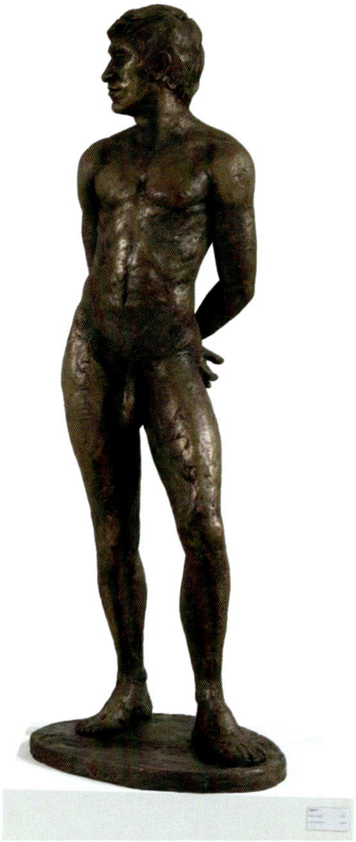

Hiromi Scintu, *Valerio.* Cold cast bronze at life-size, 162 x 50 cm (63¾ x 19½ in.). *Photo: Wah Poon.*

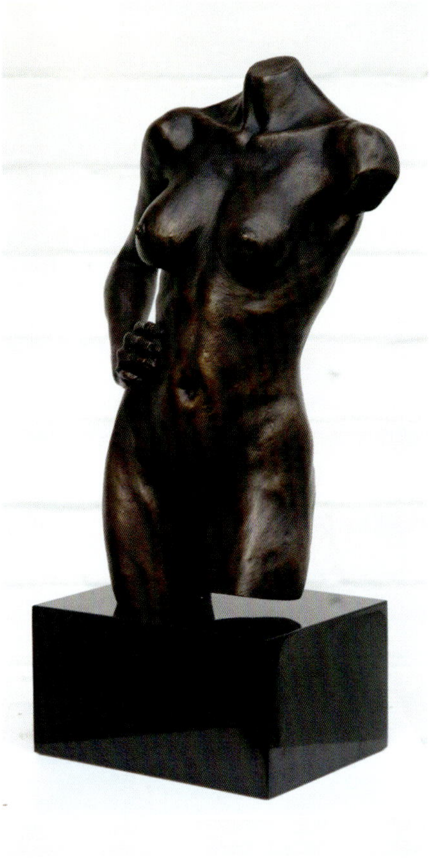

Gary Scott, *Confidence.* Cold cast bronze, 26 x 7½ cm (10¼ x 3 in.). *Photo: courtesy of the artist.*

Size

Half life-size is a good scale at which to start learning figure modelling. Measurement is made easier by working to a simple scale – in this case it is a matter of dividing all the measurements you take from the model by two.

One-third life-size figures can be rather fiddly and it is hard to block out the big shapes at this scale, but for commercial purposes this size can be quite saleable, being suitable for domestic settings. Three-quarter life is a very nice size to do, perhaps for your second or third life study.

Life-size is best to try when you are quite confident of the shapes, anatomy and proportions of the figure, having done a few smaller ones. A life-size figure uses a lot of clay, the armature requires some proper welding, and a lot of issues arise just because of the weight and volume of clay you are trying to manipulate.

Choosing the Pose

Choose a pose that is interesting to you and shows as many parts of the body as possible. Ideally this would be standing, with the arms or legs not crossed. A bit of contra-posture (as in the images on the opposite page – hips and shoulders at opposite angles, so you get a lovely shape up the spine) is quite good during the learning process, as it helps you to study the structure of the body and how it moves.

The Modelling Process

We are now going to look at a few different areas that you need to consider throughout the modelling process. We will cover one section at a time and then look at how to put them all together to create your sculpture. Some knowledge of anatomical terms is needed to start the measuring process, so have your anatomy book to hand (see my recommended books on p. 126).

Proportion and Measurement

Always remember that your eye is the key tool for judging measurement and proportion. Using a ruler or callipers is purely a check for your eye, to train and tune it, or to help your eye get to the root of an issue that is proving difficult. However, taking measurements at regular intervals is important, especially when you are less experienced, as it can help you notice the development of an error in the modelling proportions early on, and therefore save you huge amounts of time. If you step back and look properly at your work at regular intervals, you are much more likely to see where and when measurements are really needed.

As with armature making (see pp. 44–3), taking measurements from your model is key to getting the proportions right in your piece and to ensuring that the whole sculpture hangs together in a realistic way. There are two types of measurement: calculation measurements and proportional measurements. Both are very useful.

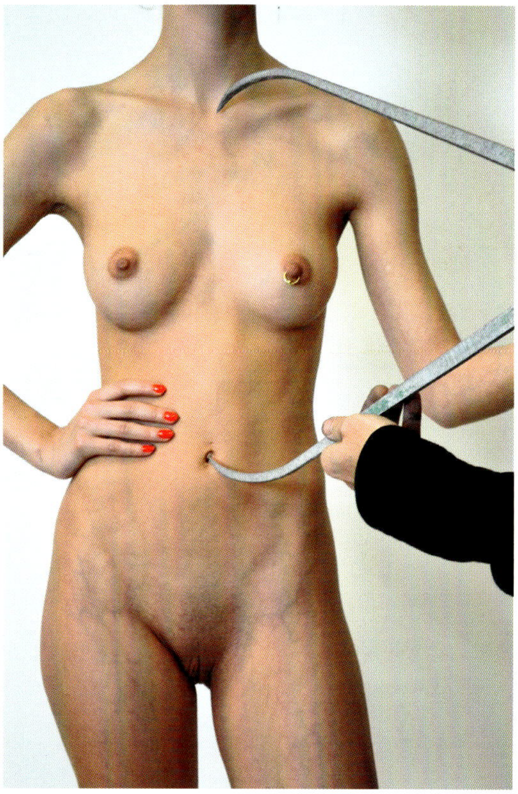

Measuring the model from sternum notch to navel.

Calculation Measurements – Creating a Scale

Before building the armature, we have already established that we are doing a sculpture that is half the size of the model, so any measurement on the model will need to be divided by two in order to get the equivalent measurement for the sculpture.

Tips for Measuring

- When measuring heights, make sure that you are at eye level with the measuring point.
- You can place a ruler or straight edge on a spirit level to ensure accurate measurements.
- Take measurements in metric units, as it is less complicated than feet and inches. As the carpenter's saying goes, 'measure twice and cut once' – be very alert to errors in your measuring.
- Be accurate. A few millimetres here or there can be a large amount when scaled up or down and can make all the difference to something looking right or not.

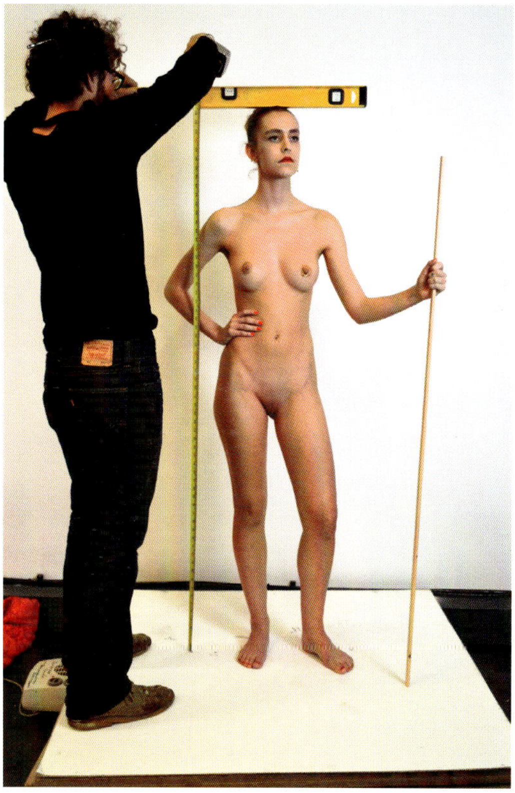

Place a spirit level on the model's head to get an accurate height measurement.

- When measuring from the ground, invert the callipers so that the point is touching the ground.

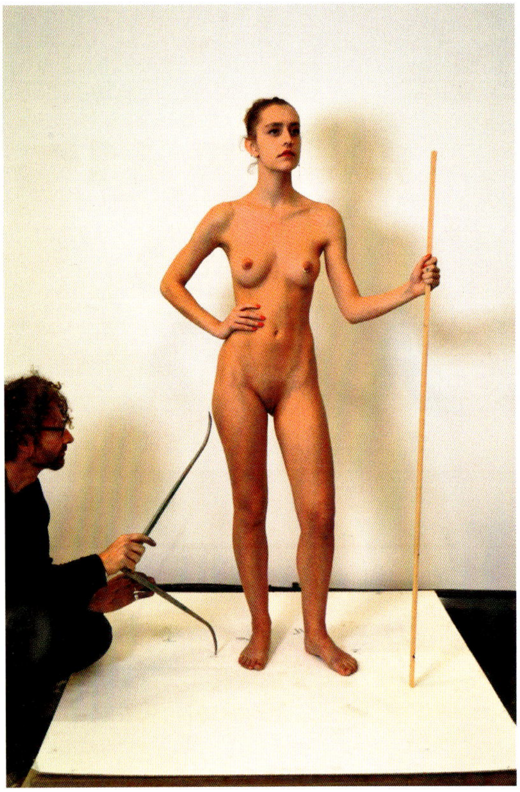

Invert the callipers to get an accurate reading when measuring from the ground (in this case, ground to hipbone).

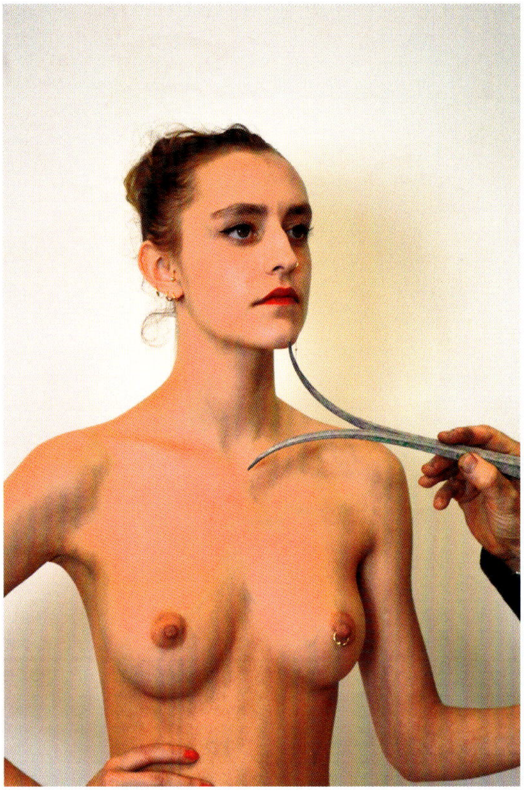

Measuring sternum notch to chin.

- Use the measurements not only for modelling your sculpture, but also to check that the model returns to the original pose after a break.
- Go back and re-measure on the model from time to time. The very process of measuring will help you notice other features as your sculpture progresses.
- A bony protrusion is the best point from which to take measurements, as it is easily pinpointed and is the least changeable.
- It can be useful to put matchsticks or cocktail sticks in your sculpture to denote points that you have measured, so as to not to lose them.

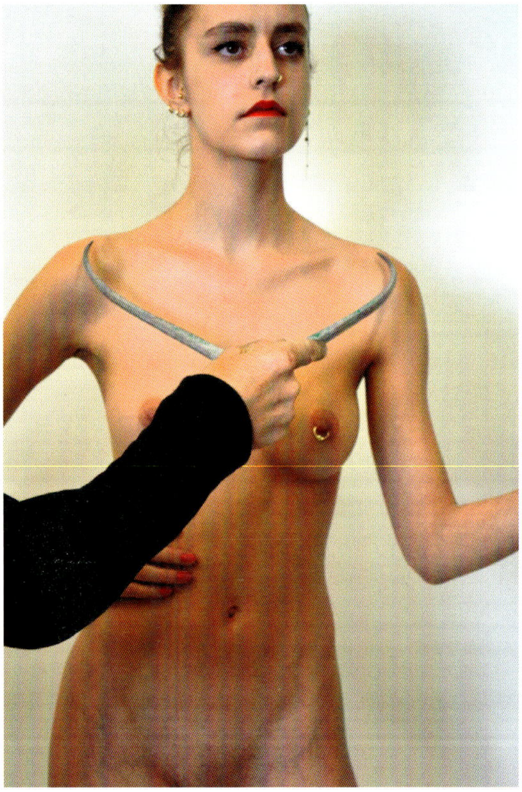

Measuring shoulder bone to shoulder bone.

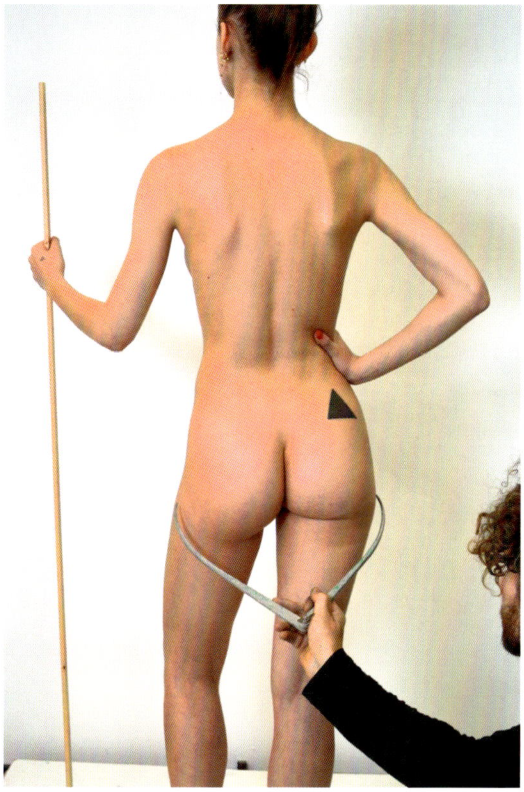

Some width measurements are easier to take from the back, in this case hipbone to hipbone.

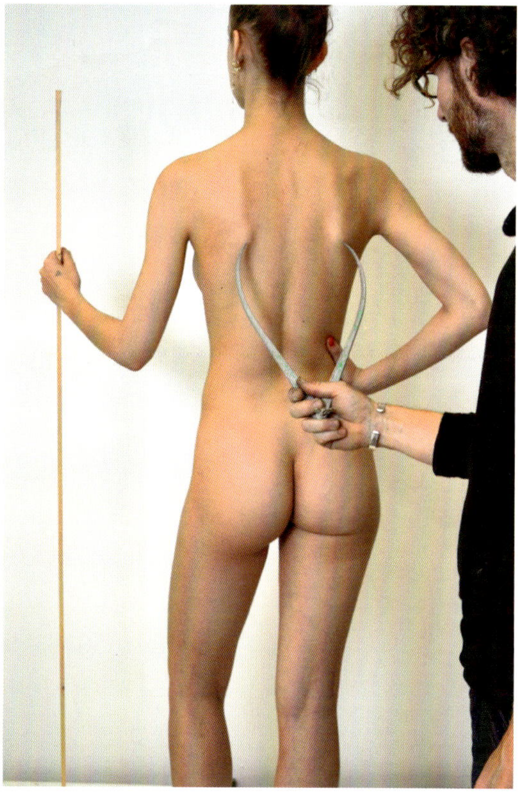

Measuring shoulder blade to shoulder blade.

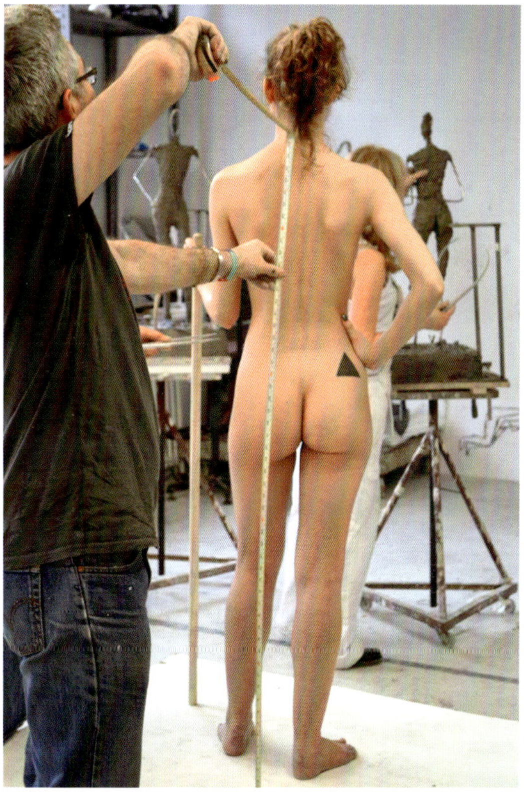

Measuring from the ground to the seventh vertebra.

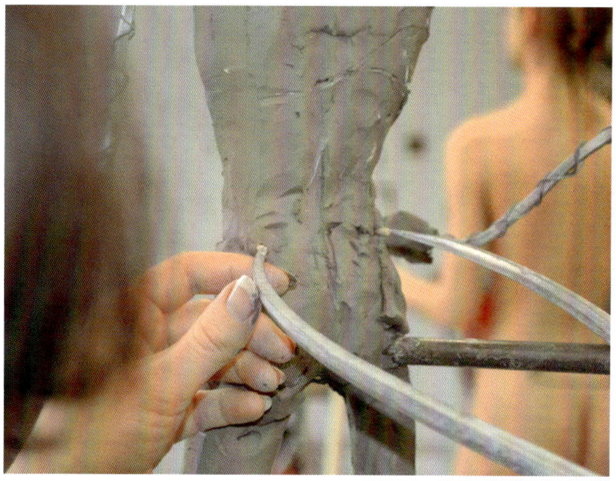

Matchsticks can be placed at points on the sculpture to help with the measurement process.

Table of useful measurements

There are many useful measurements you can take to keep your sculpture on track, but the chart opposite lists the ones most commonly used – you will discover many more for yourself.

Proportional Measurements

Proportional measurement involves measuring parts of the body in relation to other parts. It is very good for making sure that the sculpture is working together as a whole.

It is important to use both types of measuring. Proportional measurements are more intuitive than the calculation type; you identify more useful points and attune your eye to detailed forms on the figure while you are actually taking the measurements.

An example of a proportional measurement would be the number of times the head of the model (measured from the hairline to the centre of the chin) could be divided into the length of the body (measured from the sternum notch to the ground). The average person is seven-and-a-half heads tall, including the head. By taking note of the points reached by the lower end of each measurement, going down the body in relation to anatomical points (e.g. sternum, navel, crotch, knee) or prominent features (e.g. a shadow, skin fold, change of texture), you can check the accuracy of these points in relation to each other.

Another example would be to take the width of the waist (find the narrowest point) and then see how many times it can be divided into the length of the figure from sternum notch to the ground.

Children and adults have different proportions and there is plenty of information on this topic in drawing books, anatomy books and on the internet, so you can study this if you are interested, but the most important thing is to take real measurements, as this will inform both your eye and your sculpture.

Point of Measurement	Measurement on Model	Measurement Divided by 2 for Your Sculpture
Vertical Front Measurements		
Ground to top of head (highest point)		
Ground to sternum notch		
Ground to navel		
Ground to crotch		
Ground to knee		
Ground to left elbow		
Chin to sternum notch		
Sternum notch to crotch		
Width Measurements		
Width across shoulder bones		
Widest point of rib cage		
Pelvic bones		
Hip bones		
Centre of knees		
Vertical Back Measurements		
Ground to seventh vertebra		

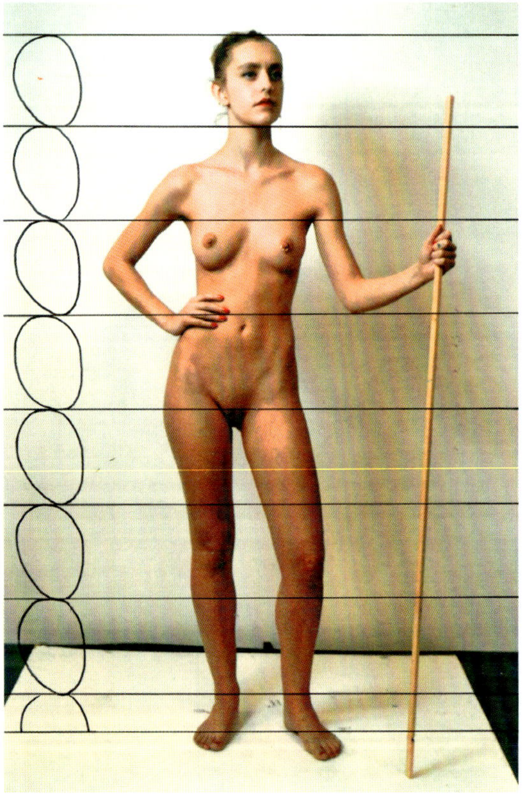

Diagram of proportional measurements.

Anatomy

Anatomy in its own right and for its own sake is a beautiful and amazing subject, but for most sculptors using the figure, it is just part of the essential building blocks that form the full meaning of their work. Some people get rather carried away with anatomy, but be aware that trying to make the anatomy perfectly realistic can take over from the character and the expression of the piece.

It is sometimes thought to be old-fashioned or 'traditional' to consider anatomy important, but it would seem odd to me to use a form to express something if you have no understanding of the form itself. Your aim should be to learn anatomy so well that you forget about it. Just as you are not thinking specifically of your words when speaking a sentence, but still using some part of your mind to make conscious choices about the words you use, so anatomy should not be foremost in your mind when you are sculpting, even as every mark you make is partly informed by it.

When using your model or anatomy studies as a reference, you must remember that it is only a reference. You are never going to put in every vein, pore and sinew. What you put in and what you choose to leave out is the key. You are an artist, not a photocopier.

Anatomy for artists is such a big subject that many books have been and will be written about it. My three recommended titles are given in the Further Reading list on p. 126. Other useful tools for understanding anatomy can be purchased, such as skeletons, and flayed heads or figures.

☛ EXERCISE 1

As the first exercise, I suggest that you do separate studies, drawing from anatomy books and from the model. Look at the book and the model and make sure you really understand where everything joins, what the form of each muscle is and, most importantly, what the high points and the planes of the muscle are. When you think you have got it, draw it all from memory. When you come to sculpt, you should not have to think about it or be distracted by it.

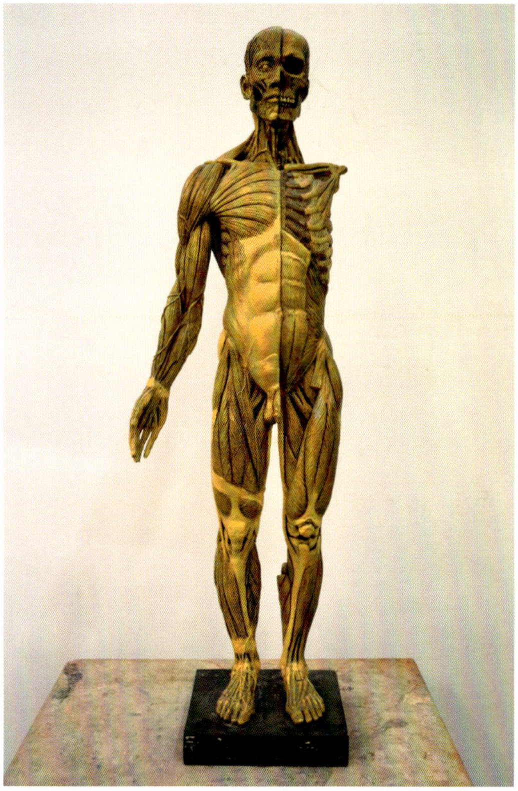

A flayed figure.

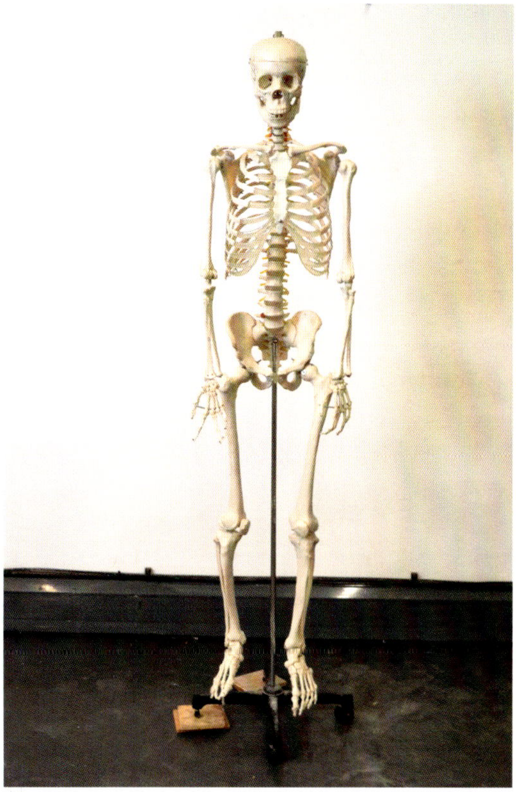

A skeleton.

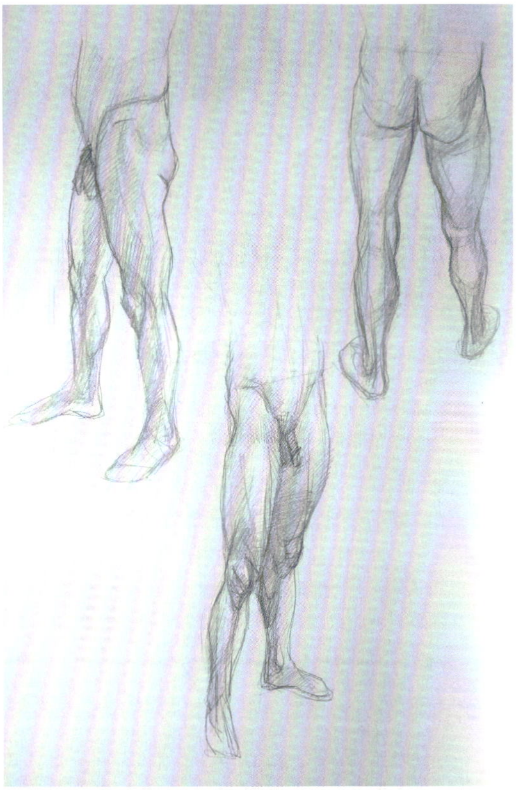

Leg studies by Eigil Nordstrøm. *Courtesy of the artist.*

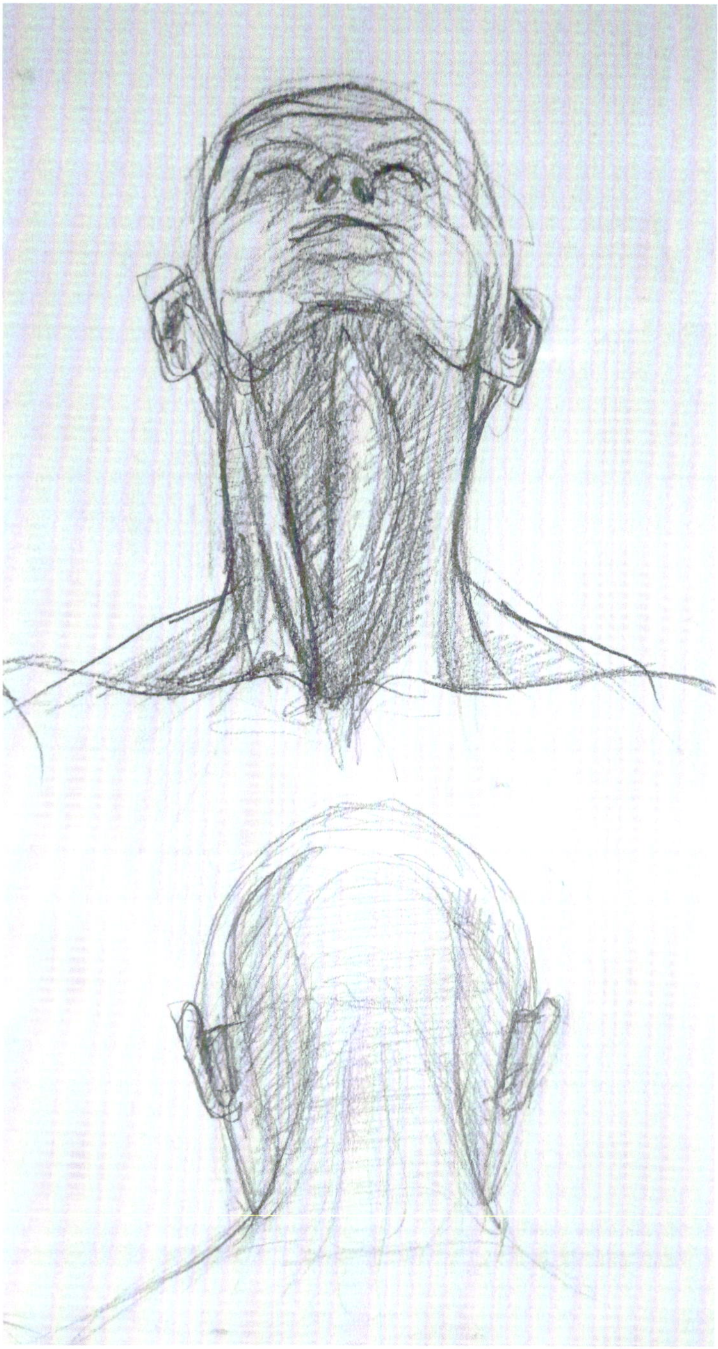

Neck and head studies by Eigil Nordstrøm. *Courtesy of the artist.*

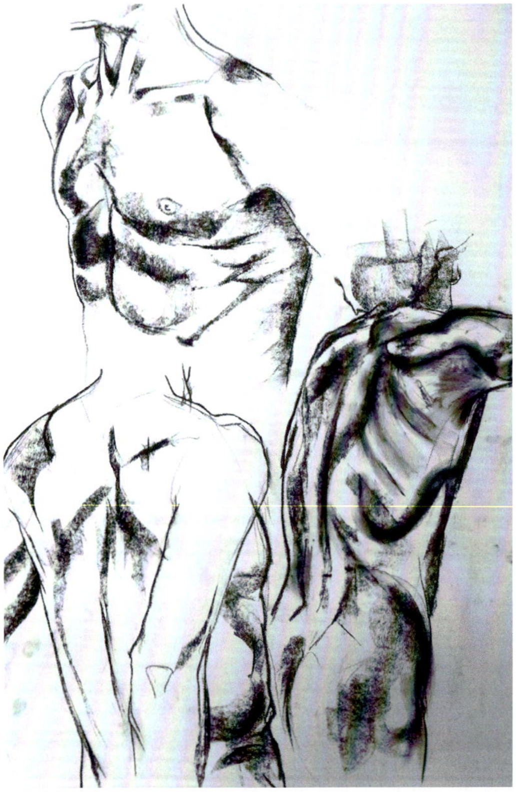

Torso studies by Melodie Cook. *Courtesy of the artist.*

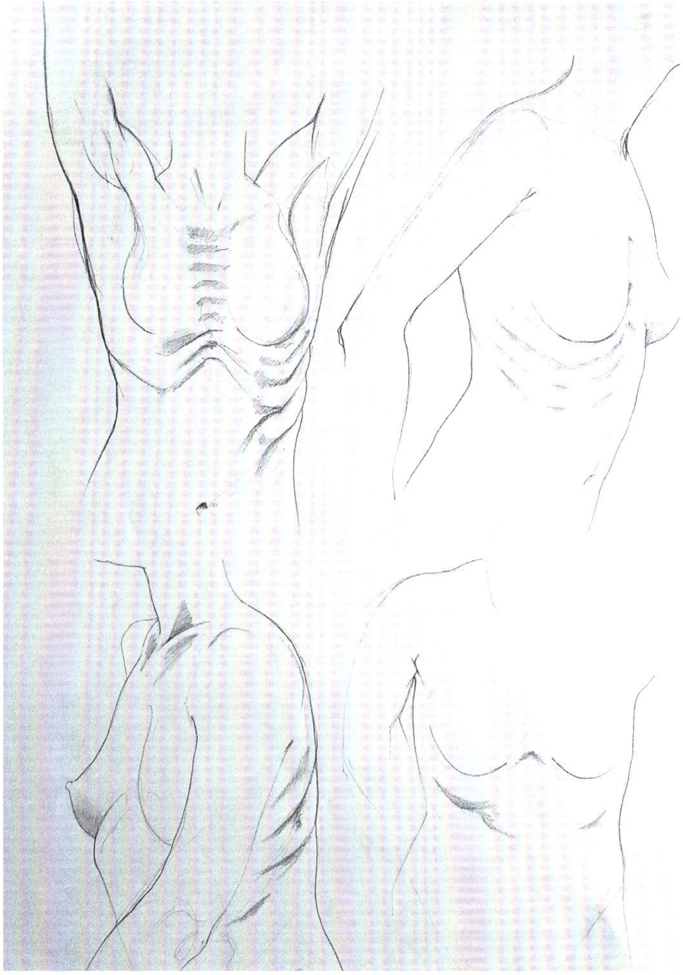

Female torso studies by Melodie Cook. *Courtesy of the artist.*

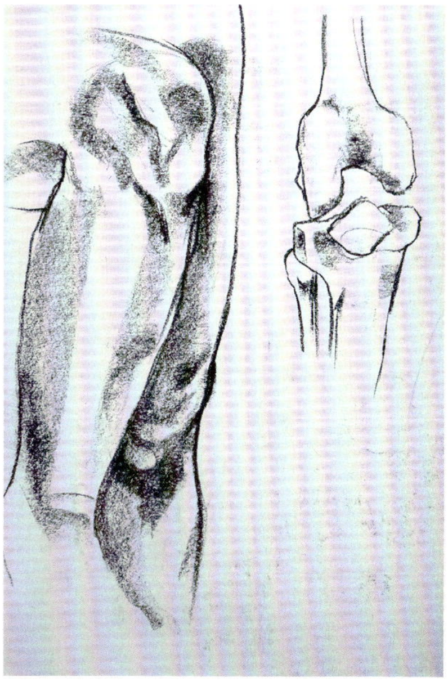

Knee studies by Melodie Cook. *Courtesy of the artist.*

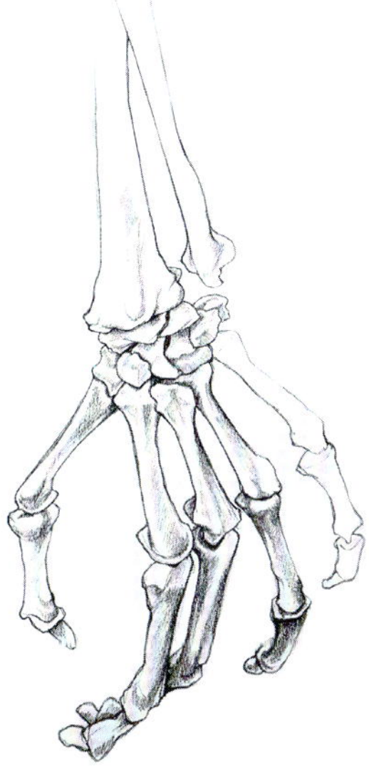

Bones of the hand study by Melodie Cook. *Courtesy of the artist.*

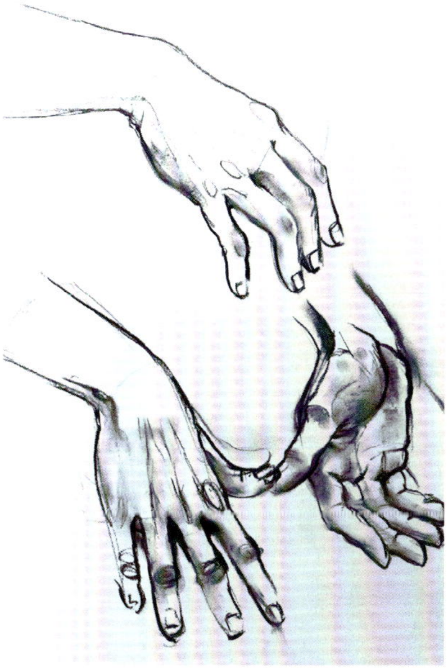

Hand studies by Melodie Cook. *Courtesy of the artist.*

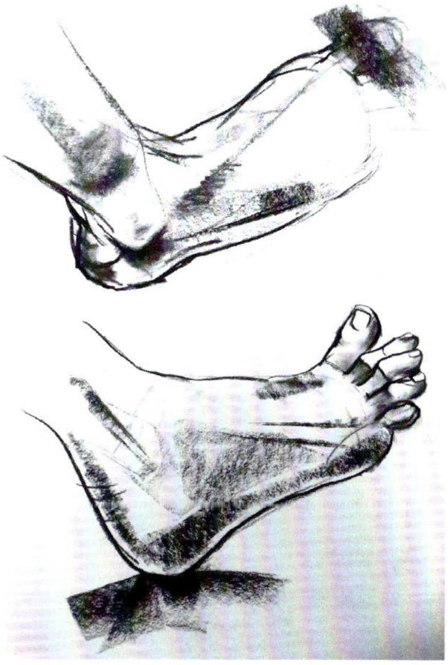

Foot studies by Melodie Cook. *Courtesy of the artist.*

☛ EXERCISE 2

An excellent exercise is to sculpt a figure from scratch, starting with the armature, modelling the bones and the whole skeletal structure, then putting on the muscle groups (the book by Bruno Lucchesi detailed in the Further Reading list on p. 126 shows this process). It is important to work precisely and methodically when doing this exercise, studying the structure and detail of each layer.

☛ EXERCISE 3

It is most important when considering anatomy to look at detail but not to lose sight of the bigger picture. As in the example of the head on p. 72, it is very important to see the jigsaw of forms that makes up the whole figure. You can view the sculpture as being made up of hundreds of lumps and bumps, and this can be useful for study purposes, but this is not really what our eyes see – it is in fact the larger planes, or jigsaw pieces, that make a sculpture powerful and effective (see p. 82 for more on planes).

This exercise can only be done if the model will let you draw on them with eyeliner or something similar. Mark out the jigsaw of forms as you see it, then draw again, trying to get the pieces as big as you can. Have quite a few goes, making the pieces different sizes, from quite small to large. Each time you create a jigsaw piece, put a dot on the highest (that is, the most raised) point of the form.

I cannot overemphasise how useful this exercise will be for you in understanding the key forms of the body and how they fit together. Do this exercise with the whole figure if you get the chance. If you are unable to draw on the model, look carefully and imagine the pieces, noting the highest points.

☛ EXERCISE 4

A slightly different exercise related to Exercise 3 involves putting the model in the pose you intend to use and then looking at the largest structures – head, shoulders, chest and pelvis. Do a quick, simple drawing with horizontal lines showing how each of these parts relates to the other, as shown in the photo above.

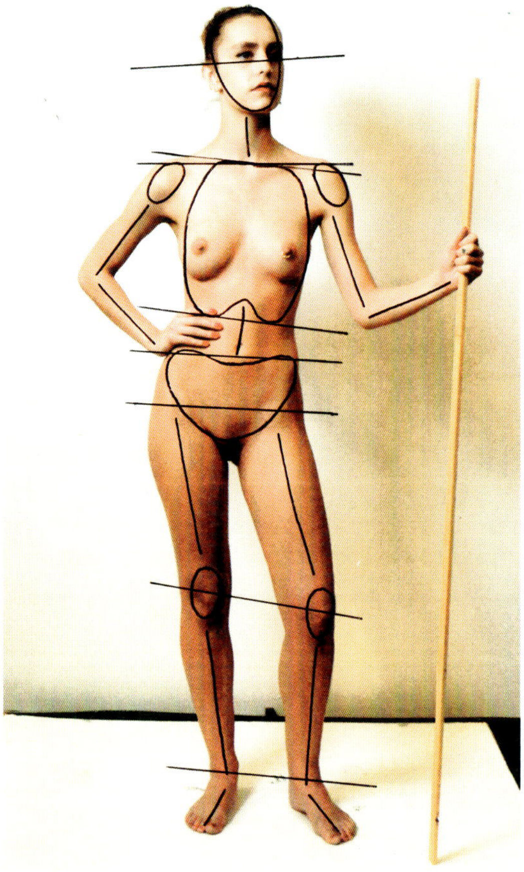

This shows the relationship between the main body parts – head, shoulders, chest and pelvis.

Architecture, Line, Geometry and Pose

These aspects are fundamental for sculpture – getting them wrong is like putting all the words in your sentence in a completely illogical order. Architecture, line, geometry and pose are really four ways of saying the same thing. (Note these concepts are discussed in more detail in Chapter 5, p. 79).

There are three different considerations:

- The silhouette
- The internal flow lines, created through planes, recesses and texture
- The extended linear structure – where the external lines flow to, the geometry.

Using a Plumb Line

Understanding the architecture of the figure involves the use of a plumb line, a weighted string used for vertical reference. Make sure you have a decent one – it is best to buy one, but you could tie something like a large bolt to a thin piece of string. When you are plumb lining it is important to make sure that your position in relation to the base on which the model is standing is the same as your position in relation to the base of your sculpture, otherwise the difference in angle will affect the results.

Ensure that your arm holding the plumb line is straight out in front of you, that the line is long enough to go from the top of the model right to the ground, and that you are standing far enough away. The plumb line must be completely still to get an accurate reading.

Stand directly in front of the model, about 2 m (6 ft) away, facing the straight edge of the base. Start by holding the plumb line so that it runs through the centre of the model's sternum notch and see what points it lines up with on the way down and up. Then stand about 1m (3 ft) in front of your sculpture, in exactly the same orientation (lined up with the front of the base) and do the same thing. In this way you can check the angles and architecture of the piece are working. You can really plumb line from any point, but as with the measuring, it is good to work from fixed points on the figure such as bony nodules. See p. 63 for images of plumb-lining.

The Silhouette

To see the silhouette you need to create a grid-like structure, horizontally and vertically, relating different points to each other. You can do this by using a plumb line for the verticals and a straight edge for the horizontals, looking at the model and creating a grid in your mind's eye. You could also take a photo and draw on it, as I have done in the examples here, and on p. 62. I have done this only for the purpose of illustration in this book and would normally do it by eye.

For each vertical line, decide on a useful starting point on the model (e.g. sternum notch, shoulder, elbow), hold up the plumb line and look at the points and negative spaces (if any) where the plumb line falls. Then move to stand in exactly the same place in relation to your sculpture and check that the same points are aligned.

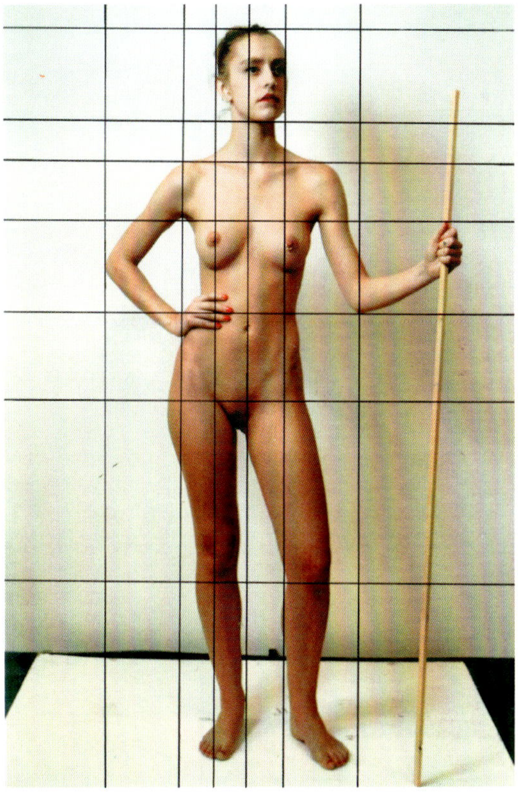

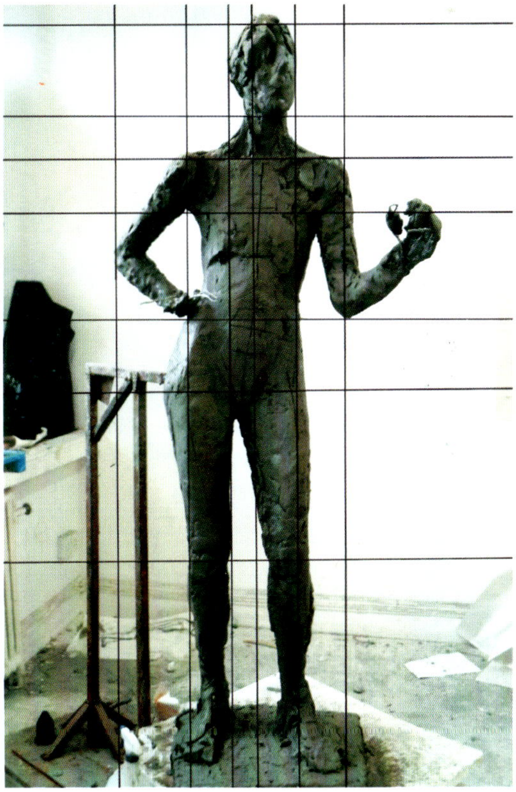

This shows how you can grid up the model and sculpture using your eye, a plumb line and a straight edge, drawn on a photo here for the purpose of demonstration.

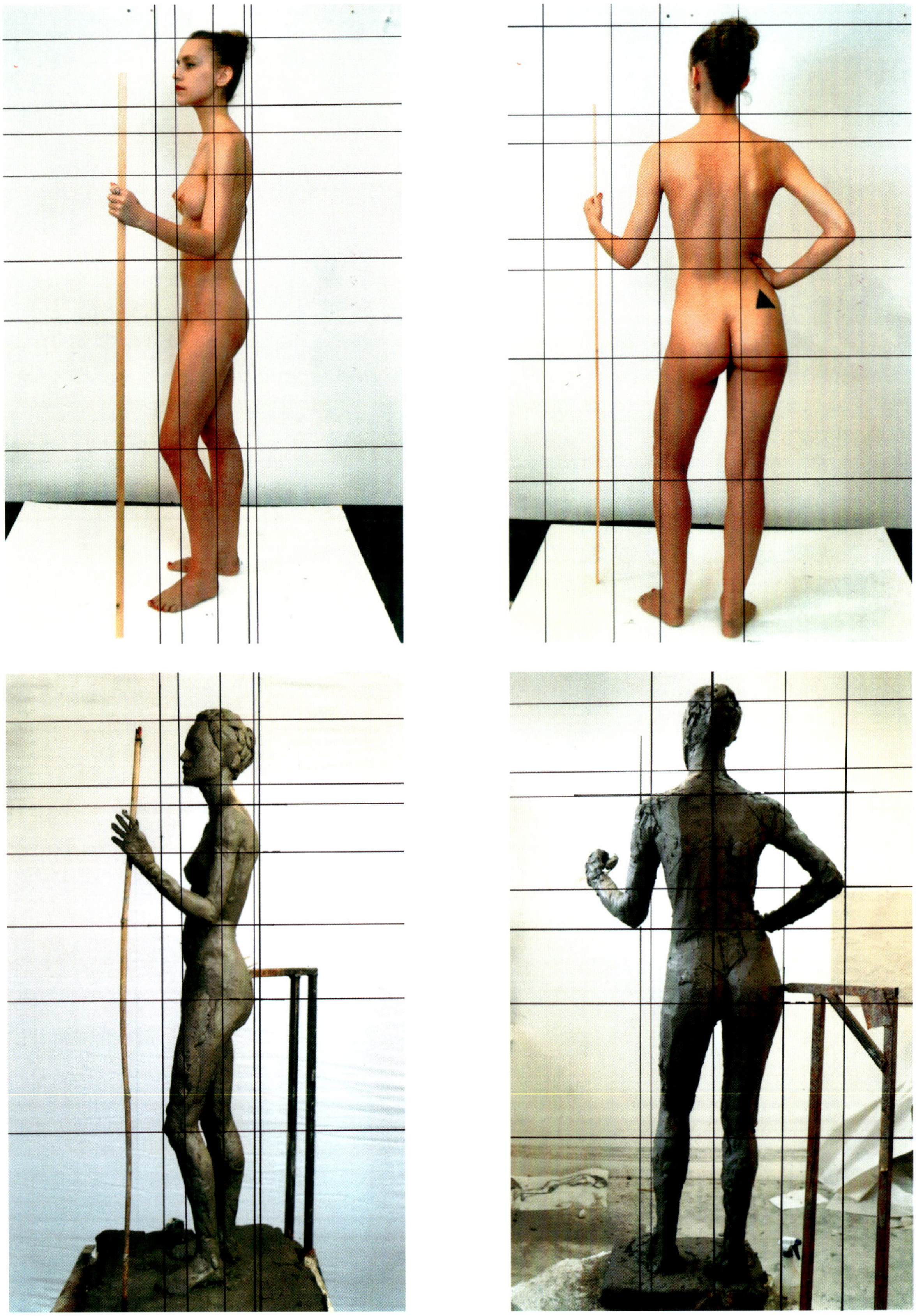

Again, this shows how you can grid up the model and sculpture using your eye, a plumb line and a straight edge.

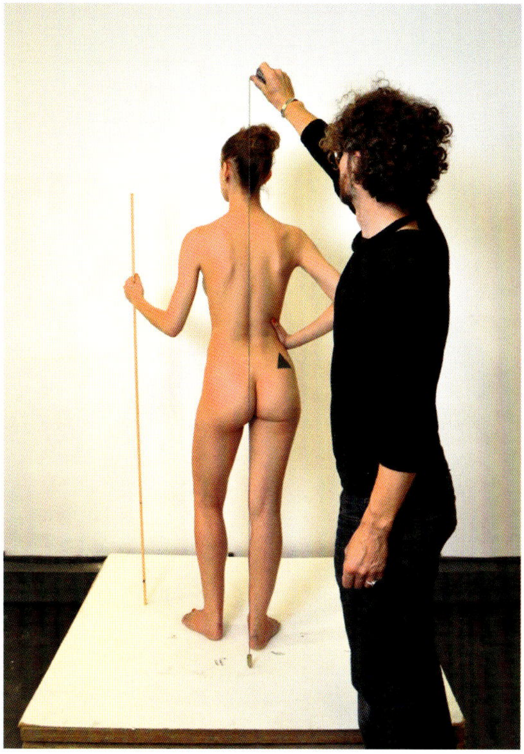

John shows a useful plumb line down the centre of the back (he would normally be standing square to the board, but for the purpose of this photo he has stood to the side).

For horizontals, stand away from the model and, either by eye or with a straight edge (held horizontally), gather information about how points lie in relation to each other across the figure. Then check this on your sculpture. Some people find this easy to do by eye, but a spirit level can be useful to ensure accuracy

You can repeat the same process all around the model.

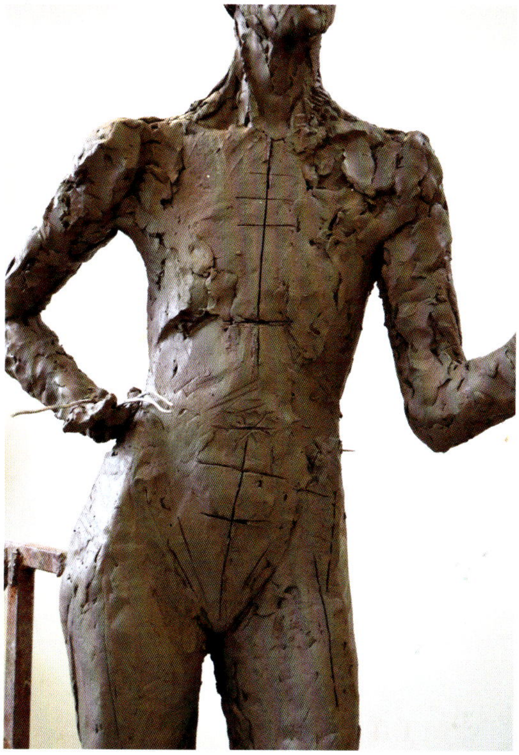

Lines drawn on the sculpture help to show how the angle of the shoulders, ribcage and hips changes down the figure.

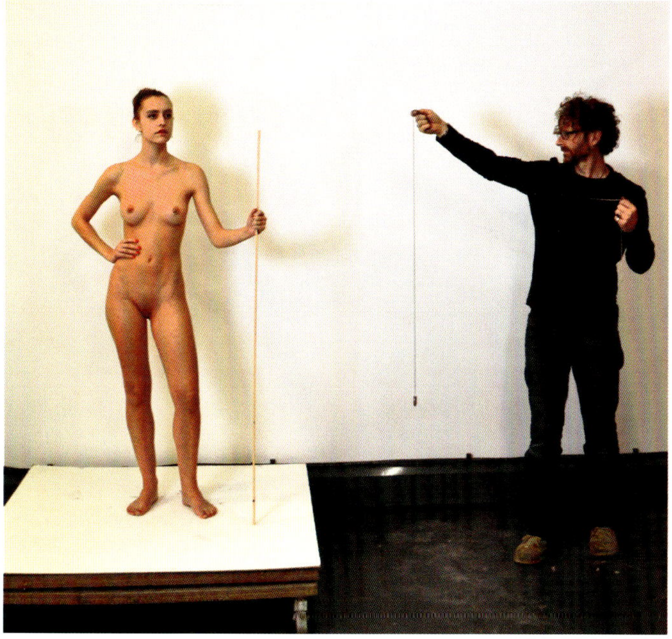

John plumb lines the model from the side.

You can also plumb line from actual points on the model – see p. 64 – then mark the point on the baseboard. You can then measure sideways on the board to the nearest useful point. Divide the measurement by two (as it is a half life-size figure) and check it on your sculpture.

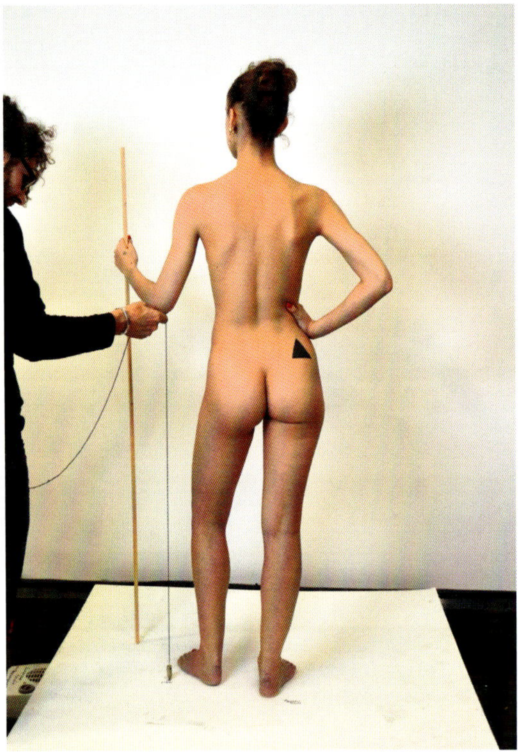

Plumb lining a point vertically from the elbow and marking the point on the base board.

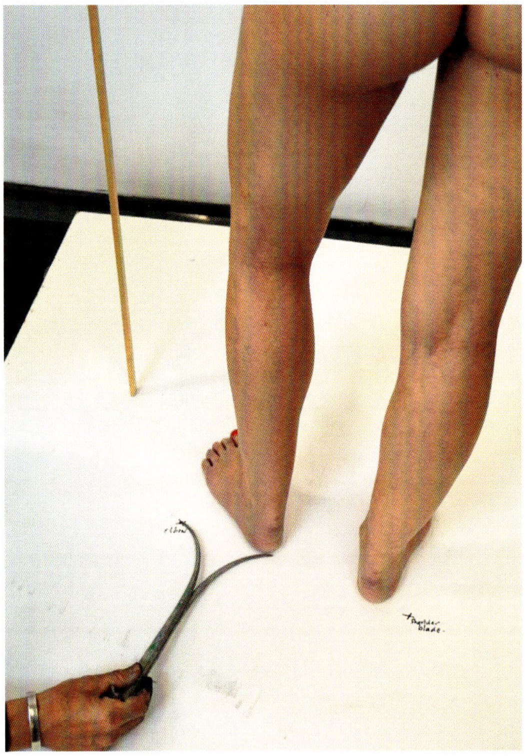

Measuring on the base board from the point marked for the elbow to the side of the foot. Ensure you choose an obvious fixed point when taking this measurement.

The Internal Flow Lines

If you look at any pose carefully, you will normally find that you can draw one line to express its main directional characteristics – this is the primary flow line. In a few instances you will find two flow lines that are equally important (such as in a crucifixion pose). Sometimes a primary line will be directly contradicted by a second line, as in the photo opposite, and this can be a key element of the pose. Looking again, you can find subsidiary lines that qualify the primary line – these are the secondary flow lines.

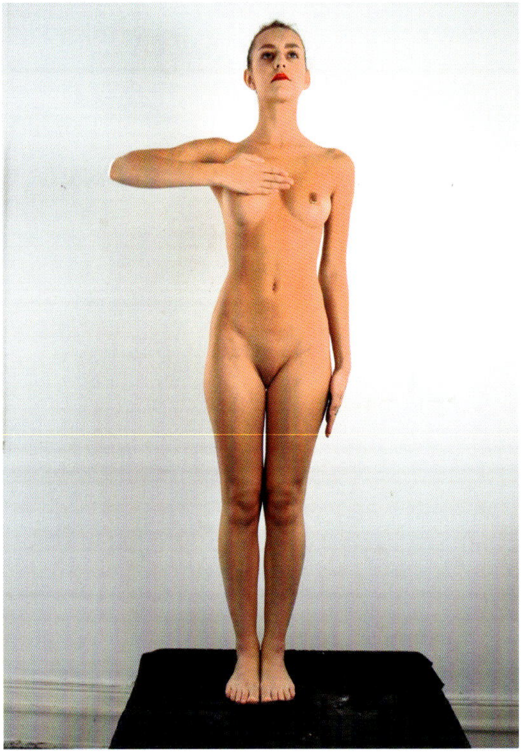

An example of a contradictory pose.

Primary Flow Lines

Right at the beginning of the sculpture it is important to see the main internal flow lines through the pose. It can be very helpful to draw this a number of times before you start the sculpture, or express it using one or more pieces of wire.

Secondary Flow Lines

These are slightly less obvious than the main flow lines, but are equally important. They are made up of contour lines and internal lines, created through shadows in hollows, shadows caused by planes, and skin texture. These draw your eyes in different ways around the figure and it is really important to get them right.

The Extended Linear Structure

This is vital for the whole feel of the piece. Our minds and eyes are actually absorbing far more than we give them credit for most of the time, picking up flow lines and subtleties in form and colour, joining lines together to create patterns that have a huge effect on the brain and the messages it sends to the rest of our bodies, evoking various feelings and responses.

In the photos below, see how the external and internal lines of the model's pose are flowing, creating patterns and geometry that have their own meaning. This is actually one of the most important and powerful areas that we pick up on when we see an artwork and is totally related to how it affects us. With the pose we are using for this half life-size study, the extended linear structure is not particularly obvious or dramatic, but as every mark you make has an effect, and each tiny line or mark contributes to the character, feeling and effect of the piece, you need to be aware of this structure even when it is subtle. An excellent example of a pose with an obvious extended linear structure can be found on p. 81.

Texture

Texture is often misunderstood as meaning surface texture, which is not really proper sculptural texture at all. Texture applied to the surface very rarely works, unless done for a specific reason and with great skill. Texture starts the moment the clay is applied and is a result of the whole modelling process – it is often the result of what you don't do, what you leave untouched. We will talk a lot more about texture in Chapter 6.

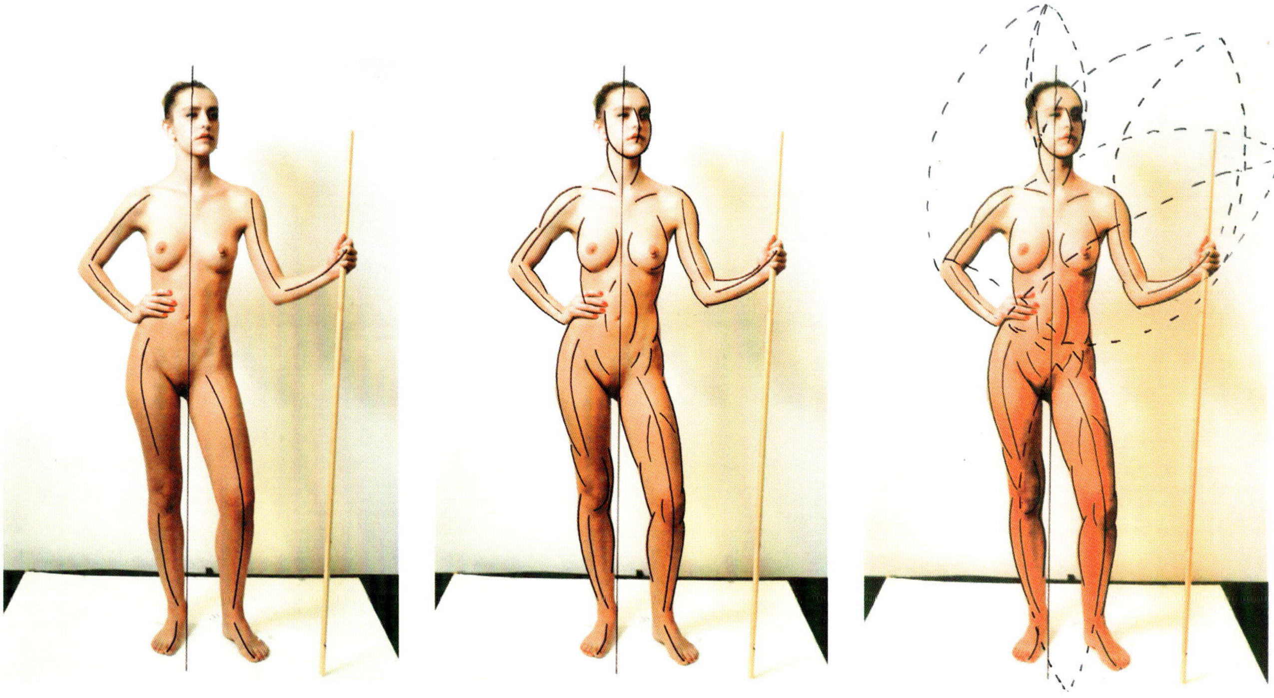

This shows the primary flow lines through the pose.

This shows the main contour lines and the internal lines, created through planes, recesses and texture.

This shows the extended linear structure.

Putting It All Together

- Construct an armature using the process described in Chapter 3, including the clay base. Bend it into the correct position for the pose, measuring the points at which the armature bends in relation to one other and the base. When measuring, always remember that the armature wire is running down the centre of the forms.

- Place a 2 cm (¾ in.) blob of clay on the head of the armature to denote the final high point of the figure. Referring to your table of measurements for the sculpture (see p. 56), measure the full height of the figure down to the clay base ('Ground to top of head' in the table), altering the base height if necessary. These two points are now fixed for the duration of the modelling process.

- Put small pieces of clay at crucial points measured on the figure – i.e. sternum notch, navel, crotch, knee.

- Start building up the form, working on the whole pose at the same time, constantly doing vertical and horizontal measurements and plumb lining, maintaining the flow, movement and angles all the way through. Put the clay on in smallish pieces, but make them large enough to describe a whole form with a single piece, both in terms of volume and anatomical structure.

- In the early stages, keep well within the final bulk of your sculpture. Don't build up too thickly all over, but build out at various points (e.g. the hips and shoulders) to show what the final width at those points will be – these act as a useful reference points.

- It is vital to work the whole sculpture at the same time. At any point the whole piece should be at the same stage – do not leave heads, hands and feet until the end, otherwise they will look like they have been stuck on. Model them at the same time as the rest, bearing in mind that the finest parts may have to be modelled in a wax-based medium (see pp. 68–72 for modelling hands, feet and heads).

- Check your basic measurements at least three times a day, if not more. You would be amazed how quickly something can go wrong. I always measure a point both upwards and downwards to check that it is correct, i.e. to check the navel point, I measure from ground to navel and then also from sternum notch to navel – you find a lot of inconsistencies that need resolving doing this!

- Continually check your geometry using your eye and a plumb line.

- Stand well back from your work at least every 10–15 minutes. This is the only way of seeing your sculpture and ensuring that all is going according to plan, that no part is too big compared to the rest, and that the angles are correct. Not standing back is as daft as trying to see the whole mountain while standing halfway up it.

- Build the head quickly as you do the rest of the figure, ensuring that the angles and planes are working with the rest of the body.

- Be aware of not overworking the clay, as the texture is so important. Do not smooth it off to finish it, or you will kill it stone dead.

- Towards the end, stand back more and more often. People tend to get caught up in the detail towards the end. They get all comfortable on a stool and start finishing the sculpture off – literally!

- Check the tonal colouring. Standing right back, look at your model. Look for the big dark areas and what stands out as being darkest, and check that your sculpture reflects this.

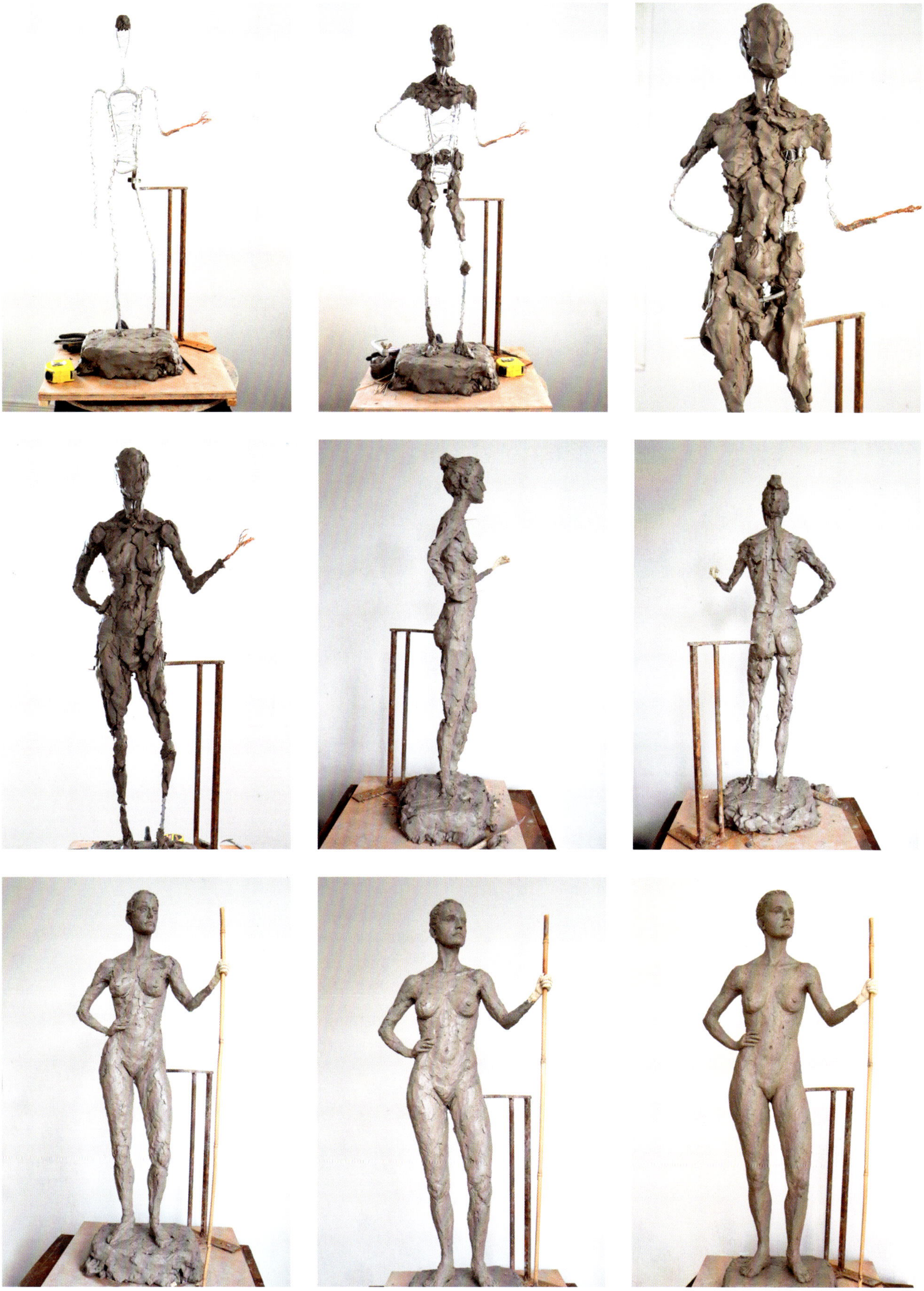

The development and build-up of a figure, as described in the 'Putting It All Together' section.

Modelling Hands and Feet

As with the head, hands and feet must not be modelled as a separate part of the figure – model them right at the beginning, work on them at the same time as the rest of the figure, and give them as much attention as other parts, like the knees.

Tips for Modelling Hands

- Crucially, note that the outside and inside edges of the fingers all go to a point in front of the hand. If you do not get these lines in the fingers right, the hands will look like a bunch of bananas.

- The top line of the fingertips, the knuckles and the base of the fingers all follow the same curved line

- Just like the rest of the figure, the hand is not flat. There are quite strong planes running all through it, especially the back of the hand when viewed from above.

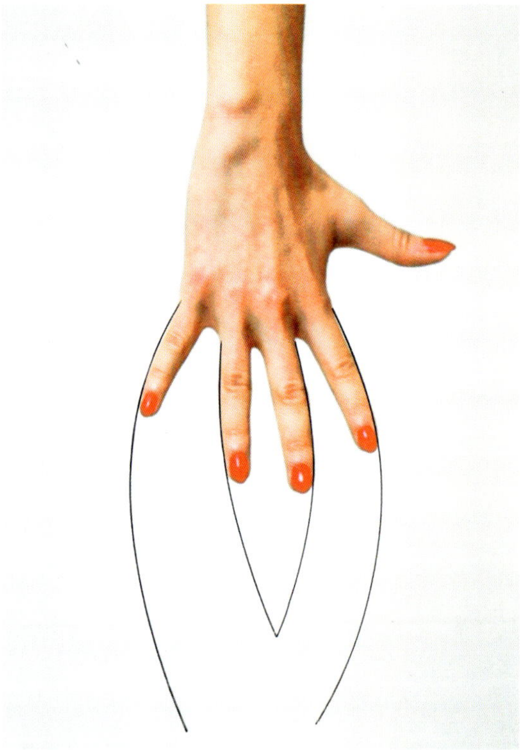

The fingers curve to a point even when they are spread.

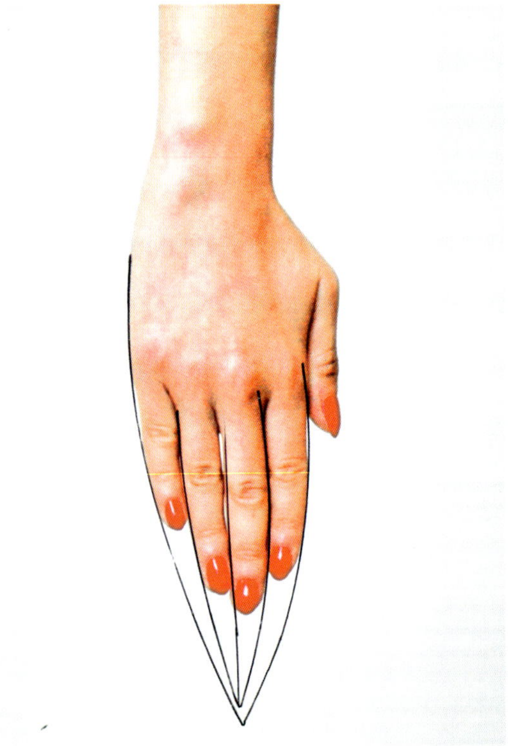

The fingers curve to a point.

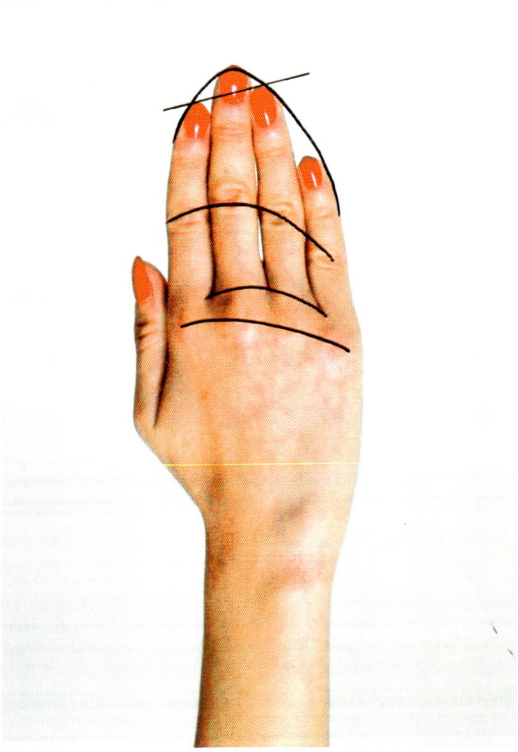

This shows the relationship between the knuckles and the tips of the fingers.

Tips for Modelling Feet

- Much the same as the hands, the lines of the feet curve inwards and the tips of the toes, knuckles and bottom of the toes follow a curved line.
- Note that the gaps between the toes are not all the same thickness and tonal colour.
- The dark undercuts are very important to note, and to create on your sculpture. These give the feet life. Note the strong shapes on the bottom of the feet in the photo at the bottom of this page.

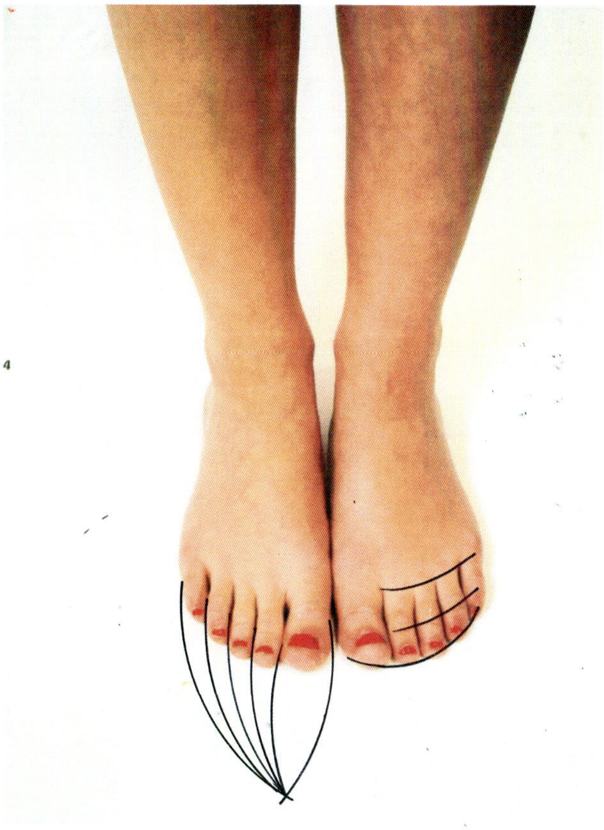

This shows how the toes curve to a point and the relationship between the toe joints and tips.

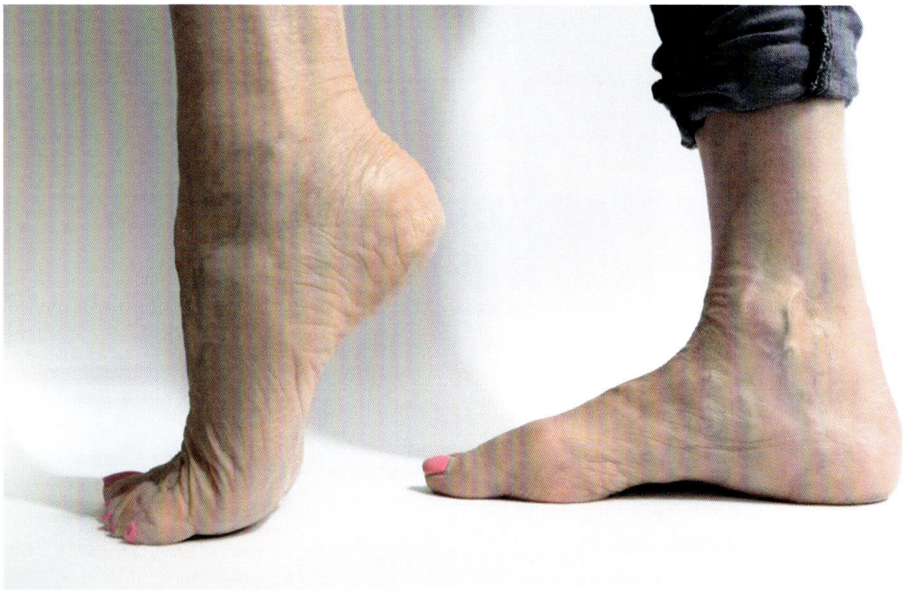

Note the strong shapes made by the feet.

Modelling a Portrait Head

In order to be comfortable with modelling the head at the same time as other body parts, it is almost essential to have done some portrait head studies at life size. Learning to model a head is really a book in its own right, but the following summary covers the main points:

1. Clamp your bust peg (see p. 49) onto your modelling stand and ensure that the centre of your bust peg and your model's head are both at your eye level.

2. Decide which is going to be the front of your head. I suggest you align the front with one of the straight edges of your board.

3. Roughly and quickly, using large lumps of clay, build up a basic head structure, keeping well within the final dimensions of the finished head.

4. Start taking a series of measurements, giving you accurate proportions and also enabling you to build up a kind of grid, making it far easier for your eye to see what is going on between these points. Insert matchsticks or cocktail sticks to keep these points of measurement.

When measuring, always cover the tips of the callipers or dividers so as not to hurt the model and adjust the callipers or dividers away from the model's face.

Remember that measurements are not a substitute for your eyes – you must look first and just measure to confirm what your eyes are telling you. As you take the measurements, adjust the shape of your clay head to account for them.

- Start with the measurement running from the centre of the neck to the chin (on the model) and the centre of the bust peg to the chin on the sculpture, to ensure that you do not build the face too close to the bust peg. Otherwise, when you come to build in the angle of the neck, you will hit the bust peg around the sternum notch area.
- Ensure that you are not building the head too low down on the bust peg and that it is sitting comfortably over the wire frame.
- Measure vertically from the chin to the hairline and note how far back the hairline is in relation to the chin in a horizontal dimension.
- Measure from the chin to the sternum notch.
- Measure from the chin to the furthest point on the back of the head.

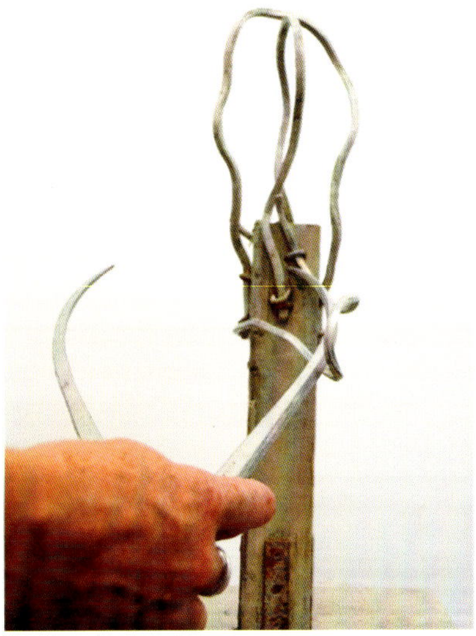

Note how far out from the bust peg the chin needs to be.

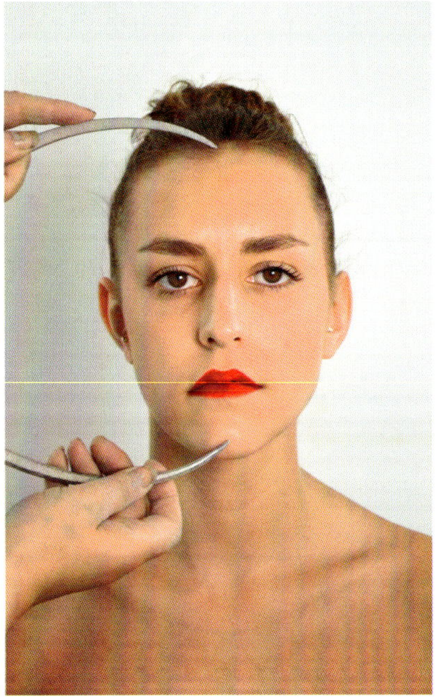

Measuring from chin to hairline.

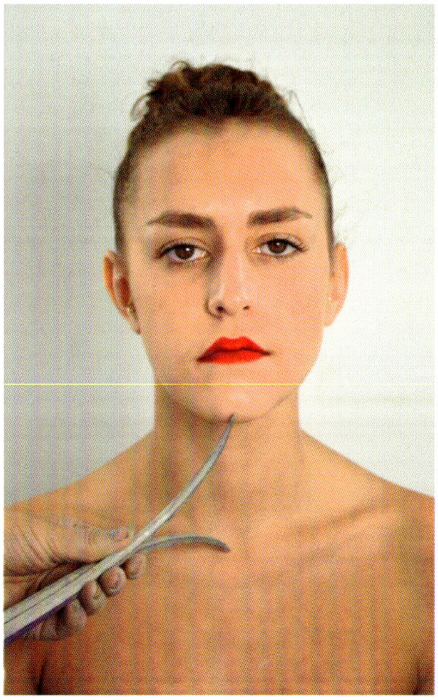

Measuring from chin to sternum notch.

- The next point of measurement is actually composed of three measurements. This is a critical measurement as it is giving a third dimension to the grid that we are building up.

a. First, from underneath, measure the distance between the two points where the earlobe touches the head (notice how you cannot pull your callipers forward at this point, only down, as the head dips in towards the ears past the swell of the cheeks).

b. With callipers, measure from the chin to the same point of the ear and rotate the callipers to draw an arc on your sculpture showing the position of the ear. Do it on both sides.

c. Measure from the hairline to the same point of the ear and draw another arc, on both sides.

d. The point where the two arcs intersect is the point vertically where the ear is positioned (see right).

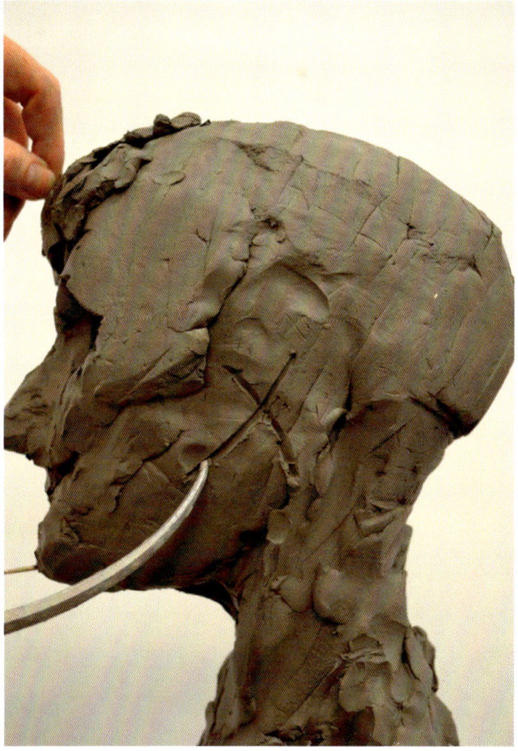

Finding the ear point using two measurements.

5. Now you have a basic grid built up on the head within these measurements. Turn the head constantly, checking the profile, standing back, getting the overall shape correct. Build up every part to the same level, and put in neck, ears, shoulders and so on.

6. Now we will do some measurement for the features:

- Re-check the chin-to-hairline measurement.
- Using dividers, very carefully measure from the chin to the point between the eyes to check their height.
- Measure from the chin to the base of the nose.
- Measure from the chin to the centre of the mouth.
- Measure the width from the outside of one eye to the outside of the other, then the same for the inside points. (Note: make sure the model closes their eyes for this and be very careful). There is normally one eye width between eyes.

7. Using these new measurements, and constantly checking these and the previous ones, build up the likeness.

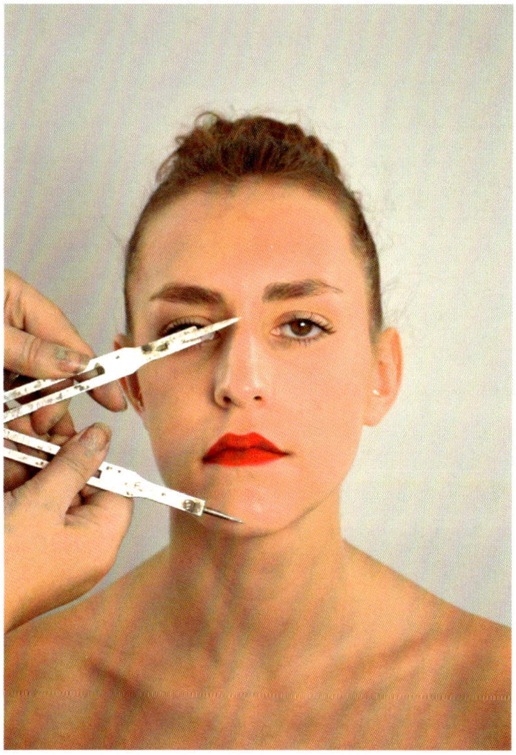

Carefully measuring from the chin to the point between the eyes, using dividers.

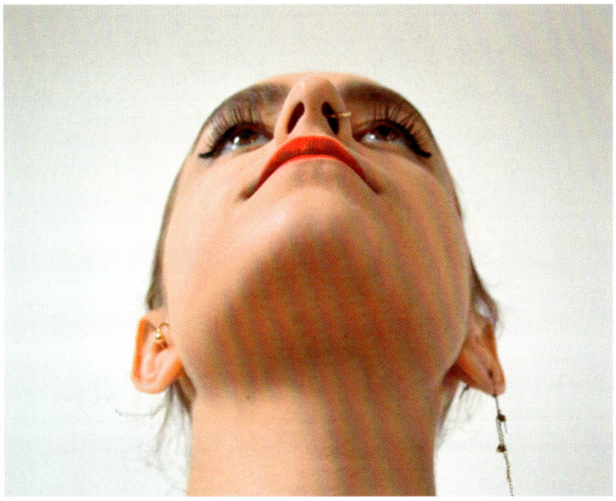

This view from beneath shows the section of the head is curved, not flat.

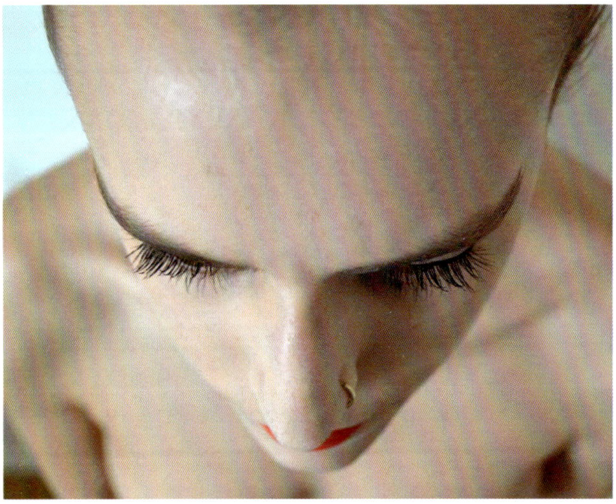

This view from the top also shows that the section of the head is curved.

8. It is vital to look at the model and your sculpture from underneath and from above. The main area where people make a mistake is in giving a flat front to the head. In the photos above, see how rounded the section of the head is – the mouth and the eyebrows are not flat, they are curved.

9. As we discussed ion p. 60, the head is made up of a jigsaw of forms. It can be very useful to look at these and draw them for yourself on the model, marking the high points as shown in the photo on the right. Ensure that you are not too distracted by the smaller lumps and bumps, but focus on the larger jigsaw structure.

10. One of the main distinctions between 'amateur' and 'professional' portrait sculptures is the richness of the forms. Note in the photo left how much depth there is between the form of the cheek closest to the mouth and the corner of the mouth.

11. As with the rest of the figure, keep the texture lively.

12. Look really closely at the detail of the forms. For example, the eyelid is not just one thickness and depth all the way along. It has subtle forms and changes that are important in keeping the liveliness of the sculpture.

13. A strange and frequent mistake made when modelling heads is continuing to add clay to get the richness and roundness of the forms. More often than not when creating a raised form, you actually need to take clay away around it, rather than adding clay onto it. Be very aware of this as you are modelling.

14. As always, keep standing back and looking.

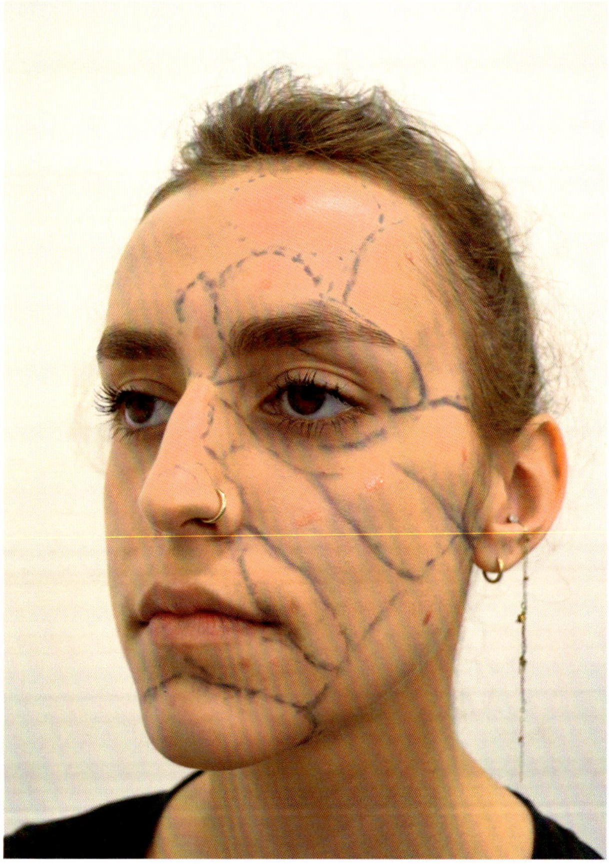

A useful exercise is drawing the jigsaw of forms that make up the head, pinpointing the high points of each form with a red dot.

EXERCISES

- Draw on the model's face doing the jigsaw exercise.
- Sculpt very large, detailed fragments, studying the eye, the nose and the mouth, in order to understand fully the forms that make up these parts.
- Do three detailed heads, taking your time over them, but also do at least three quick portraits (two hours maximum). By doing these quick studies, you learn how to capture freshness and character in the piece, at the same time as gaining an understanding of the larger forms of the portrait head.

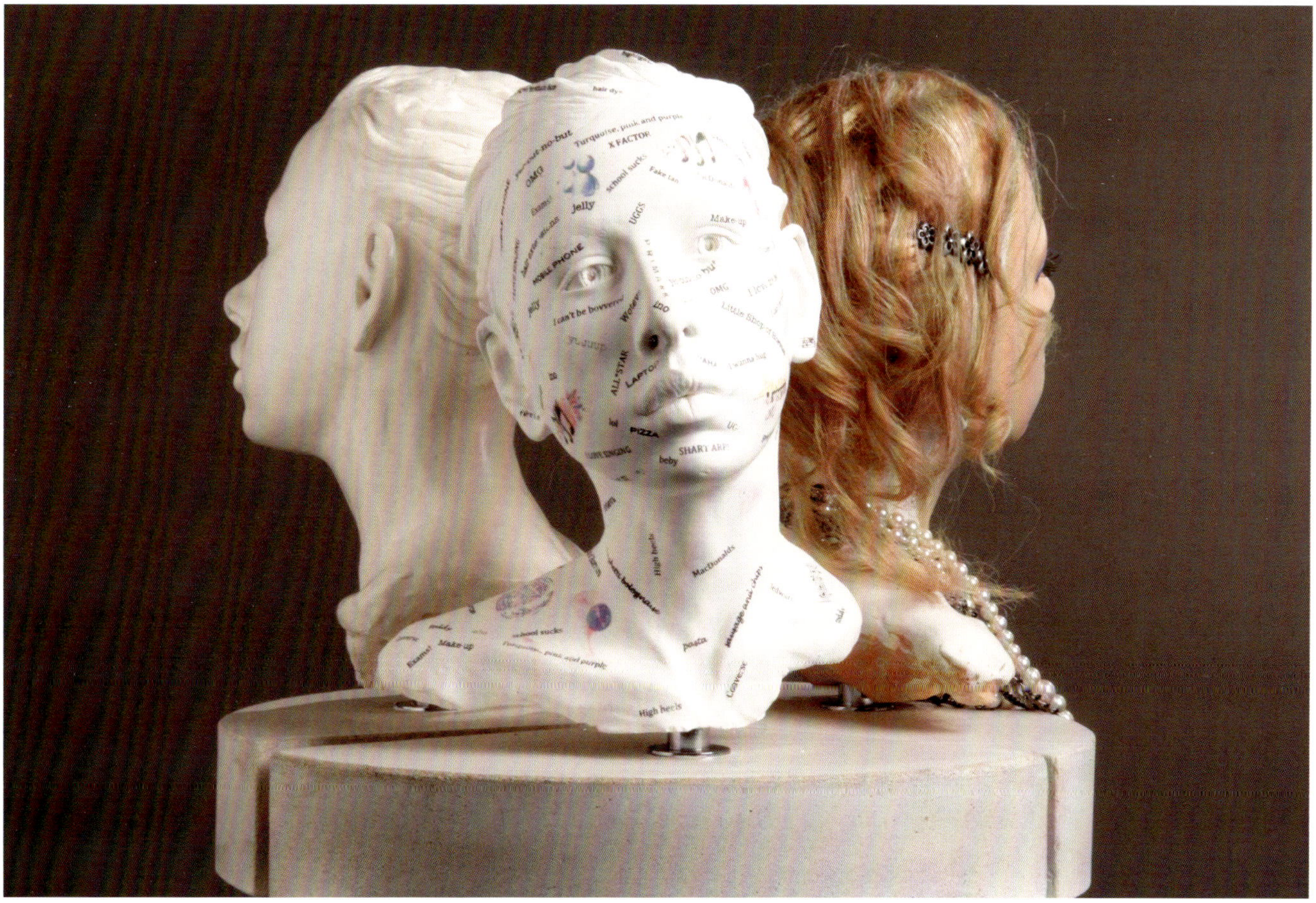

Billie Bond, *Purity, Culture & Art.* Plaster, hair and other materials, 44 x 50 x 50 cm ($17\frac{1}{3}$ x $19\frac{2}{3}$ x $19\frac{2}{3}$ in.). *Photo: Billie Bond.*

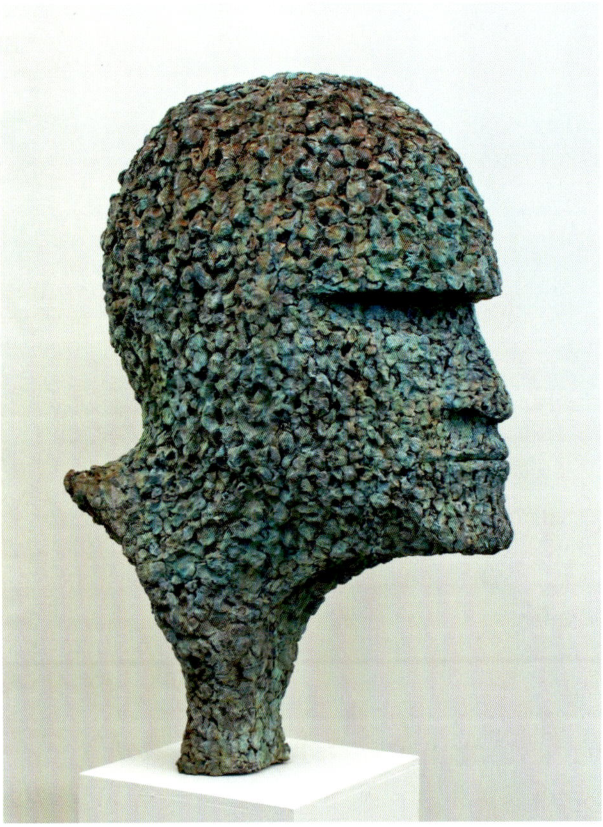

Michael Speller, *Presence.* Bronze, 154 x 95 x 80 cm (60½ x 37½ x 31½ in.). *Photo: courtesy of the artist.*

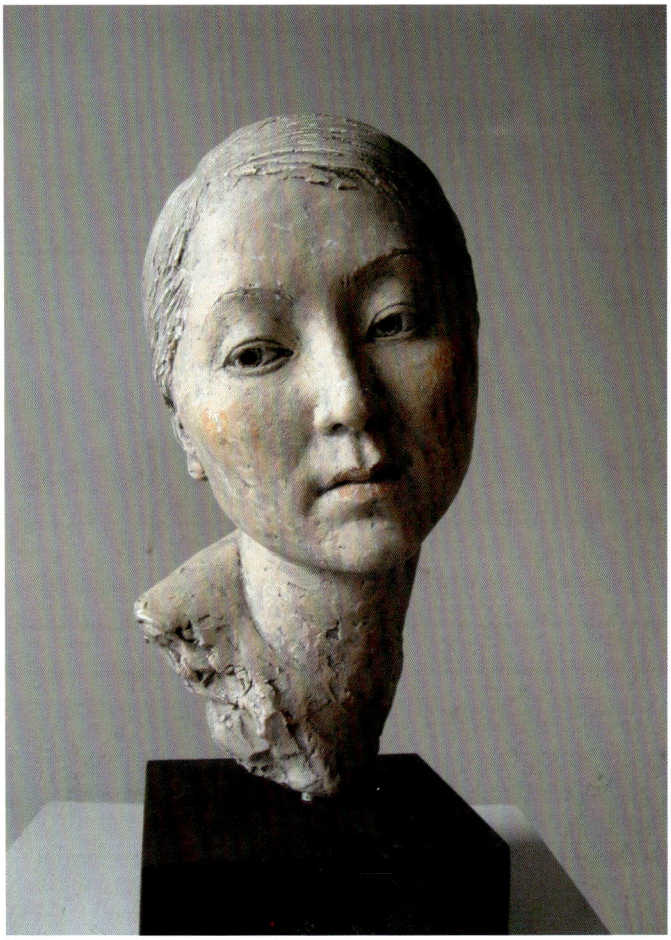

Suzie Zamit, *Aya.* Coloured plaster life-size, height 25 cm (9¾ in.). *Photo: courtesy of the artist.*

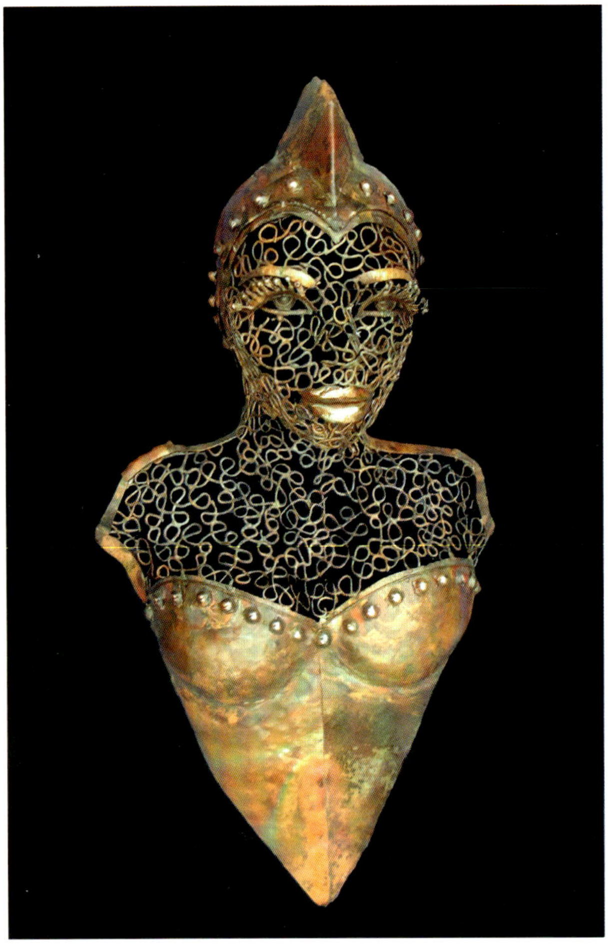

Jill Simpson, *Warrior woman.* Beaten and brazed copper, 55 x 37 x 12 cm (21½ x 14½ x 4¾ in.). *Photo: courtesy of the artist.*

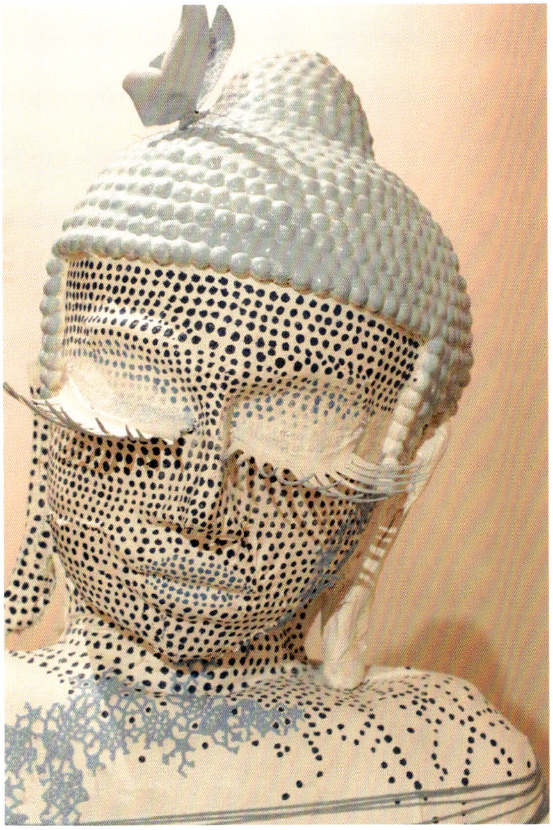

Jessica Nyssen, *'My Buddha' Belief.* Recycled cloth, canvas paint, 100 x 70 cm (39½ x 27½ in.). *Photo: Artur Nizicki.*

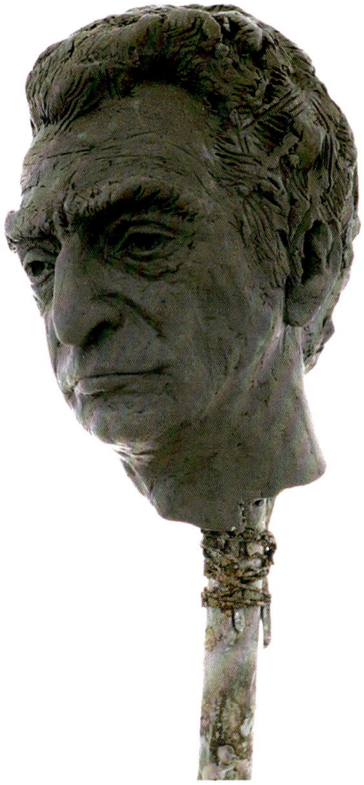

Hiromi Scintu, *Dad.* Clay, 30 x 12 cm (11¾ x 4¾ in.). *Photo: courtesy of the artist.*

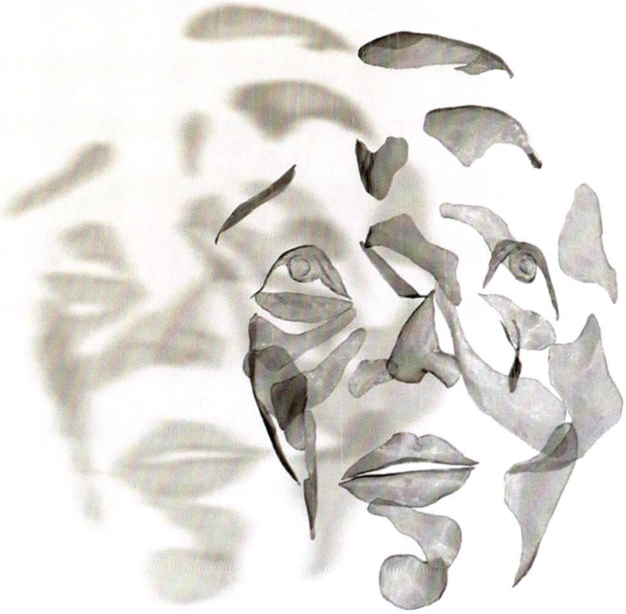

Silja Truus, *Air.* Stainless steel mesh, nylon thread, 37 x 25 x 18 cm (14½ x 10 x 7 in.). *Photo: courtesy of the artist.*

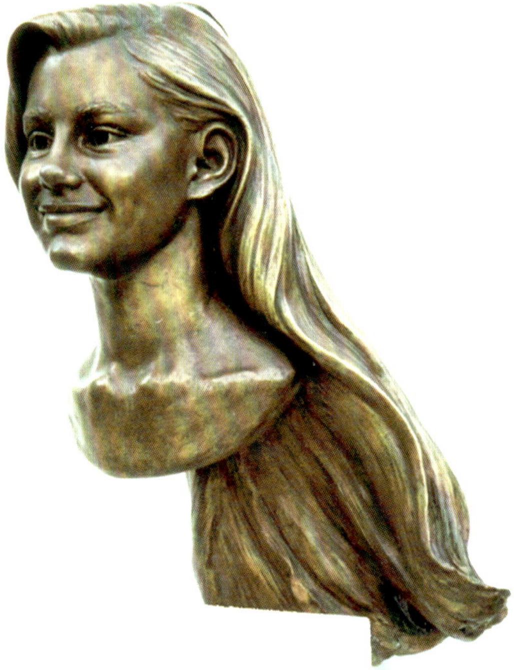

Tanya Russell, *Isobelle.* Bronze life-size, 60 x 33 cm ($23^{2}/_{3}$ x 13 in.). *Photo: courtesy of the artist.*

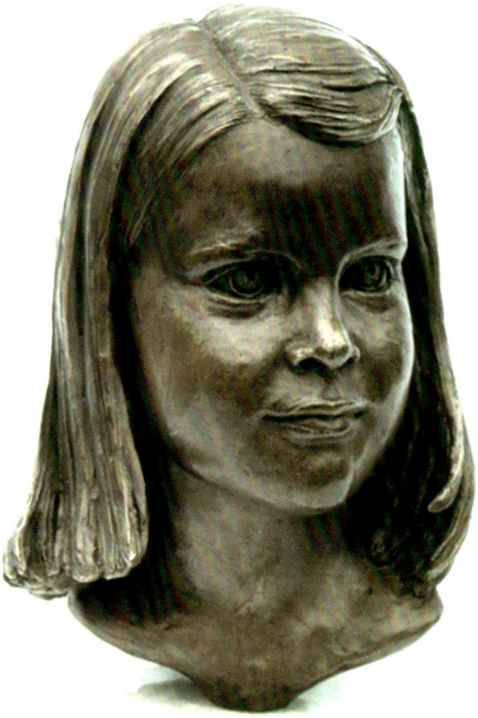

Tanya Russell, *Rachel.* Bronze life-size, 33 x 22 cm (13 x 8¾ in.). *Photo: courtesy of the artist.*

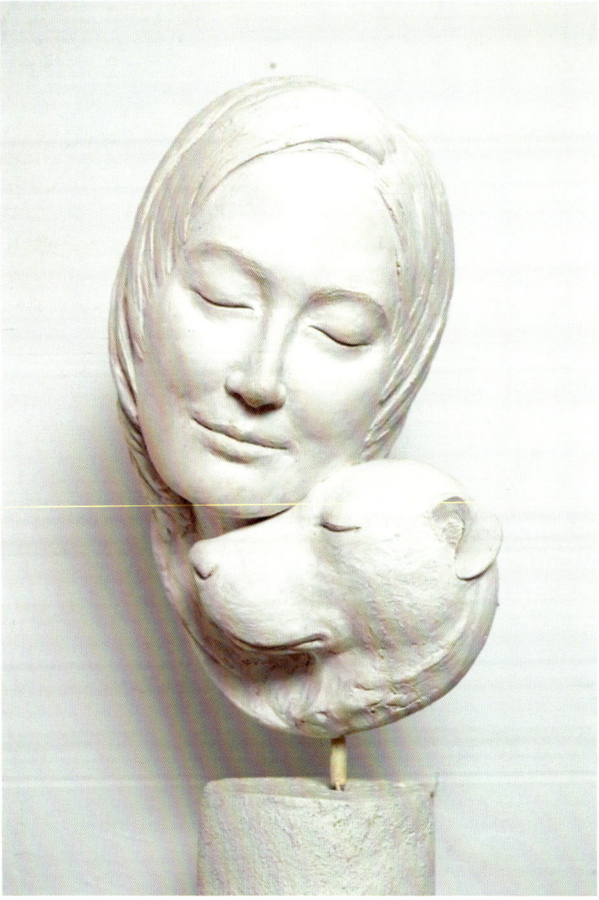

Tanya Russell, *Love is love.* Marble composite life-size, 42 x 25 cm (16½ x 10 in.). *Photo: courtesy of the artist.*

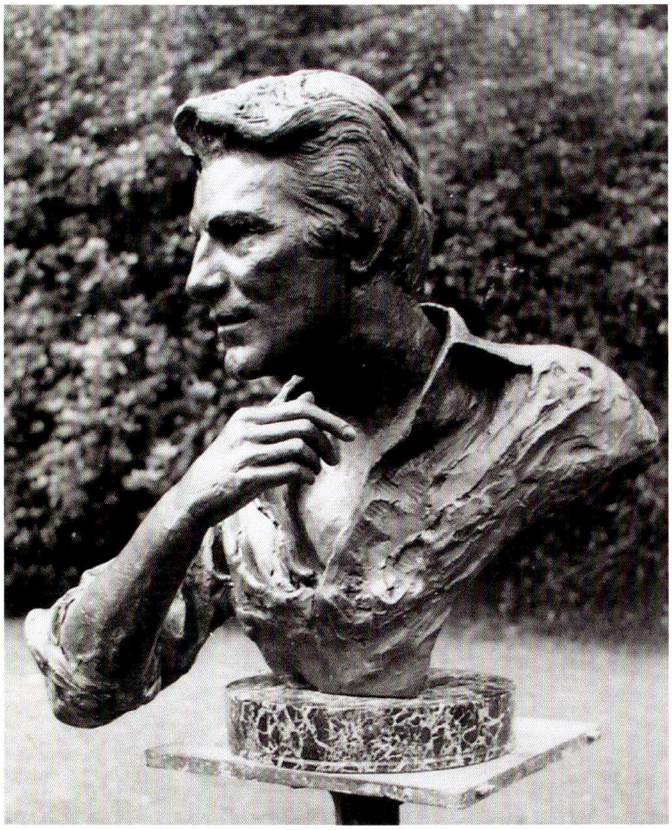

Lorne McKean, *The Earl of Lichfield.* Bronze life-size, 63 x 58 cm (24 x 22¾ in.). *Photo: courtesy of the artist.*

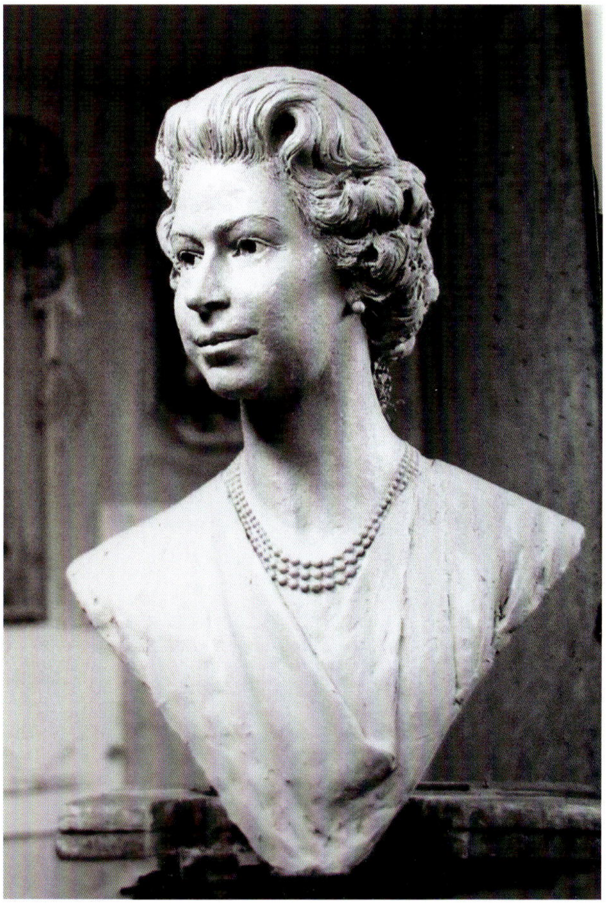

Lorne McKean, *HM The Queen.* Clay life-size commissioned for Drapers Hall, London, 66 x 52 cm (26 x 20½ in.). *Photo: courtesy of the artist.*

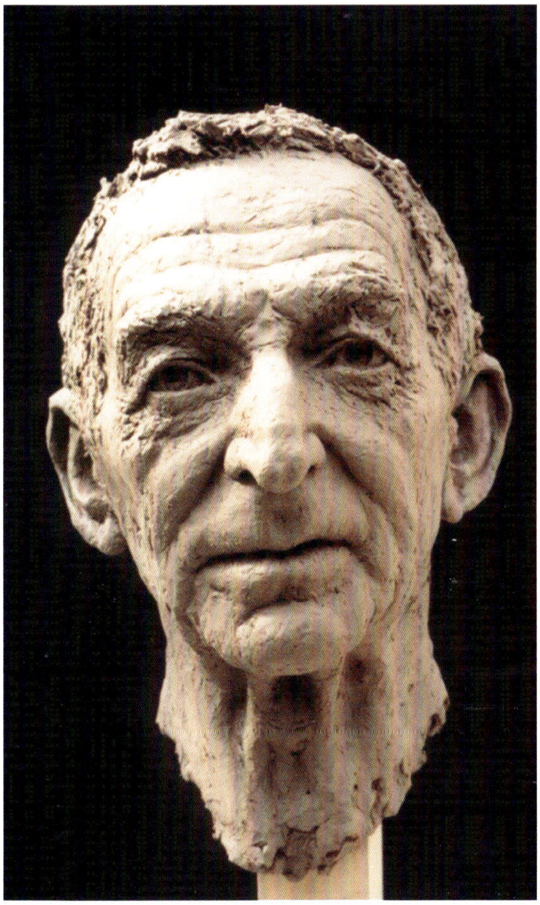

Suzie Zamit, *Dave Corran.* Original clay life-size, height 27 cm (9½ in.). *Photo: courtesy of the artist.*

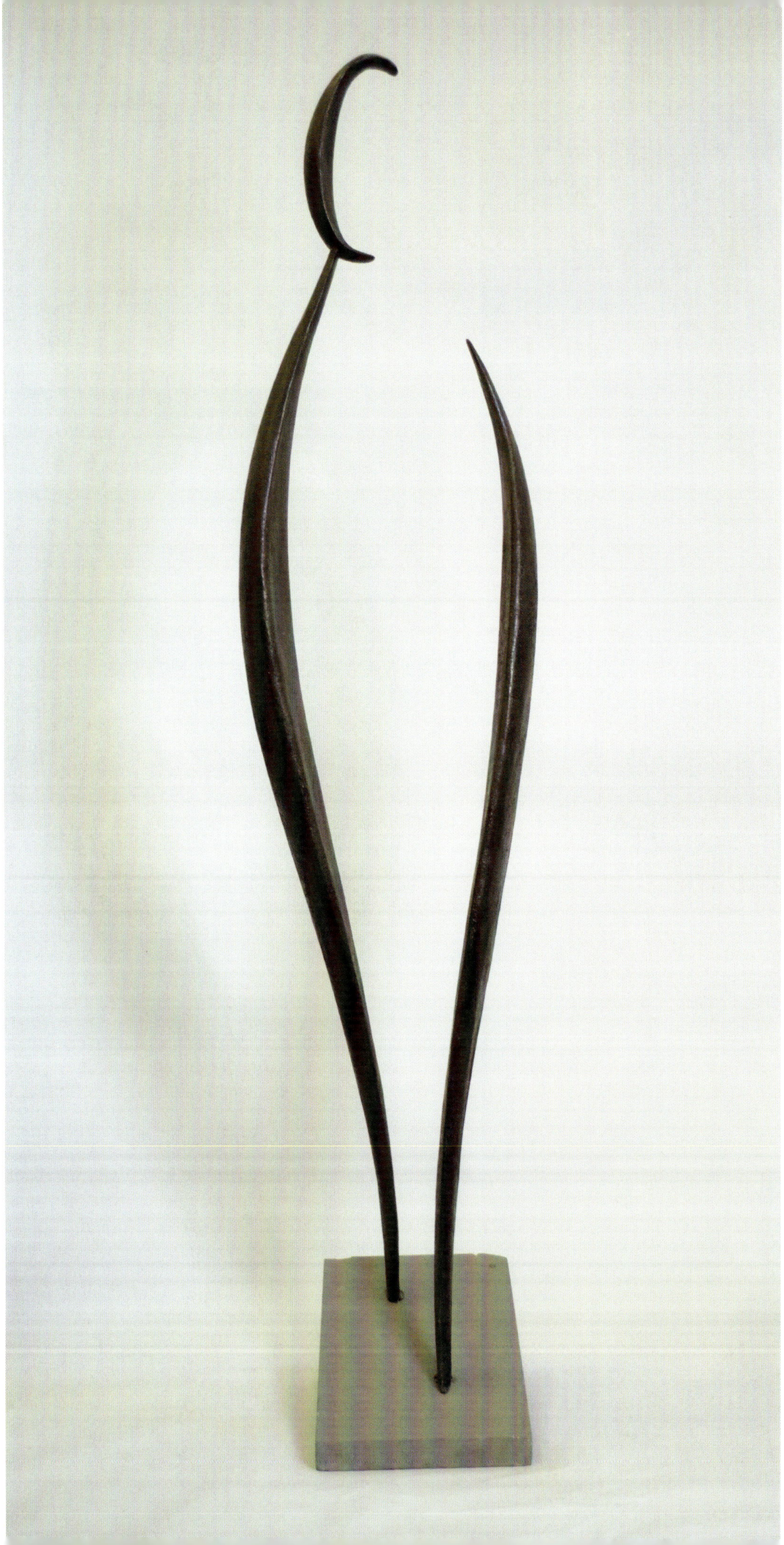

Tanya Russell, *Spirit of Being*.
Bronze commissioned for a private garden, 200 x 46 cm (84.5 x 18 in.).
Photo: courtesy of the artist.

5

THE ABSTRACTED FIGURE

What is the Abstracted Figure?

Abstraction involves reducing the form down to its core components, where you get rid of everything superfluous until you are left with the pure essence of your expression. The abstracted figure shares much common ground with the expressive figure, covered in Chapter 6, but if the latter is a poem, the former is a haiku, with the formal components reduced to a minimum.

Sculpture can be semi-abstracted, in which case the original 'real' object is still discernable, or fully abstracted, when no realistic semblance of the original form remains. As always, one is not intrinsically better than the other – it is all about your intention.

Artists from every culture have been abstracting forms for thousands of years, from Neolithic stone carvings onwards, so it is a very natural perceptive process for us.

I do not subscribe to the idea that the 'photographic' representation of life is more 'real' than the abstract. If you ask someone to describe an amazing personal experience, they will rarely describe it like a photograph, with every detail in place. They will describe it in a much more abstract way – much of the detail is omitted, not least because much of it is not even perceived during the experience. In describing our experiences, what comes across is the essence of the subject rather than the photographic specifics, and although our perception of the world is uniquely individual, these essential elements allow the experience to be shared and recognised by others.

Emotional or internal experiences are also 'real' and often exist for us in simple abstract forms: in colours, shapes or rhythms.

Abstraction is not about distorting form. When you write a haiku or speak in a very concise way, you choose every word, intonation and rhythm with extreme care, as every part must echo and contribute to the whole to be effective. So with abstract sculpture you do not just throw in a distorted form because you like the form or want to be different. You choose every form, material, texture and so on with great care, as every part will either enhance or dilute the whole.

Although abstraction can come about through both formal and conceptual intentions, concepts are a rich source of abstraction because they are often abstract by their very nature. Universal concepts, such as those related to the human condition, are easy to connect with even when expressed in abstract form.

There are two ways of approaching an abstracted figure:

1. A purely formal exercise, starting with a physical form, then reducing and exaggerating it to explore the effect that the form has on us, physically, emotionally and mentally, and by doing so arriving at a successful abstracted form.

2. Starting with a concept or emotional feeling and using abstraction as a language to echo the concept or feeling and find its pure physical manifestation.

In this chapter I am going to set out some broad concepts of abstraction and a suggested exercise for each area. Abstraction is a very personal thing and it comes in many forms, so I think it would be a mistake to be more prescriptive here, as it could stifle your own original creative expression. The exercises will be useful for setting you on track and showing you what is possible – it is then up to you to create whatever you will.

Whole movements of abstraction, such as cubism, fauvism and lyrical abstraction, have come about through ideology, social movements and personal revelation. This chapter looks at the broad concepts behind some of them and you can explore many others yourself.

Concepts of Abstraction

The language we use for abstraction is the same as for expressive and realistic figures, in that we are still working with form, planes, texture, colour and so on. Here, we look again at these different elements from a purely formal view in order to maximise the potential of every aspect of your visual language. We mainly start with the figure and make decisions formally to manipulate chosen elements such as line, form and tone, to accentuate the sculpture's intrinsic formal properties, thereby influencing its emotional and conceptual effect.

Line (Internal and External)

As mentioned in Chapter 4 (p. 64–5), there are three types of line:

- **The primary flow lines**, running through the form.

- **The secondary flow lines**, which in a drawing are fixed, but on a sculpture are constantly shifting and made up of infinite contours.

- **The extended linear structure.** A sculpture inhabits a space much greater than its actual physical edges. The size of this boundary is determined by the piece and contributes hugely to the feeling it conveys. Sculptures that are about internal, introspective subjects, such as care or pain, tend to create an internal space through the lines and planes within the sculpture, which is smaller than the sculpture itself. This draws the viewer's eye inwards. Sculptures about outward, dramatic or more exuberant subjects create spaces larger than themselves, drawing the eye outwards and giving the viewer a sense of opening up.

All these aspects of line and geometry are vital in abstracting a form – our eye reads line, internal and external, without us even realising it.

The next exercise looks at these three types of line in turn. For the purpose of this exercise you will be asked to draw these lines, as this makes it easier for you to see their impact. Clearly these lines are equally transferable to three-dimensional sculpture – you just encounter more lines as you move around the piece and the aspect changes.

☛ EXERCISE 1

1. Using a model, find a pose that particularly appeals because of its linear flow, and photograph it.

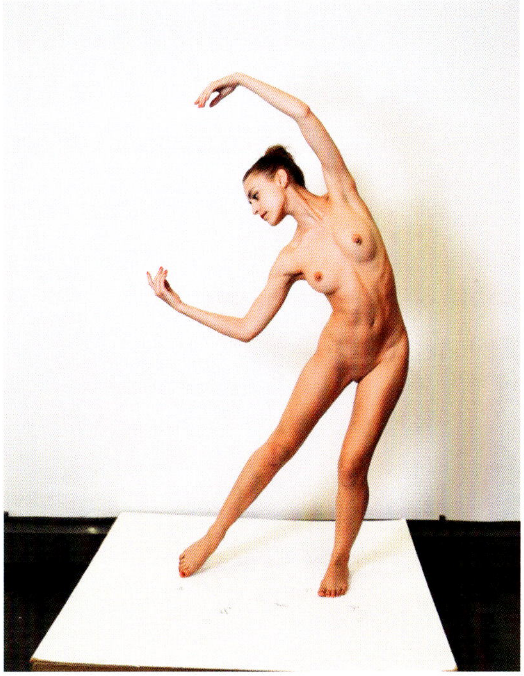

This pose shows the linear structure well.

2. Print out the image and take some time looking at it, considering the key internal lines that, for you, reflect the main characteristics of the pose, i.e. the curve of the spine, the angles of the arms and legs.

3. Place a sheet of acetate over the top of the image. First draw the primary internal structural lines, as seen in the image above right. These will often follow the form of the skeleton – arms, legs, spine. Remember that you are making artistic choices based on the inherent structure so you are not making things up, but choosing which lines to follow and which to ignore.

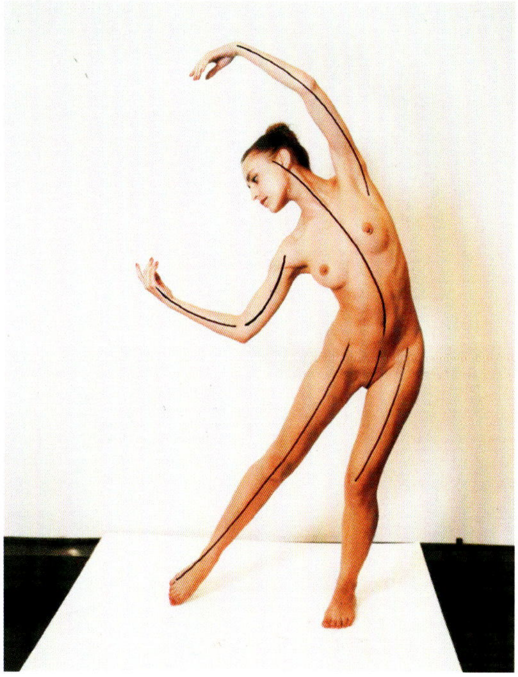

Here are the primary internal structural lines.

4. Next draw the supporting secondary internal lines to reinforce the strength of the primary flow lines (see image below). These are often smaller lines that show the contour of muscles, ligaments and so on. Each tiny line is important – be very accurate as to the angle, direction and end point of each.

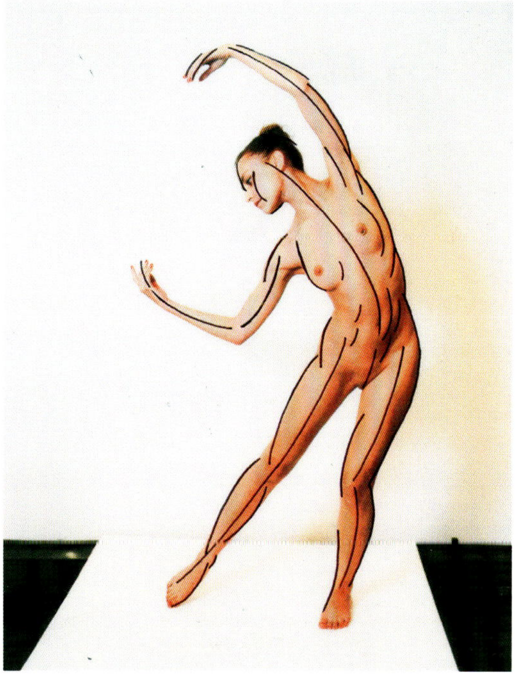

These are the secondary internal structural lines.

5. To mark the extended linear structure on the photograph, it is important first to determine your focal point, and then to make choices about which are the strongest external lines to complement your focus. There are many lines that make up one direction – for example, one leg extension line can be pulled out visually by the line in the other leg. All the internal lines will also be contributing to this external linear structure and can emphasise one direction by repetition.

   Our eyes and brains are amazing tools – they are assimilating all of this information. In the images here, not all the extensions or lines have been drawn in, as each artist will, to some degree, make personal choices as to which lines to accentuate or ignore. Some of the lines that have been curved one way could in fact be interpreted and curved the other way to tie in with a different structure. Experiment with this and do a few different versions to see which works best for you.

   The study and drawing that you have done will become the basis for your abstract sculpture, as abstraction is purely about enhancing the essence of what is there. Consider your drawing: what kind of form and feeling does it give you? Ensure to enhance these attributes in the sculptural form.

6. Place another sheet of acetate over the photo and your first sheet of acetate, then re-draw your flow lines, exaggerating the angles and flow and the relationship of the lines to one another. Start with your primary internal lines then move on to secondary internal and contour lines, always being aware of the effect of your extended linear structure. You will find that simple shapes and forms emerge, such as the straight lines and circles in the illustration on the right. You might need to lift off your last image and work on it separately at some point, as the lines can start to get confusing.

7. Once you have drawn your study, it is time to take it into three-dimensional form, using wire. Repeat the stages above, exploring the three types of flow line. Do the exercise several times, looking at it from all sides and experimenting with different approaches.

8. Now try this using other mediums – clay, for example, is great for getting good internal lines.

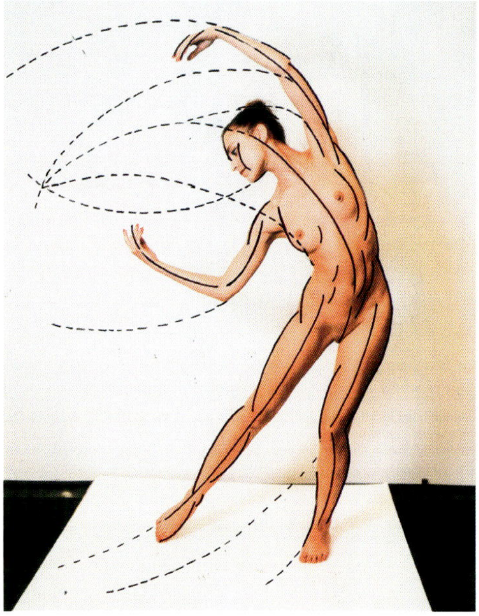

This shows the extended linear structure.

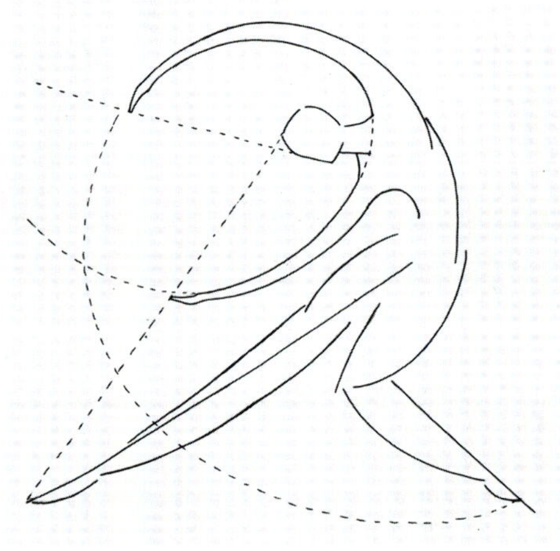

Here the internal and external lines are abstracted and exaggerated.

Planes

Planes refer to the large forms in a figure, like the architecture of a house. You can create a simple house out of about nine planes. Likewise, the big planes on a sculpture carry a lot of the simple power and expression of the piece. If you find that you are getting bogged down in detail, remember it is vitally important to look back at the large planes you need to create within your piece.

In the examples on p. 84, a simple pose has been represented, but you will find that you can express almost any pose in very few planes, often more powerfully than when you put in more detail.

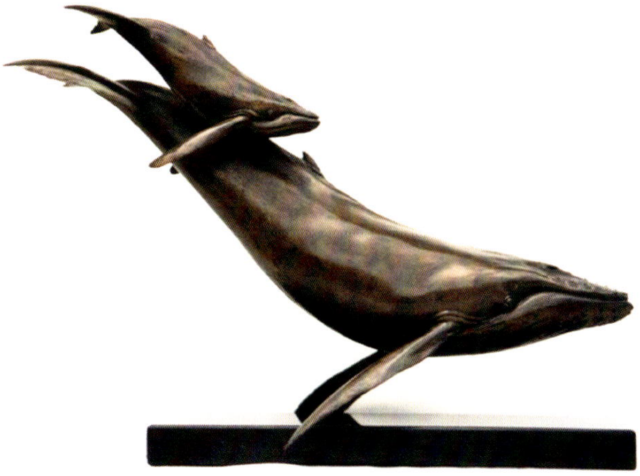

Tanya Russell, *Humpback Whales.* Cold cast bronze, 32 x 33 cm (12⅔ x 13 in.).
Photo: courtesy of the artist.

A good example of the importance of line in figurative sculpture.

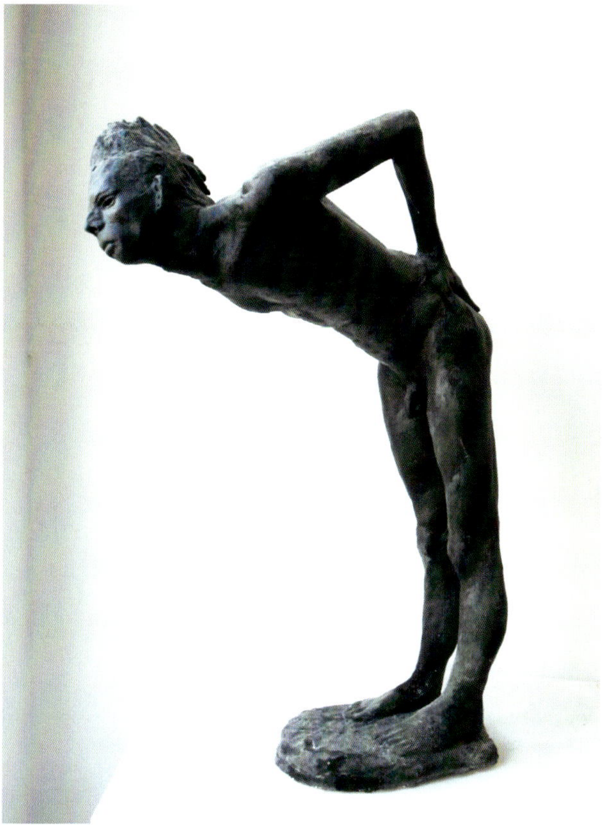

Chloe Leaper, *Curiosity.* Cold cast bronze, 70 x 45 cm (27⅔ x 17¾ in.).
Photo: courtesy of the artist.

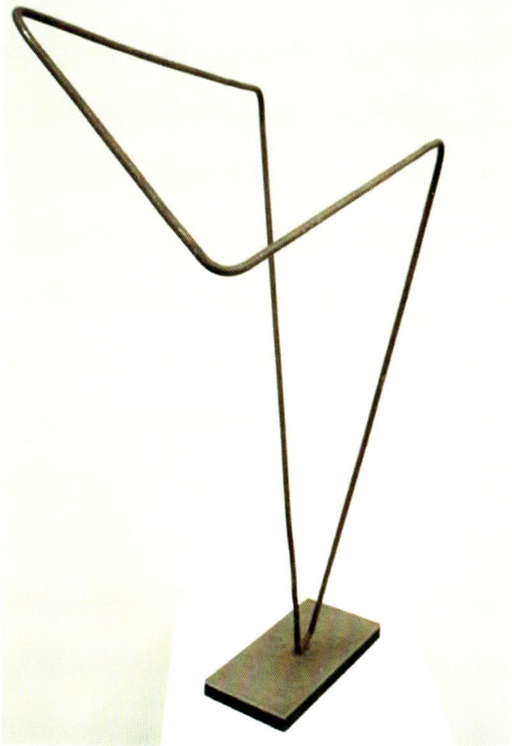

Chloe Leaper, *Curiosity Abstract.* Steel, 70 x 45 cm (27⅔ x 17¾ in.).
Photo: courtesy of the artist.

In this piece, Chloe has taken the original Curiosity sculpture and reduced it to its simplest lines.

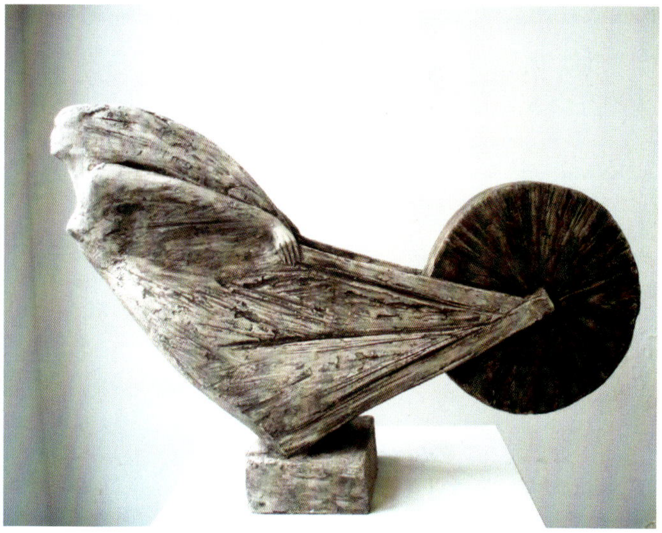

Chloe Leaper, *Longing (Gretchen and the Spinning Wheel).* Plaster, 55 x 34 cm (21¾ x 13½ in.). *Photo: courtesy of the artist.*

EXERCISE 2

Place your model in a simple pose, as shown in the example below.

Using only a large square box tool or a piece of timber approximately 5 x 2.5 cm (2 x 1 in.) and clay, create the pose in as few planes as possible. Take about seven minutes to do this.

Do the exercise again, in a different pose if you like, but trying to get fewer and fewer planes in your sculpture. You may also like to try this with a head.

Note how successful reducing the number of planes can be in sculpture. Also note the lovely dynamic marks you are making with your simple tool – do not lose these marks, as they are probably very expressive!

In the images below, Art Academy student Gary Scott has taken a maquette and abstracted it using the main planes of the form, in another maquette and then in a finished work.

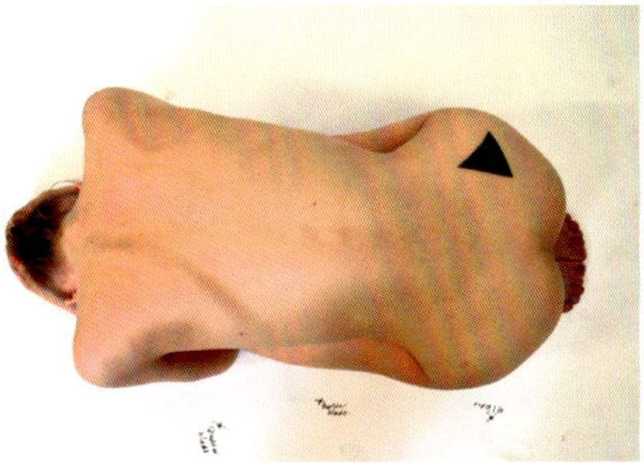

The model in a simple pose that accentuates the planes.

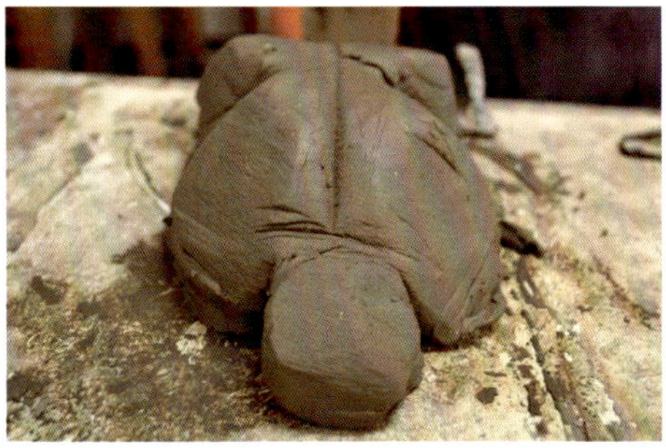

A seven-minute exercise sculpting the above pose in clay using a minimal number of planes.

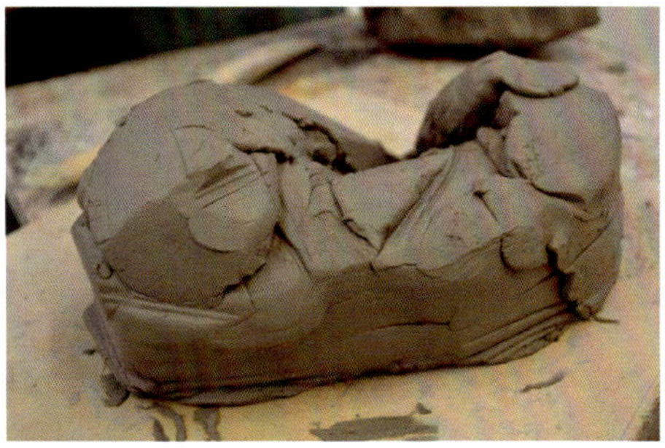

This planes exercise, involving sculpting the model in a foetal pose, illustrates the mark-making that occurs.

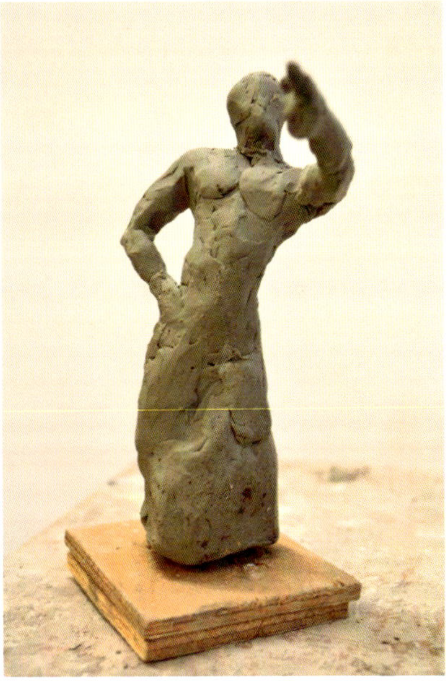

The initial maquette in Chavant.

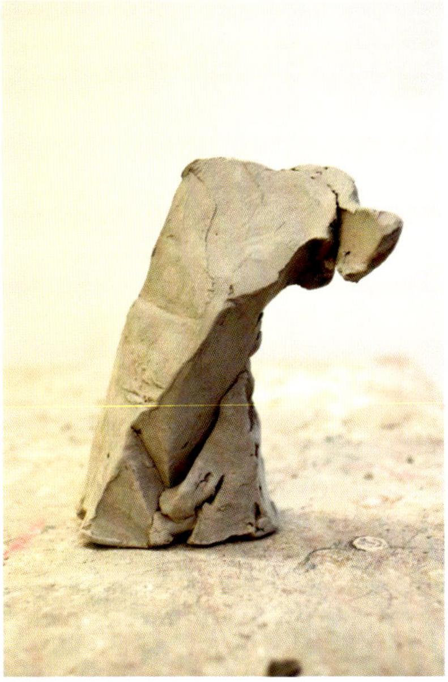

Abstracting the planes in clay.

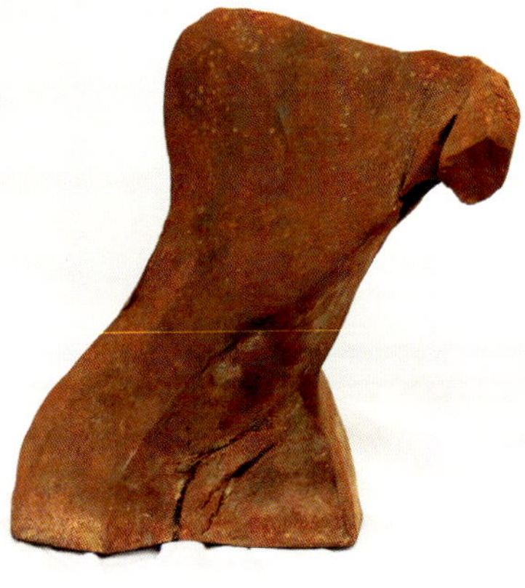

Gary Scott, *Iron Man*. Iron resin, 24 x 18 cm (9½ x 7 in.). *Photo: Jo Scott Images.*

The finished work.

Geometric Abstraction

Geometric abstraction is simply breaking down a pose into its simple geometric components. In a sculpture, this can mean reducing the form to its pure geometric shapes or just alluding to them. Even if you are not intending to create obvious geometric shapes, it can be very useful to see the large and small shapes within a pose, tuning your eye to its forms and structure.

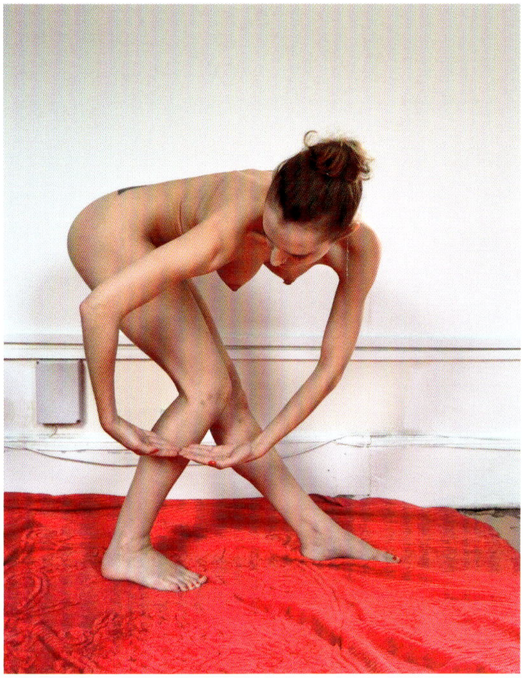

The model in a pose that is good for abstracting into simple geometric forms.

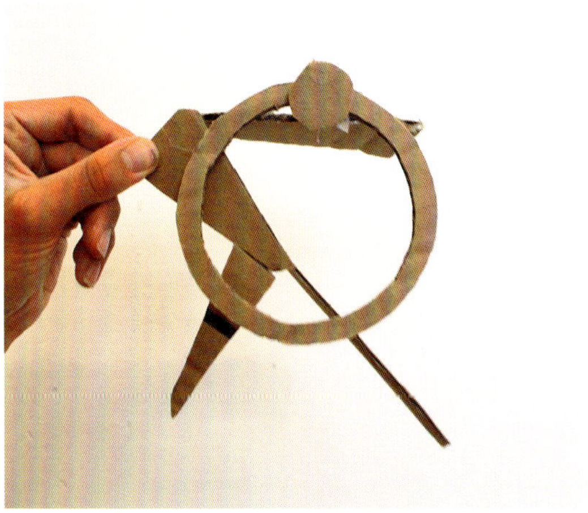

The above pose abstracted into simple geometric forms, made by Jessica Wetherly in cardboard.

☛ EXERCISE 3

1. Ask your model to take a pose conducive to geometric abstraction. Working in cardboard, reduce the forms in the pose to their simplest geometric shapes.

2. Extend this into other mediums. Try it initially without blending the forms – you can then go on to be subtler with the shapes, alluding to the geometry. You can even draw on the surface of the medium for an interesting effect.

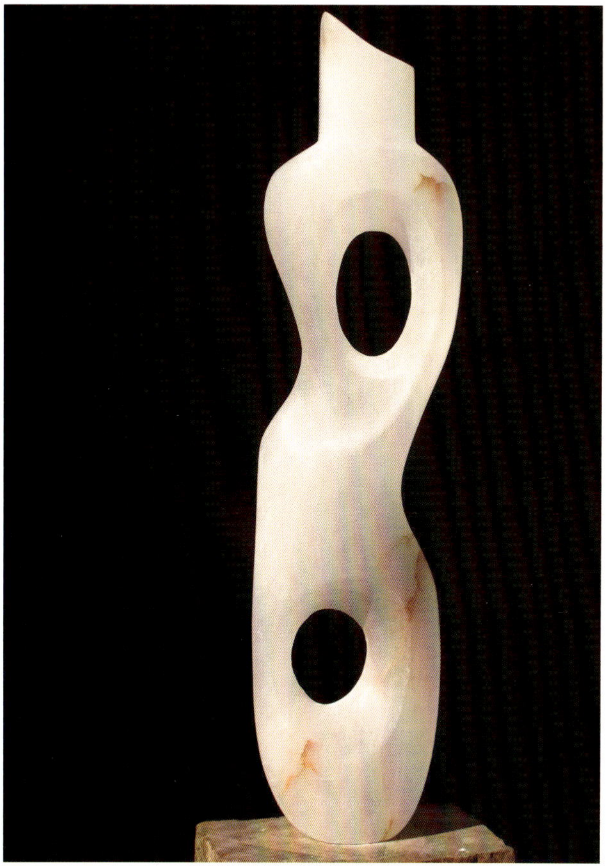

Paz Perlman, *Sacred Feminine*. Alabaster, 60 x 16 cm (23⅔ x 6⅓ in.). *Photo: Jo Confino.*

The joy and harmony of the female form is stripped to its essence.

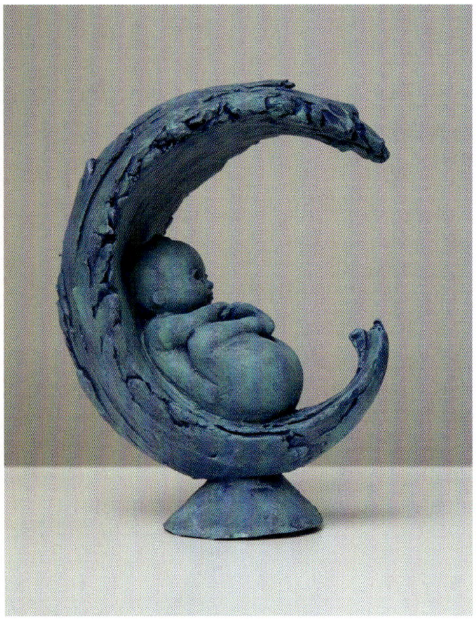

Hiromi Scintu, *Birth*. Crystacal and wood, 14 x 20 cm (5½ x 8 in.). *Photo: Wah Poon.*

This piece is a part of a series of waves depicting the different stages of life, this one being birth. It was inspired by looking at my friend's baby, but the figure also unconsciously resmbles my own baby, who was born soon after.

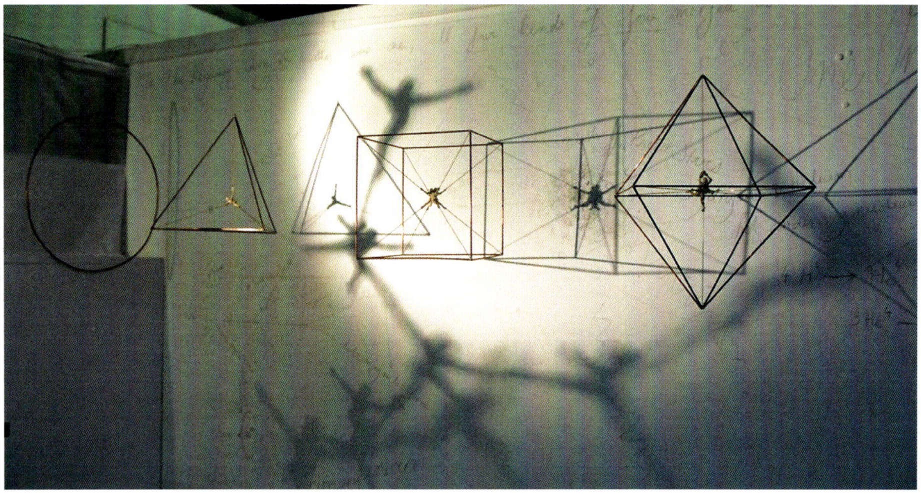

Briony Marshall, *The Emergence of Chemistry.* Installation at 401½ Studios, 2008. Mixed media (brass rod, copper tube, bioresin bronze, pencil on wall), 180 x 140 x 50 cm (71 x 55 x 19⅔ in.). *Photo: courtesy of the artist.*

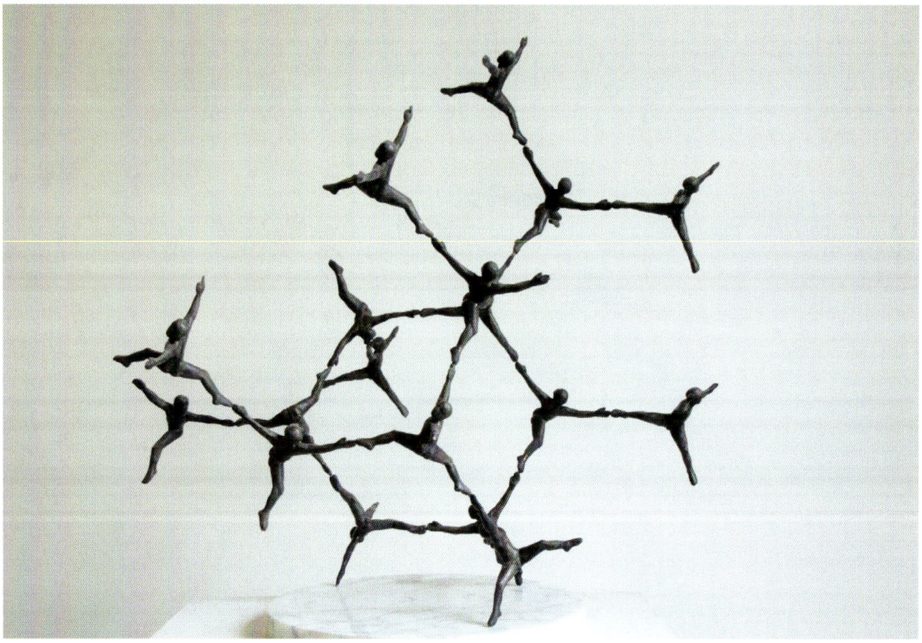

Briony Marshall, *A Dream of Society as Flawless as Diamond.* Bonded iron, 45 x 45 x 30 cm (17¾ x 17¾ x 11¾ in.). *Photo: courtesy of the artist.*

Briony Marshall often uses figures in geometric forms in her practice. In this work, the male figures form a tetrahedral lattice, such as is found in the molecular structure of diamond.

Negative Space

As sculptors, we tend to work in positive forms, as we are concerned with masses and volumes, but a vital part of any sculpture is the negative space being created. In the photo below, the negative spaces are the three triangles formed by the model's arms and legs. Our eyes read these as much as the positive shapes and they are just as expressive. They are like pauses in speech, which can be as meaningful as the words themselves.

EXERCISE 4

1. Choose a pose with your model that is all about negative spaces.

2. Using a material of your choice (card, paper, wood, clay, Plastiline), abstract the model shape to accentuate the negative spaces.

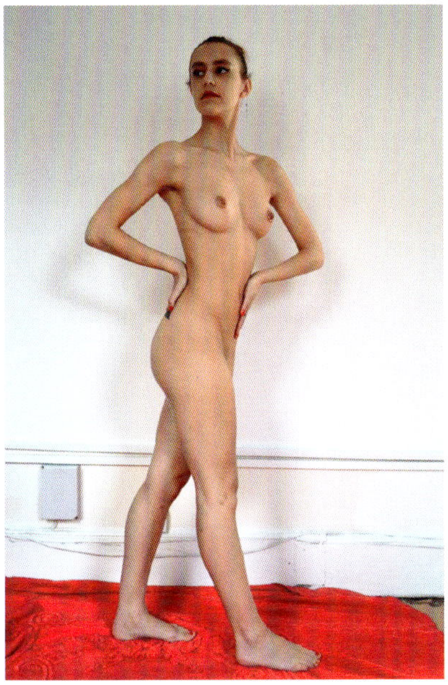

A pose illustrating negative spaces.

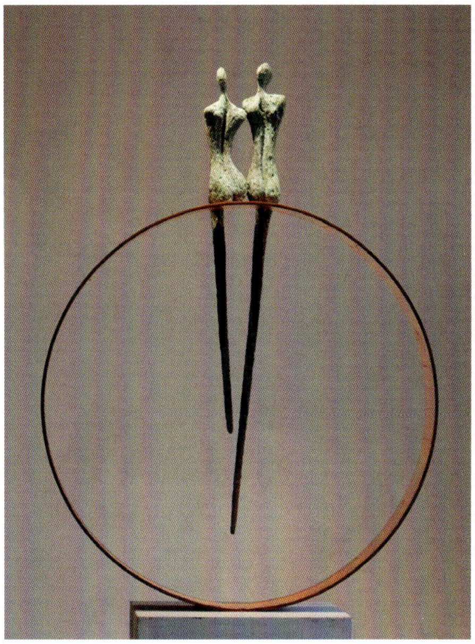

Michael Speller, *Nourish*. Bronze, 110 x 90 x 80 cm (43½ x 35½ x 31½ in.). *Photo: courtesy of the artist.*

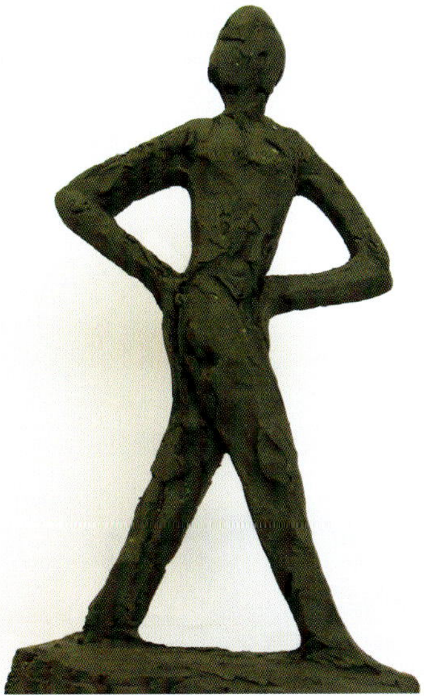

A quick exercise exploring negative spaces, based on the pose above.

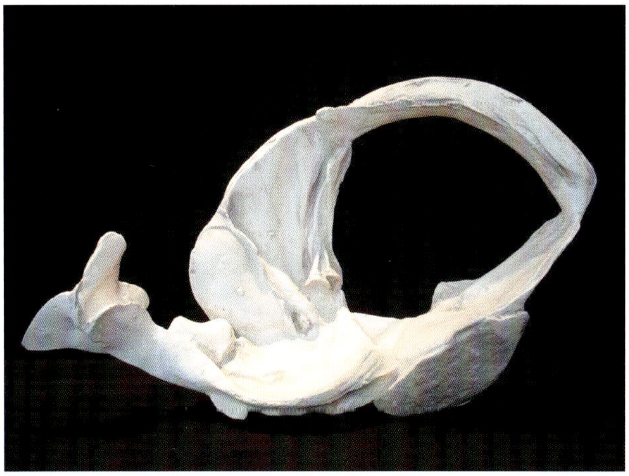

Chloe Leaper, *From the Inside Looking Out*. Plaster assemblage, 35 x 23 cm (14 x 9 in.). *Photo: courtesy of the artist.*

Chloe's sculpture is all about negative spaces.

Pure Reduction

Pure reduction is the very essence of abstraction; it involves reducing and reducing the form until only the essentials remain. If you are not careful, reduction can actually end up rather empty or crude. To avoid this you have to start with a thorough understanding of the form.

Reduction was one of the key tools of artists in the ancient Greek and Egyptian periods and in many other cultures; in modern sculpture, the work of Brancusi is an excellent example of pure reduction. In all these examples, the forms are unbelievably subtle, rich and vibrant – they are not remotely crude or empty. This is due to the artists' real expertise with the medium, understanding of the form and conscious application of process. They were only interested in bringing out the real internal essence of their subject.

Medium and technique also have a big impact on reduction – carving in stone or working in sheet steel has a tendency to reduce the forms, due to the nature of the materials.

The focus of the next exercise is a portrait. As explained you cannot reduce a form without fully understanding it first. The exercise can be done with any form, as long as you go through the steps fully.

EXERCISE 5

1. Find a willing friend or relative and ask them to pose (ideally) or take really good photos all around their head. You are doing a simple portrait study, so follow the set-up directions for a portrait head as described on pp. 70–2.
2. Draw the model from a slight distance, not focusing on the detail yet, but on the big shapes and characteristics.
3. Model a representational head, focusing and spending time understanding all the subtle forms and the main planes of the face (again, as explained on pp. 70–2).
4. Using clay, model the head three times at about 10 cm (4 in.) high, taking five minutes with each one, using different types of abstraction. In the image above right, the heads have been abstracted using planes, then texture, then reduction. This will help you to break away from the realistic study.
5. Take another bust peg and model your head structure in as simple and powerful a way as you can. There should be no raised modelling greater than 5 mm ($^{3}/_{16}$ in.) above the surface. Ensure that you capture the essence of the form and do not be afraid to leave out marks or features that do not contribute to these core qualities. Model the head, purely looking at tonal contrast, almost as if you were a painter.

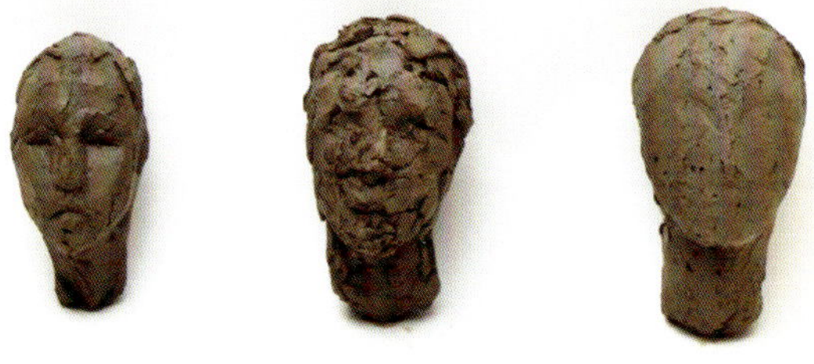

An exercise doing three five-minute sketches, approaching the abstraction in different ways, from left to right – focusing on planes, keeping the texture loose, reducing the form.

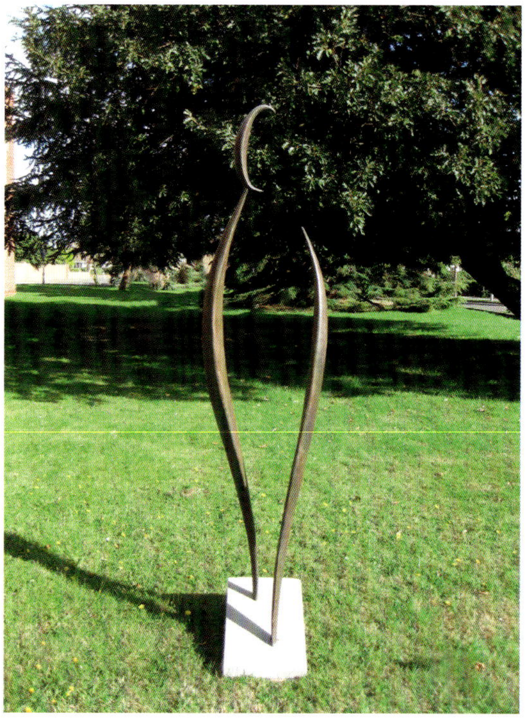

Tanya Russell, *Spirit of Being*. Bronze commissioned for a private garden, 200 x 46 cm (84.5 x 18 in.). *Photo: courtesy of the artist.*

This sculpture is an example of pure reduction.

Exaggeration/Caricature

We have already covered exaggeration and creative choices using lines and planes. This section is more about focusing on and exaggerating specific features, and the parts to be exaggerated could come either from the features of the model or the pose. Exaggeration can be achieved by making things bigger or smaller and these decisions can be made for conceptual or formal reasons, but there will tend to be a bit of both.

This is a fun exercise as it is all about being a bit wild and over-the-top, but as with all art, while having fun you must still be very careful to make conscious creative choices, taking care with each mark you make.

☛ EXERCISE 6

1. Taking your willing (but by now very tired!) model, ask them to strike a few different poses, until you find one that is exciting. If this is not possible, use a favourite photo featuring a dramatic pose.

2. Do some quick drawings experimenting with exaggerating the forms in different ways. Choose the core attributes or features of the pose and accentuate them – don't make things up or do things that look ridiculous, but exaggerate the form in such a way that it is enhanced.

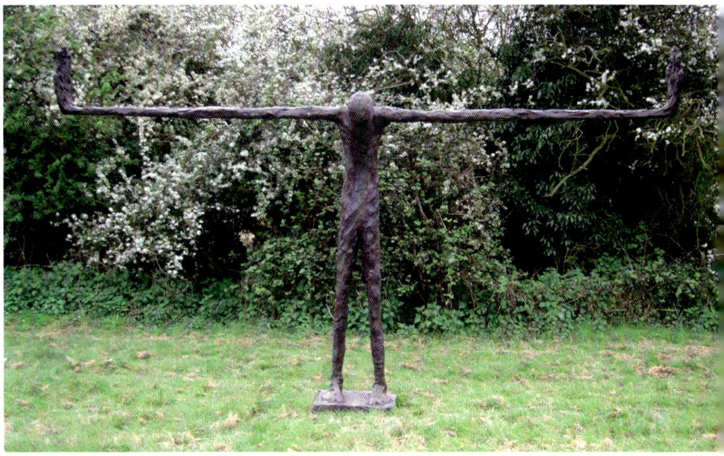

John O'Connor, *Inner space.* Cold cast slate, 270 x 420 cm (106⅓ x 165½ in.). *Photo: courtesy of the artist.*

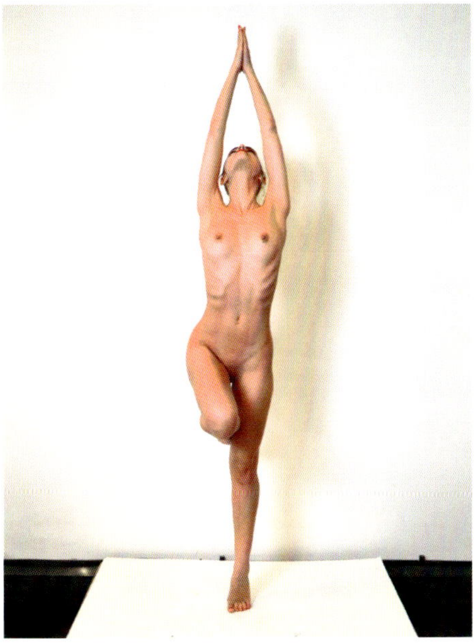

A pose that can be exaggerated.

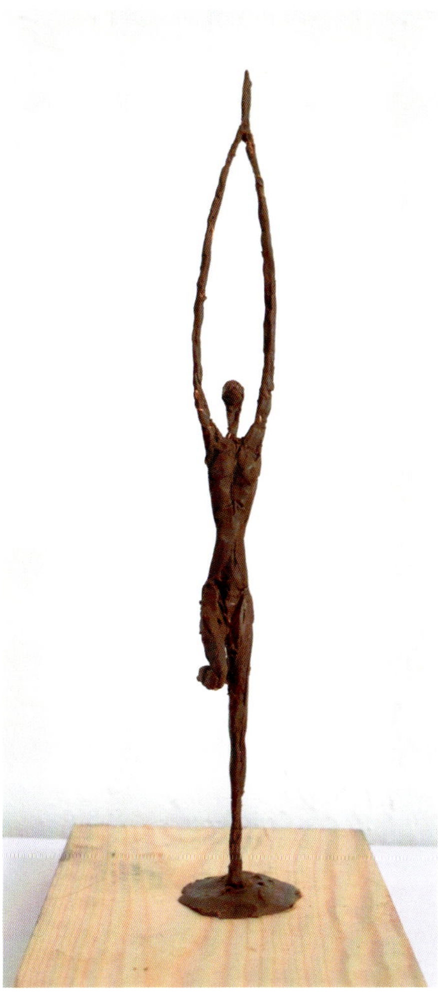

This shows one way to exaggerate the pose.

Conceptual Abstraction

In conceptual abstraction the idea determines the language of abstraction. For example, when ancient cultures tried to express the concepts and emotions associated with the fertility goddess, they emphasised the breasts (expressing nourishment and abundance), the stomach (the bringer of life) and large buttocks (again denoting fertility). These parts were therefore overly exaggerated, and there were often no arms or feet at all.

A more contemporary example of conceptual abstraction, where the texture and form are not chosen purely for their formal attributes but to express an idea, can be found in the work of George Triggs, described below. George is an alumnus of the Art Academy, where he is a visiting tutor, and is a practicing sculptor.

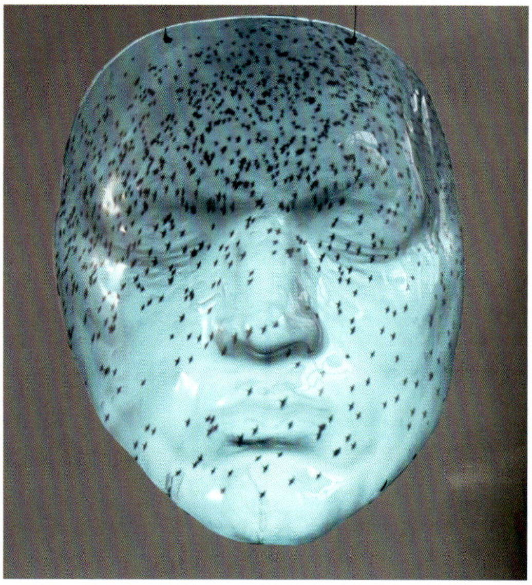

George Triggs, *Movements of the mind.* Glass and film projection, face: 66 x 55 x 50 cm (26 x 21½ x 19¾ in.). *Photo: courtesy of the artist.*

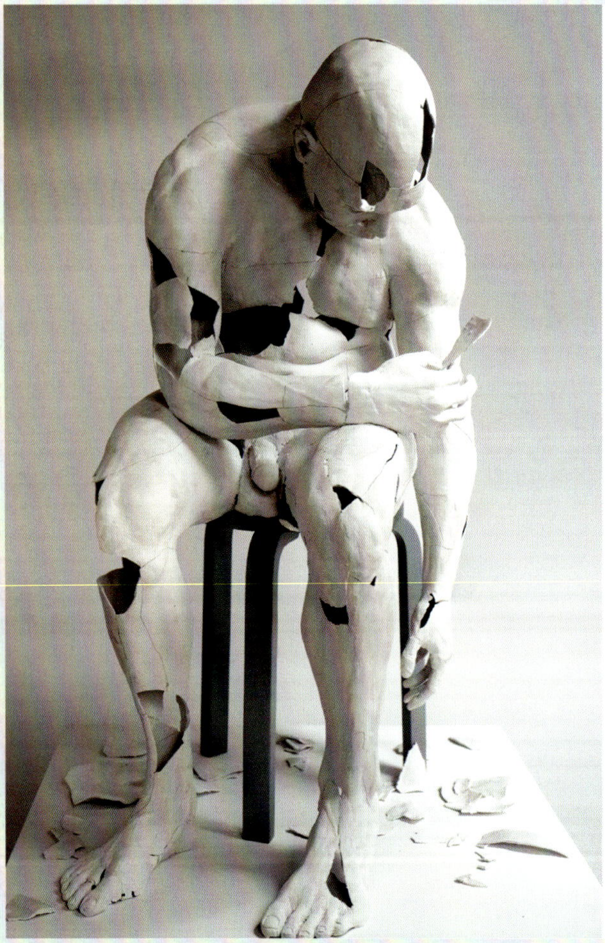

Case Study: George Triggs

Broken goes about examining the fragility, isolation and silent determination of our existence. It captures the seemingly impossible task of picking up the pieces and putting ourselves back together after a complete emotional implosion. This life-size figure is in fractured pieces slumped on a stool. It is trying to rebuild itself, examining the deterioration of its own existence, examining what it means to be broken, questioning whether it can return to life anew, questioning whether the cracks and experiences stay below the surface and whether some pieces of itself are gone forever.

Broken was created in solid clay, then cast as a hollow shell, which I then literally shattered into pieces and reassembled. Looking at all the pieces it seems like an impossible task, which made it more exciting, exhausting and inspiring. The process was a huge emotional and thought-provoking journey for me, which I feel transfers into the work.

George Triggs, ***Broken***. Painted plaster, life-size. *Photo: Ben Wisely.*

In the next example, we have a case study of Chloe Leaper's work, to explore how the concept behind the work influences the form. Chloe is a graduate of the Art Academy's Diploma course and is now a tutor and practicing sculptor.

Case Study: Chloe Leaper

My work is concerned with the exploration of space and form – sculptural, architectural and psychological. I am interested in how space and form are mentally and physiologically perceived by the viewer. I have been developing a conceptual visual language that draws upon architectural forms and narratives as metaphors for emotional and psychological states.

The concept of architectural metaphor pervades every aspect of my sculptural language. These abstract architectural elements are fused with organic forms that reference the human muscular and skeletal systems and have a tactility we instinctively understand, as it references the shapes and textures of our own bodies.

I often sculpt in plaster, as it is light, self-supporting and capable of producing organic and geometric forms. To make these forms I push found organic objects such as bones and rocks into clay and pour the plaster into the negative space they create. I make the geometric forms using clay walls as a boundary to produce the exact shapes I need.

I am fascinated by the language of form and structure, particularly archetypal relationships such as positive and negative volumes, interiority and exteriority, and the horizontal and the vertical. I am interested in utilising the inherent psychological qualities of these frameworks to express human experiences.

For example, *In Fear of Loss* (p. 94) explores feelings of grief and attachment through a compositional focus on negative space, alluding to absence and emptiness. This has been achieved through the exaggeration of the female figure's thighs to create a cradling space in which the male figure lightly lies.

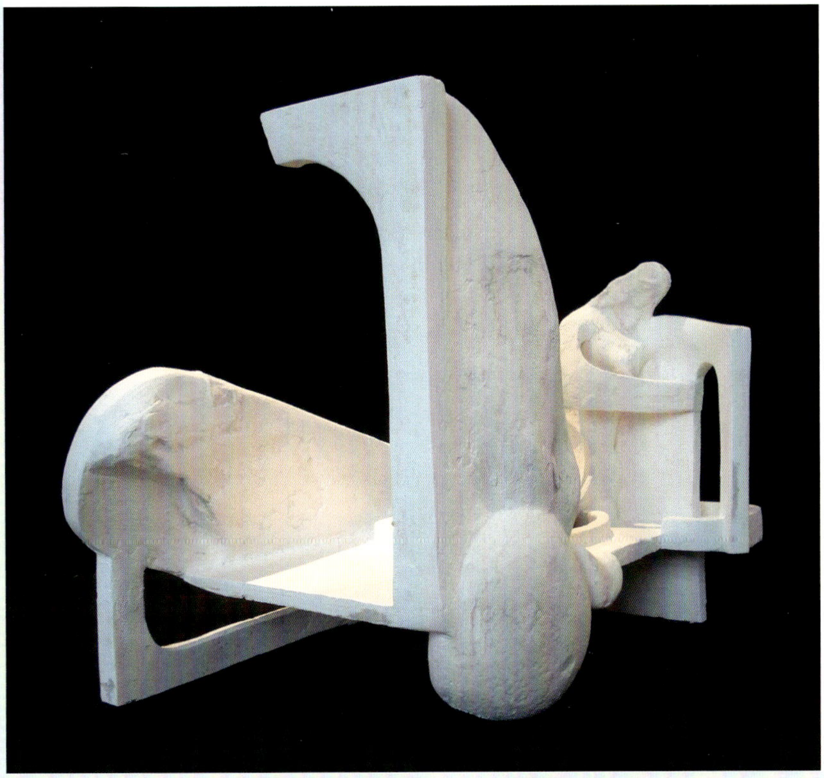

Detachment 2 (left) uses a large, open, internal space, heavily enclosed by large, flat, thigh planes which read as walls and arches. Conversely the head and upper body are made of smaller, more delicate forms. The scale change between the lower and upper body gives a sense of distance and separation. The upper body and head is in turn angled, as if turning away from the lower body. The gaze of the face is directed through a small archway, created by a suggested arm, to a space behind and beyond, signifying further mental detachment.

Chloe Leaper, ***Detachment 2.*** Plaster assemblage, 40 x 28 cm (16 x 11 in.). *Photo: courtesy of the artist.*

EXERCISE 7

1. This is a research-based exercise looking at conceptual abstraction. Choose some cultures and periods that really interest you, from ancient traditions, different cultures and contemporary culture. Research some of the core ideas and beliefs that are represented in these cultures and look at how these ideas influence abstraction in the typical sculpture of that culture.

2. Next, choose your own concept, ensure it is heartfelt, and express your concept in abstracted forms.

Material-Influenced Abstraction

Much of the language of abstract art is strongly influenced by the material the artist uses. For example, Sir Anthony Caro's work is influenced by the unique ways in which sheet steel can be manipulated and many of Barbara Hepworth's simple forms were hugely influenced by the fact that they were carved in stone or wood. The artist may choose the material because it best expresses the intention in abstract form, but the material in turn influences the form.

EXERCISE 8

1. Choose three completely different materials (e.g. cardboard, wire and fabric).

2. Using one pose, so that the effect of different materials is clear, create three sculptures using the three different materials, thinking about how to construct the form so as to use that material most effectively.

Materials, Equipment and Methods

Almost any material can be used for sculpture, but it is very important that you understand the effects of your choices on the outcome of the work, so spend time playing with materials and techniques.

What follows are some of the more obvious materials, but you can of course create your own range. Carefully note any health-and-safety instructions provided with your materials and equipment, and if in doubt obtain further information.

Plaster

MATERIALS AND EQUIPMENT

The type of plaster normally used for modelling is 'superfine', a medium-hard plaster. Fine casting plaster is too soft for modelling and Crystacal or very hard plaster is generally too tough to file down easily. Crystacal can, however, be good to use if a lot of slim forms or details are required. To mix plaster you will need:

- A bag of plaster
- Two buckets of water – one for mixing, one for washing hands and pots
- Plaster mixing pots
- Thin rubber or latex gloves (optional)

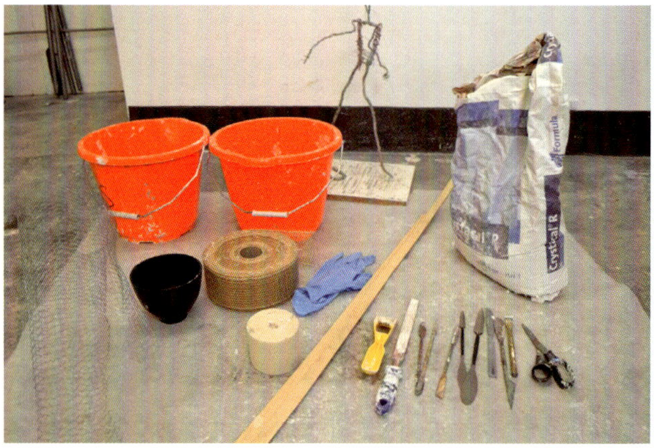

Materials and equipment you will need for mixing and sculpting with plaster.

Mixing Plaster

1. Fluff up the plaster in the bag with dry hands until it is a floury texture (never put wet hands into the plaster bag or you will get hard lumps all through it).
2. Decide what quantity of finally mixed plaster you require, then pour half that volume of water into your mixing pot.
3. Sprinkle plaster slowly and evenly into the water, until small islands appear on the top (add less if you want a runny mix and more if you need a thicker mix).
4. Carefully mix the plaster with your hands (you can use gloves for this) until it is a totally smooth liquid or paste, depending on what you are using it for. Be very wary of adding more dry plaster once you have mixed, as you will get a very lumpy consistency.

Plaster Techniques

Modelling directly

You need quite a good solid armature for this, but you probably don't want a figure iron as plaster can be used as a finished medium and coloured at the end. The armature therefore needs to be welded steel, strong aluminium or wood, depending on the structure. You can use scrim (as depicted in the photo on the right) to bulk up the form in early stages if required.

Use metal modelling tools to model the plaster, and surforms (perforated metal rasps) or files to take away excess.

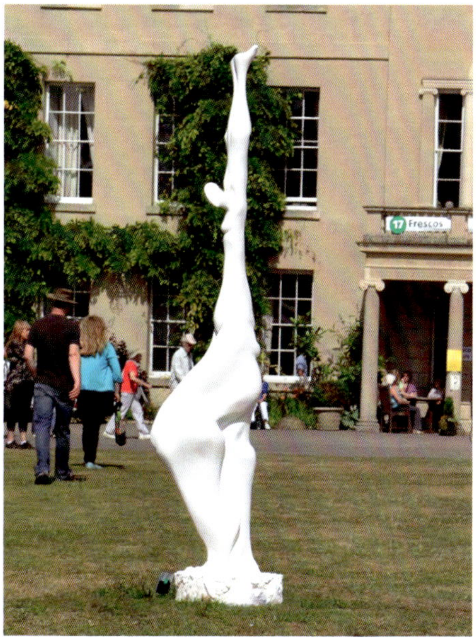

Tarek Tuma, *Levitation*. Plaster, 216 x 56 cm (85 x 22 in.). *Photo: courtesy of the artist.*

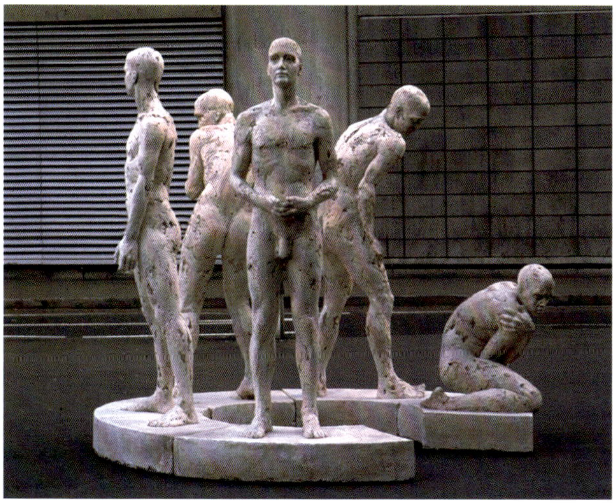

Damian Fennell, *States of Being*. Sculpture modelled directly in plaster, 210 x 201 x 201 cm (82⅔ x 79 x 79 in.). *Photo: courtesy of the artist.*

Creative plaster and scrim

This method is similar to modelling directly, but using scrim as a final medium in a creative way rather than as a bulking medium. There are two main kinds of scrim: jute scrim (a bulky hessian-type scrim) and cotton scrim (a much finer mesh). Both can be used for bulking, tying or for creative effect. Dip the scrim into your plaster mix and apply it to your armature or other support as required.

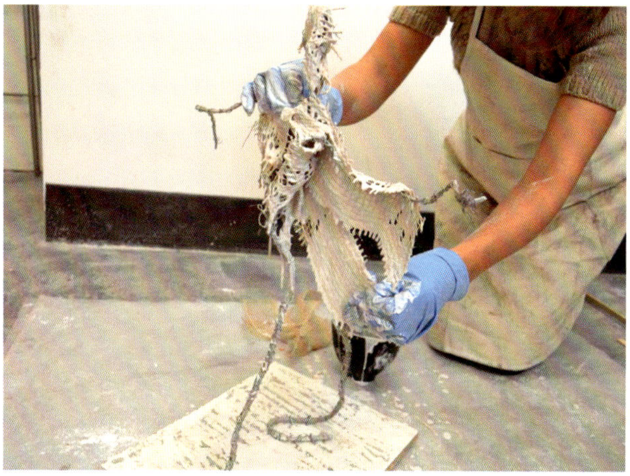

Jessica creating a sculpture using plaster and scrim.

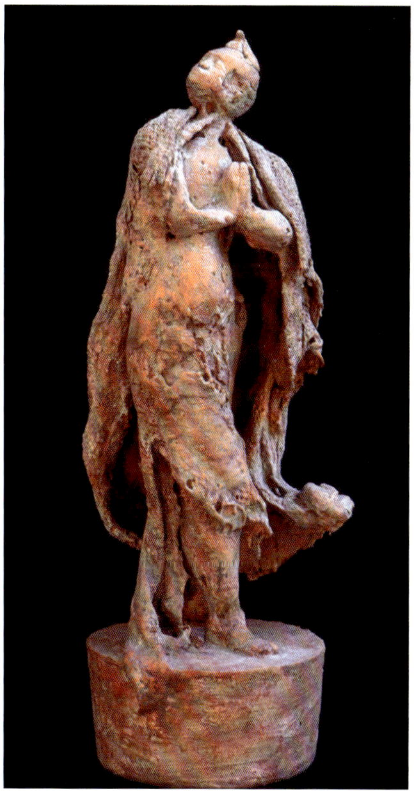

Christy Symington ARBS, *God of the House*. Pigmented plaster, in the collection of Fiona Cierach, London, 52 x 16 x 18 cm (20½ x 6⅓ x 7 in.). *Photo: Tontxi Vazquez.*

Plaster and lath

Using lengths of wood lath, you can build a structure very quickly, tying the lath together with scrim dipped in plaster.

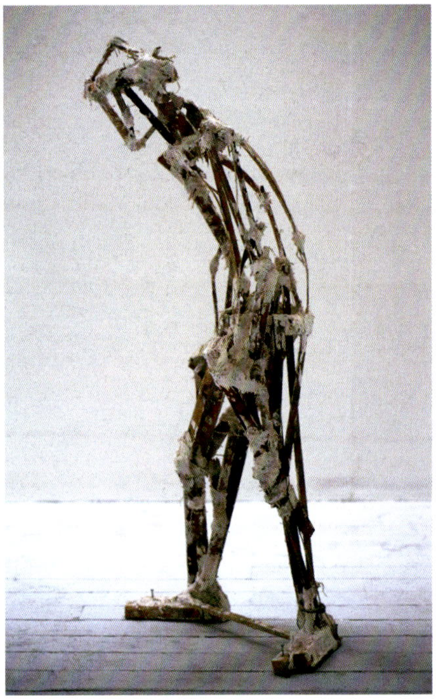

Damian Fennell, *Study for Democracy*. Lath, plaster, scrim, 110 x 35 x 30 cm (43⅓ x 13¾ x 12 in.). *Photo: courtesy of the artist.*

Plaster and found object construction

In this technique found objects, particularly natural forms, are pressed into clay to make an impression. Plaster casts made from these impressions are then assembled using liquid plaster to join them together.

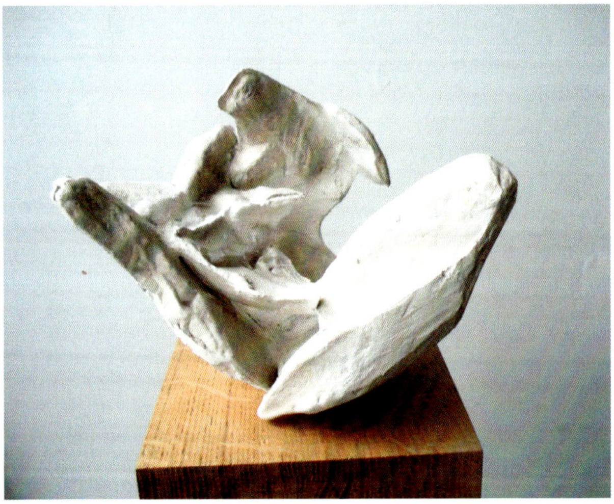

Chloe Leaper, *In Fear of Loss*. Piece created through plaster assemblage, 16 x 16 cm (6¼ x 6¼ in.). *Photo: courtesy of the artist.*

Masking Tape

Masking tape is a great medium for getting a quick creative sculptural effect. Build a simple wire sketch armature (see Chapter 6, pp. 106–10), then carefully apply masking tape, using the medium to create planes, angles and lines.

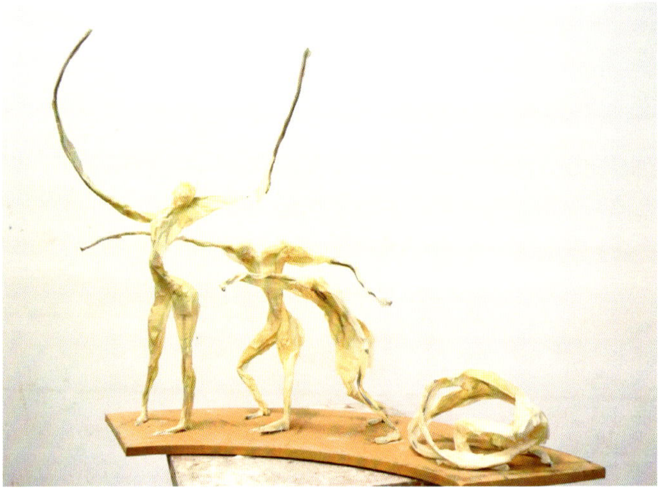

Lorna McNeill, *Flow*. Figures created using masking tape on a wire structure, 74 x 57 x 21 cm (29 x 22½ x 8⅓ in.). *Photo: courtesy of the artist.*

Wood and Glue

Attaching wood or other mediums using a glue gun is another fast, simple and effective method. Choose and assemble your pieces with care and attention.

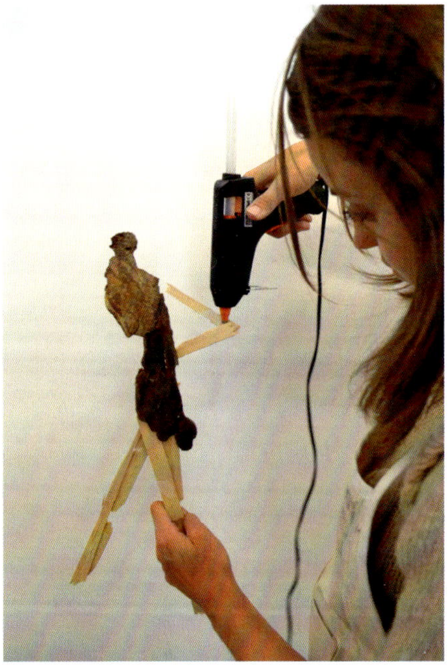

Attaching lath and bark using a glue gun.

Wire

All kinds of wire and chicken wire can be used for making sculptures – a few examples are illustrated here.

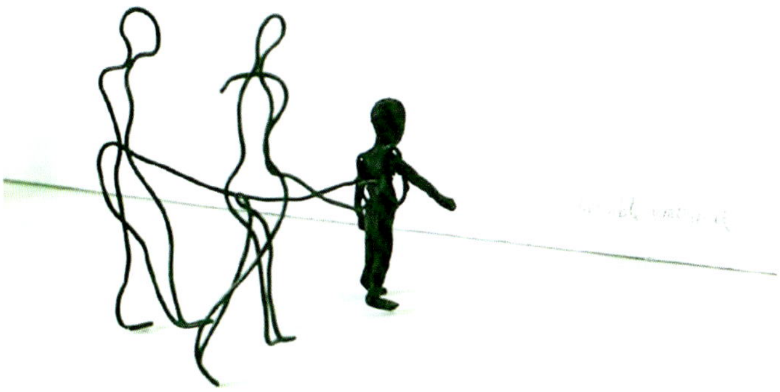

Briony Marshall, *Invisible Umbilical.* Wax and wire, 13 x 18 x 11 cm (5 x 7 x 4⅓ in.). *Photo: courtesy of the artist.*

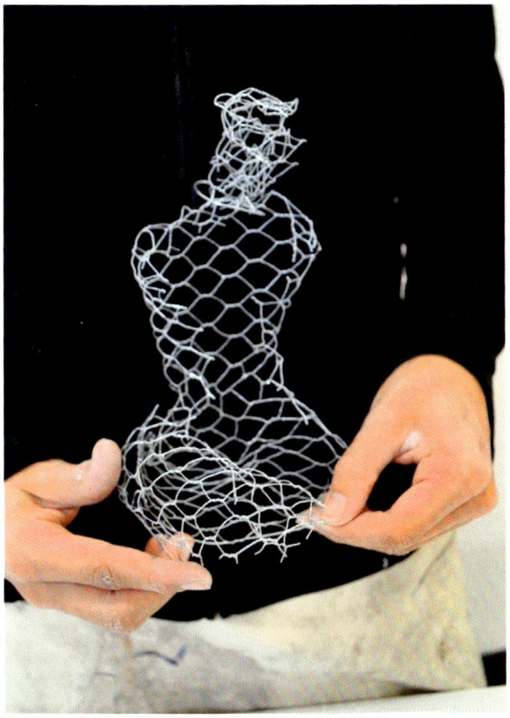

Building a figure using chicken wire.

Found Objects

Depending on the objects and the material of which they are made, these probably need to be glued, welded, braised or otherwise stuck together.

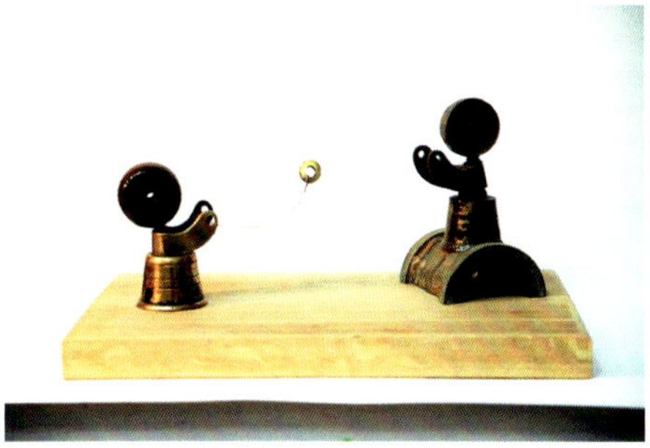

Brian Hillman, Catch. Brass, ceramic, castors, copper wire, steel washer, iron casting, English oak, 15 x 22 x 15 cm (6 x 8¾ x 6 in.). *Photo: courtesy of the artist.*

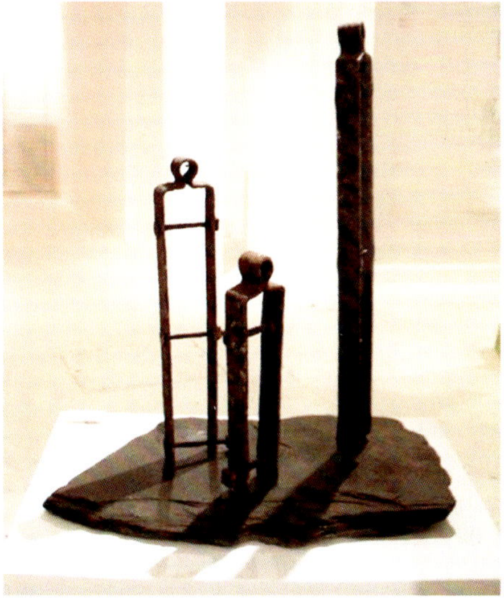

Brian Hillman, *Together.* Iron barn door hinges on Welsh slate, 70 x 50 x 55 cm (27½ x 19½ x 21½ in.). *Photo: courtesy of the artist.*

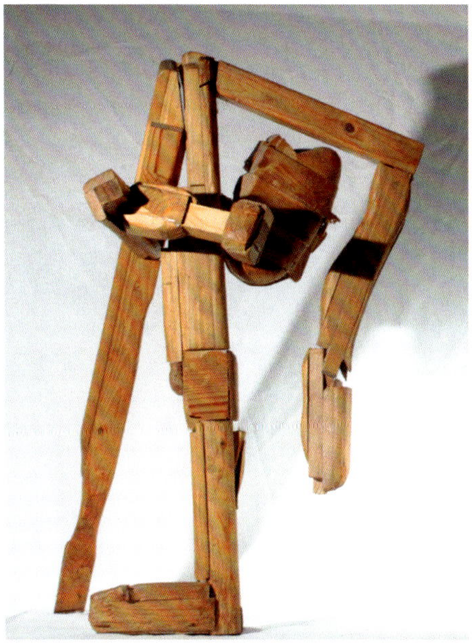

Lynne Abrahamson, *The Acrobat.* Fabricated wood, 78 x 42 x 50 cm (30¾ x 16½ x 19¾ in.). *Photo: Kevin Ball.*

Metals

This requires more expertise in techniques such as welding, grinding, drilling, casting and riveting, but as you can see from the images here, it can be amazingly effective.

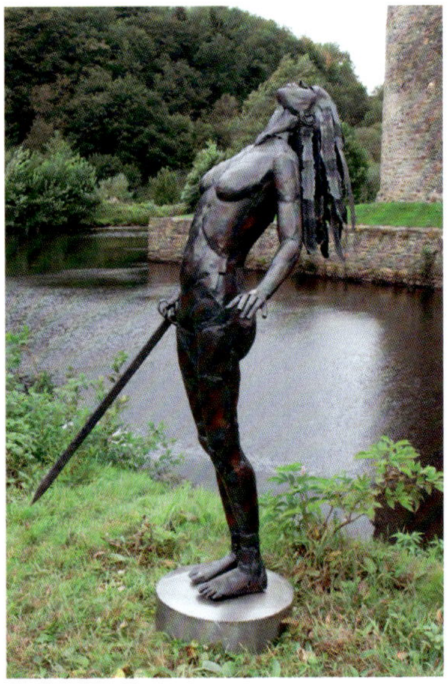

Jill Simpson, *The Lady of the Lake.* Beaten and welded mild steel, life-size, 180 x 90 x 75 cm (70¾ x 35½ x 29½ in.). *Photo: Klaus Schmoll-Clemens at Burg Baldenau, Hunolstein, Germany.*

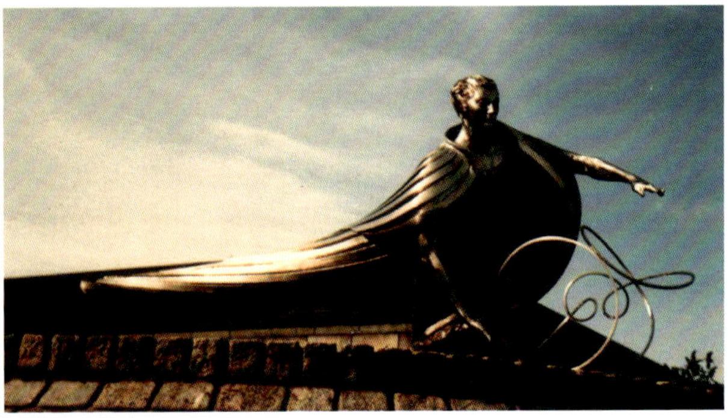

Edwin Russell, commissioned for the Scottish Blood Bank, Edinburgh. Fabricated and part-cast in stainless steel, 200 x 400 cm (78¾ x 157½ in.). *Photo: courtesy of the artist.*

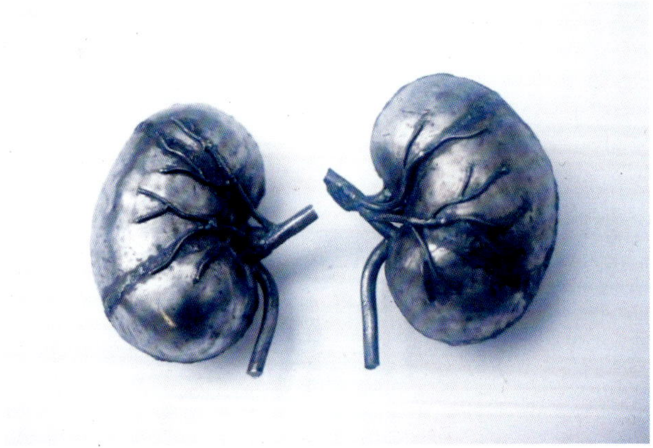

Jill Simpson, *Steel Kidneys.* Welded mild steel, 26 x 26 x 13 cm (10 x 10 x 5 in.). *Photo: courtesy of the artist.*

Carving

This is clearly a huge area that we will not seek to cover in detail. Carving can be done in wood or stone, or materials as simple as soap, breezeblock or a block of plaster. It is wise to get professional tuition in these techniques, as it makes the whole process so much easier, safer and more fulfilling.

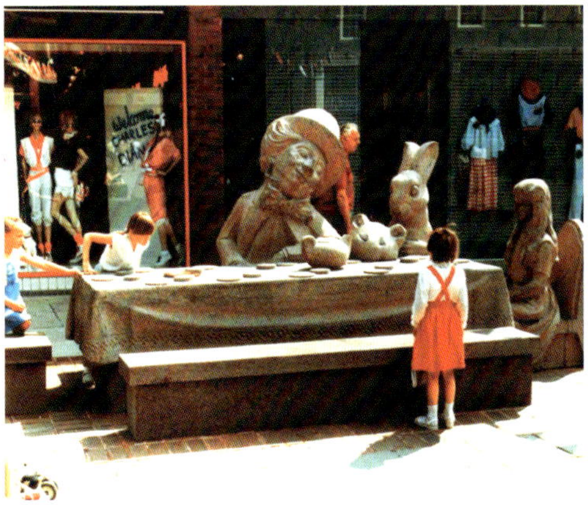

Edwin Russell, *Mad Hatters Tea Party.* Carved granite commissioned for Golden Square, Warrington, Cheshire. *Photo: courtesy of the artist.*

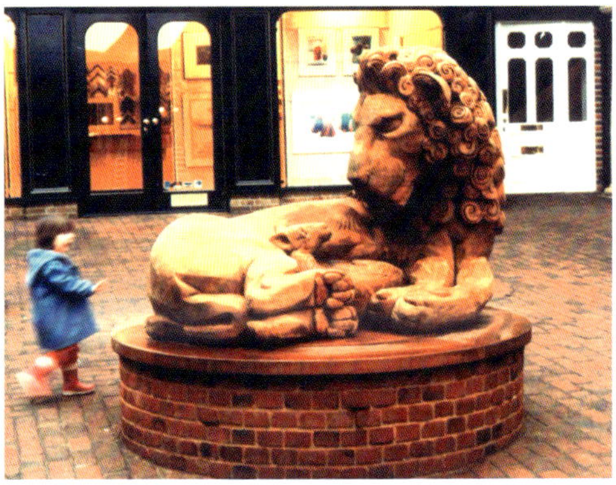

Edwin Russell, *Lion and Lamb.* Teak wood carving commissioned for Lion and Lamb Yard, Farnham, Surrey, 472 x 259 cm (186 x 102 in.). *Photo: courtesy of the artist.*

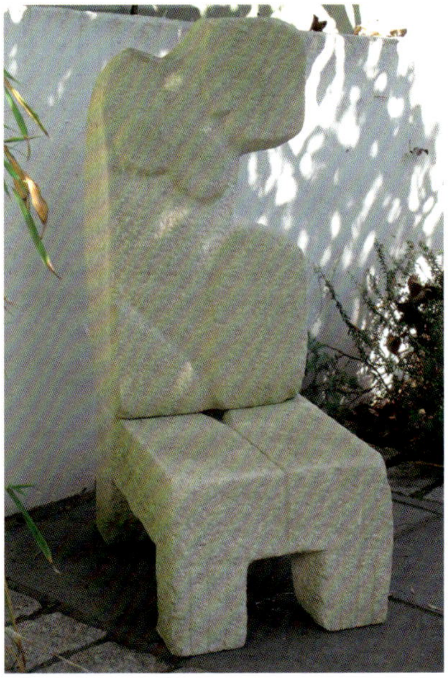

Paz Perlman, *Woman Chair.* Chalk stone, 70 x 28 cm (27⅔ x 11 in.). *Photo: courtesy of the artist.*

Relief Sculpture

Relief sculpture is a type of modelling or carving which is not fully three-dimensional.

Like all sculptures, the materials and styles for relief sculpture are almost unlimited. Generally they are fixed to walls, but they can also be on the ground or incorporated into a bigger sculpture.

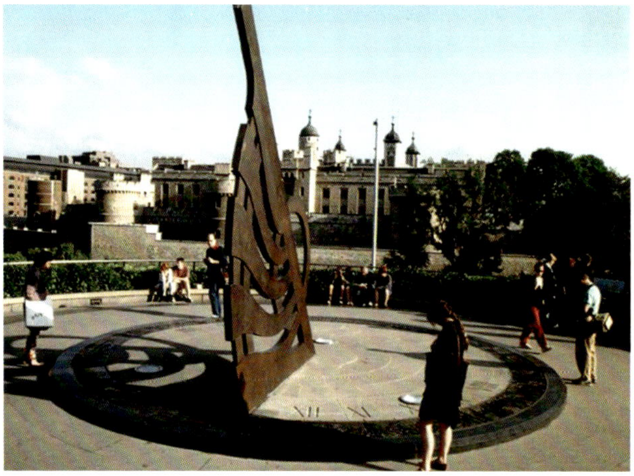

Designed by Edwin Russell and sculpted by Edwin Russell, Lorne McKean, Tanya Russell, Simon Buchanan, *History of London Transport.* Bronze, Tower Hill Sundial, above Tower Hill London Underground station, 370 x 600 cm (135¾ x 236¼ in.). *Photo: courtesy of the artists.*

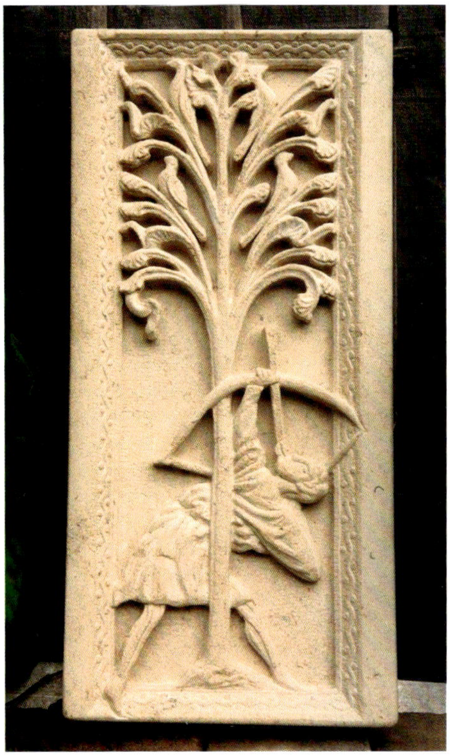

Simon Keeley, *Archer*. Relief carving in limestone, 450 x 23 cm (177¼ x 9 in.). *Photo: courtesy of the artist.*

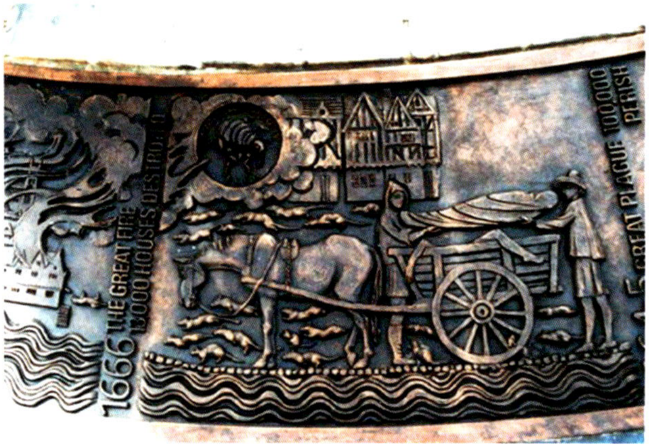

Tanya Russell, Lorne McKean, *History of London Transport* (detail). *Photo: courtesy of the artists.*

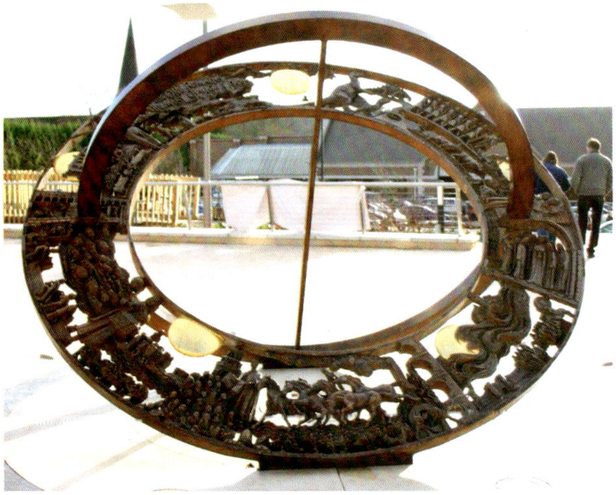

Lorne McKean and Edwin Russell, *Horsham Heritage Sundial.* Bronze, centenary semi-relief sundial commissioned by Horsham District Council (The Plaza), 300 x 550 cm (118 x 216½ in.). *Photo: courtesy of the artists.*

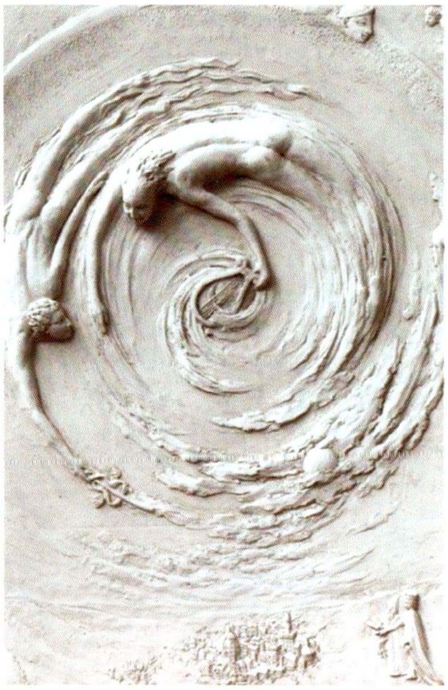

Tanya Russell, *Power should not be given without wisdom.* Relief sculpture commissioned to illustrate the 6th volume of *The Letters of Marsilio Ficino.* Translated from the Latin by members of the Language Department of the School of Economic Science. 76 x 57 cm (30 x 22½ in.). *Photo: courtesy of the artist.*

Body Casting

This is a technique made popular by Antony Gormley, which can be effective in many ways. It uses a product called alginate and sometimes plaster. Research carefully how to do it before trying, as otherwise you could seriously hurt the person you are casting from during the process. Good instructions can be found online or through sculpture materials suppliers.

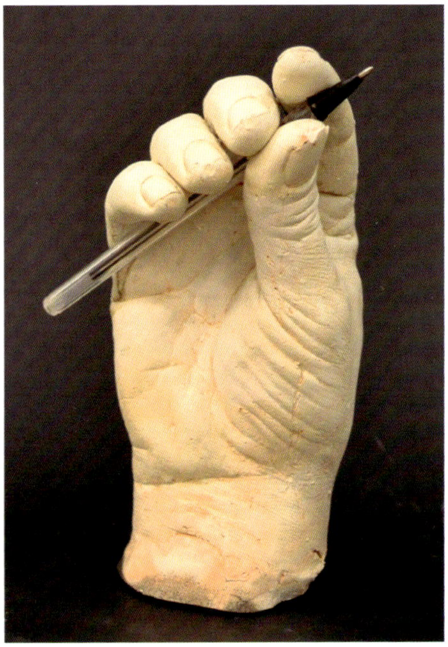

Joanne Weaver, ***Hand Writing.*** Plaster, pen, 17 x 9 x 10 cm (6½ x 3½ x 4 in.). *Photo: courtesy of the artist.*

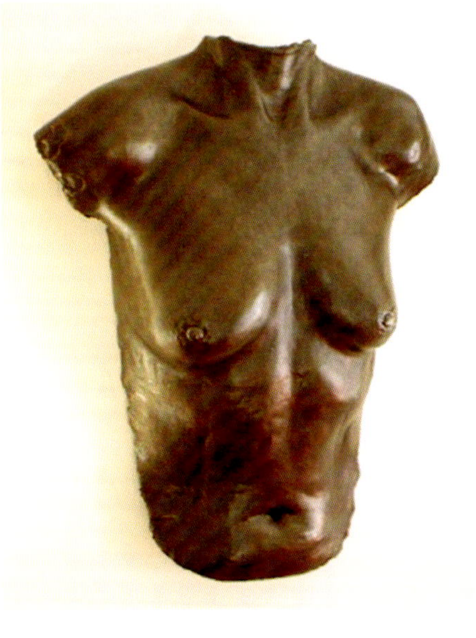

Christy Symington ARBS, ***Female Torso.*** Body cast and then cast in Crystacal plaster with bronze patina, private collection, Norfolk, UK, 55 x 35 x 15 cm (21⅔ x 13¾ x 6 in.). *Photo: Tontxi Vazquez.*

Ceramics – Fired Clay

This is another massive area of study, so I am only going to show a few examples here, as to go into any detail would take a whole book. Ceramic pieces have a lovely organic quality. Through techniques of slab building, hollowing, pinching and coiling, you can build up a hollow clay piece, which is then fired in a kiln. There are a huge variety of clays to use, and many firing techniques, colours and glazes for the surface. The main restriction of fired clay is that you cannot use an armature inside the piece. Many of the concepts and approaches covered in this book are relevant to ceramics, and many excellent publications and courses are available covering the techniques and skills required.

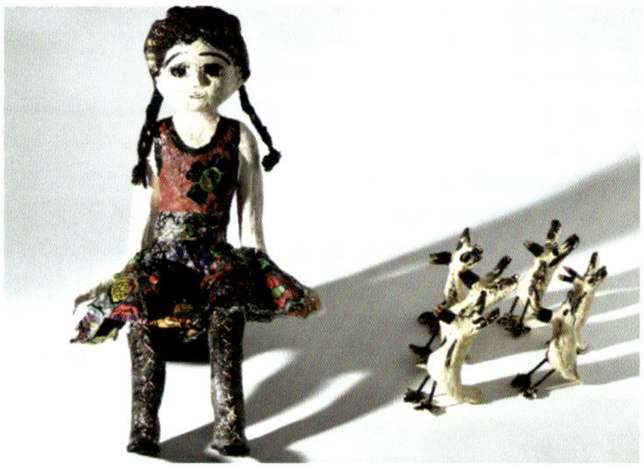

Consuelo Radclyffe, *But we do love Mary!* Stoneware clay, stains, paper, 50 x 30 x 7 cm (19½ x 2 x 2¾ in.). *Photo: Sussie Ahlburg.*

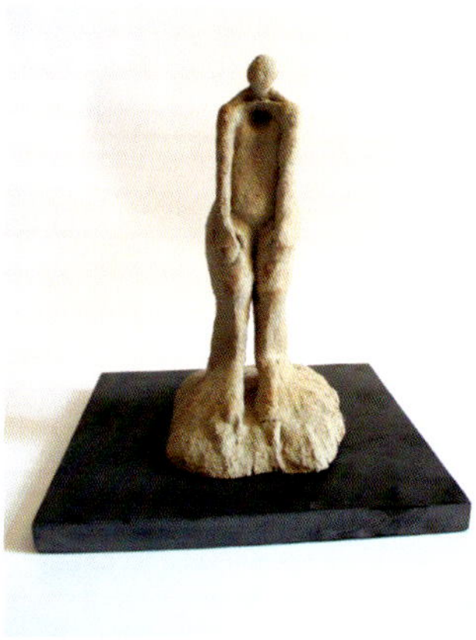

Vivienne Wallace, *240-511.* Fired crank clay, 26 x 16 cm (10¼ x 6⅓ in.). *Photo: courtesy of the artist.*

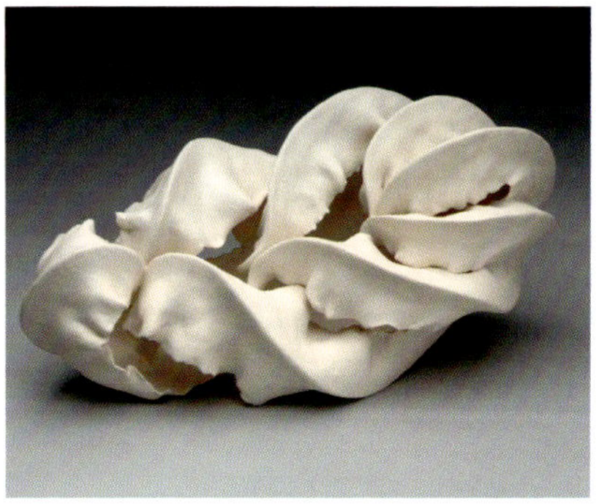

Karen Brewis, *Mother Nature.* Glazed ceramic, 20 x 38 x 16 cm (8 x 15 x 6¼ in.). *Photo: John-Paul Bland.*

Inspired by the extraordinary dried up leaves of the Cecropia Peltata or 'Trumpet Tree', which I was struck by on a visit to the Eden Project in Cornwall. These beautiful curled-up forms reminded me of infants in swaddling clothes and immediately evoked in me an overwhelming desire to nurture and protect them.

Other Materials

This list is by no means complete, so explore and experiment with other materials. In the examples below, you will see a range of materials being used.

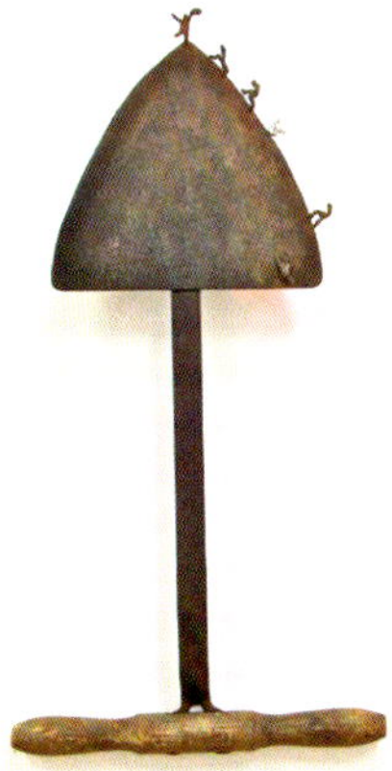

Annie Field, *On a knife edge.* Bronze figures, steel scythe with a wooden handle, 46 x 5 cm (18 x 2 in.). *Photo: courtesy of the artist.*

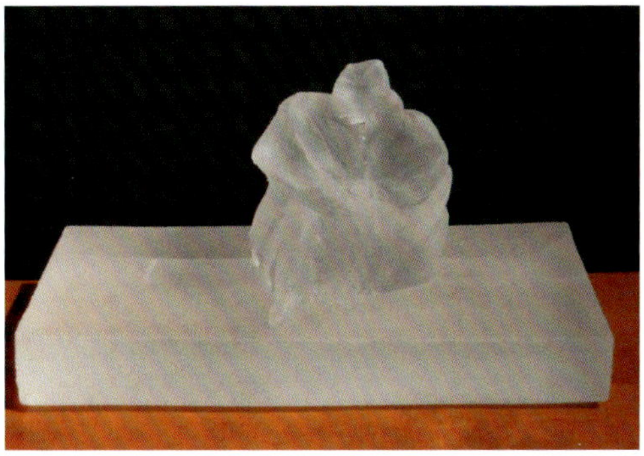

Annie Field, *Love.* Glass, 20 x 33 x 23 cm (8 x 13 x 9 in.). *Photo: courtesy of the artist.*

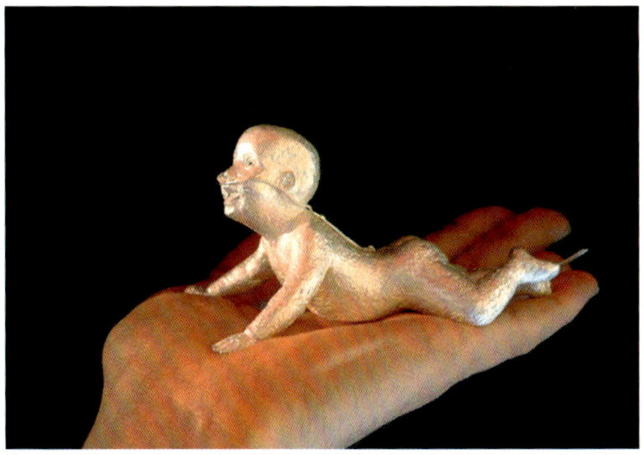

Paolo Giordanella, *Enzo.* Solid sterling silver, 6 x 12 cm (2½ x 4¾ in.). *Photo: courtesy of the artist.*

In the Easter of 2006 my son Enzo, aged only nine months, was critically ill. This period in my life served to compound an already innate belief in my heart that every life on this earth is dear to someone. Enzo has been sculpted to a delicate size that would fit in the palm of your hand, giving him a fragile appearance, and cast in the solid to a weight of half a kilo (1 lb) of sterling silver. He possess a realistic body weight for his scale, finished in a mother of pearl white patina to denote the purity and innocence of such a tiny life.

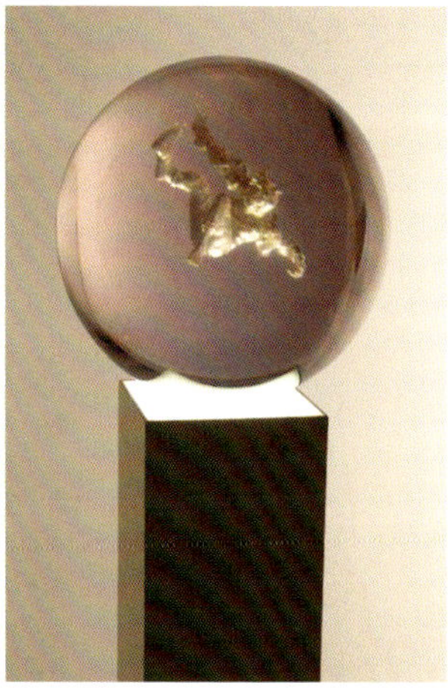

George Triggs, *Falling.* Clear resin, diameter 36 cm (14¼ in.). *Photo: courtesy of the artist.*

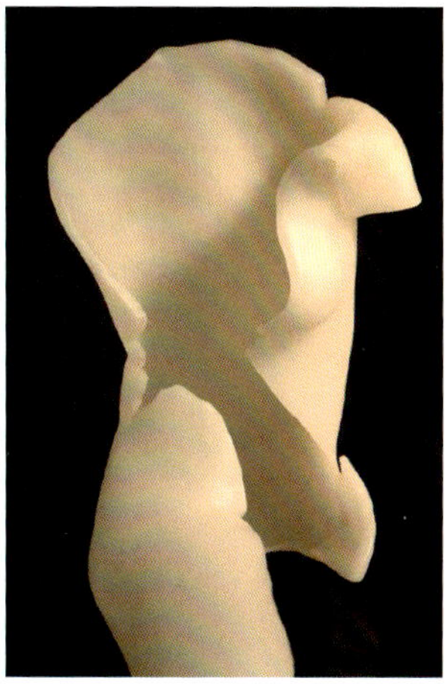

Paolo Giordanella, *Wax Study.* Crystalline wax, height 20 cm (8 in.). *Photo: courtesy of the artist.*

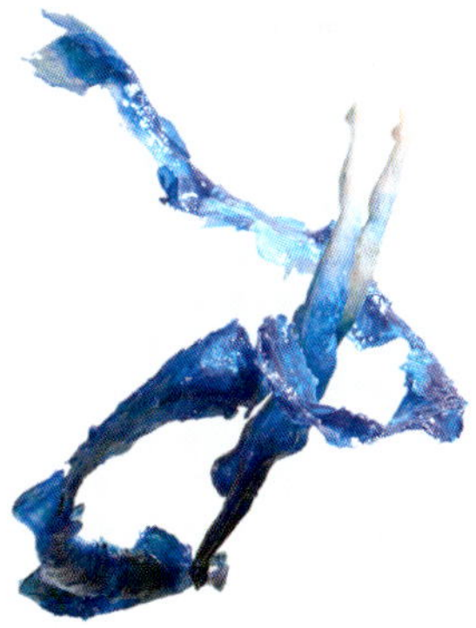

Hiromi Scintu, *Deeper than Indigo.* Crystal resin with pigments 50 x 60 cm (19¾ x 23½ in.). *Photo: Wah Poon.*

Deeper than Indigo *is an expression to explain going deeper into faith, as a swimmer dives further and further down into the deep. Indigo is a strong pigment that can be used to dye clothes over and over again to attain the deepest of blues.*

Putting It Into Practice

We have covered quite a range of styles, techniques and materials, but the next and most important step is to apply all of this knowledge to creating your own abstract work. Explore your interests, experiment with styles, forms and mediums, be objective, brave, passionate, natural and spontaneous.

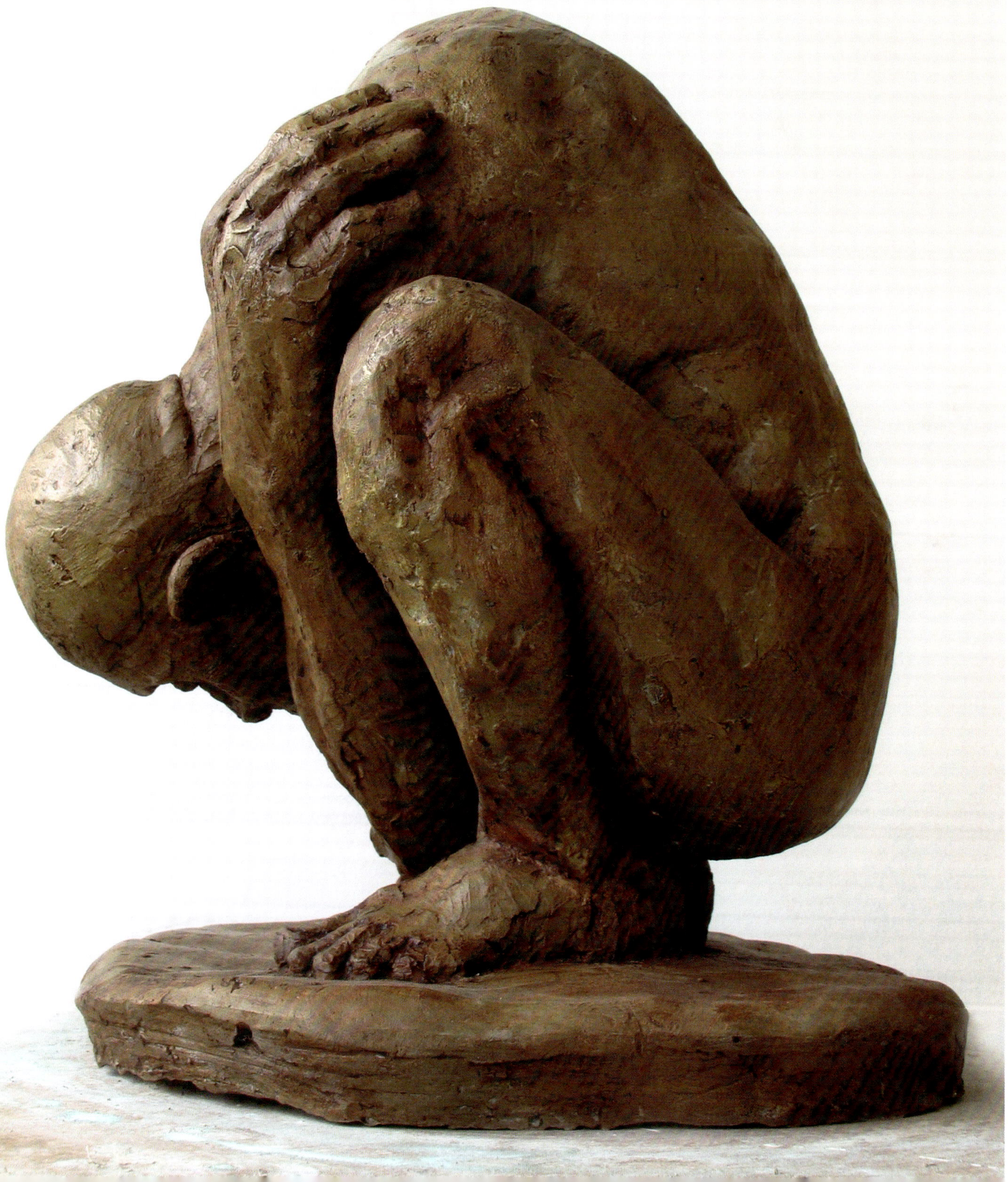

Pete Sherrard, *Mouse.* Brass resin, 32 x 33 x 30 cm (12½ x 13 x 12 in.). *Photo: Pete Sherrard.*

This sculpture is about loss, death and how we deal with grief. The man is holding a dead mouse in his hand (not shown in the photo).

6

THE EXPRESSIVE FIGURE

What is the Expressive Figure?
Making Maquettes
Exercises for the Expressive Figure
Creating the Sculpture

What is the Expressive Figure?

The expressive figure is one where you start, not from the form but with something you wish to express, and then give form to that expression. If the realistic figure was a study essay and the abstract figure a haiku, the expressive figure is like a poem – each word, intonation and rhythm being carefully chosen for the purpose of expressing the poet's intention, whether this be a feeling, concept, expression of character or an experience.

The inspiration for the expressive figure can arise in many ways, often when you see or experience something that is special to you. Sometimes this involves 'the moment' – a gesture or movement that reveals the character or special qualities of someone you are intentionally observing, or a fleeting but amazingly revealing moment in your daily life. It is very important at this point to remember the experience clearly, and not to mess around with it or add things to it, because that moment was absolutely real, complete and original.

The expressive figure can also originate from something more abstract. You may have been considering a concept for some time or have been exploring something of particular interest. Gradually a concrete message, form and intention will arise.

The inspiration may be a fleeting moment or the culmination of a longer process, but there is a moment where it crystallises and you feel it almost as part of your being – this is the time to let it manifest itself in form. It is not simplistic, as it can have layers (like a musical chord, in which many notes make a single sound).

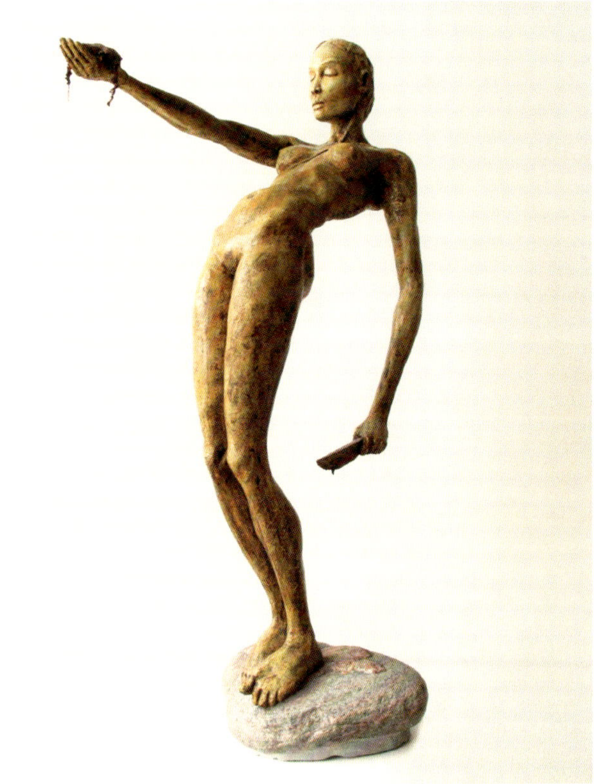

Pete Sherrard, *Fragile.* Ash resin, stone base, 60 x 25 x 15 cm (23½ x 10 x 6 in.). *Photo: Pete Sherrard.*

This sculpture represents the idea of the fragility of relationships and how, sometimes, we will try almost anything to keep them going, even if it is at the expense of our own wellbeing. The girl has cut her own heart out and is presenting it to someone. It's a desperate gesture. It's futile. The benefit will only last for a very short time ...

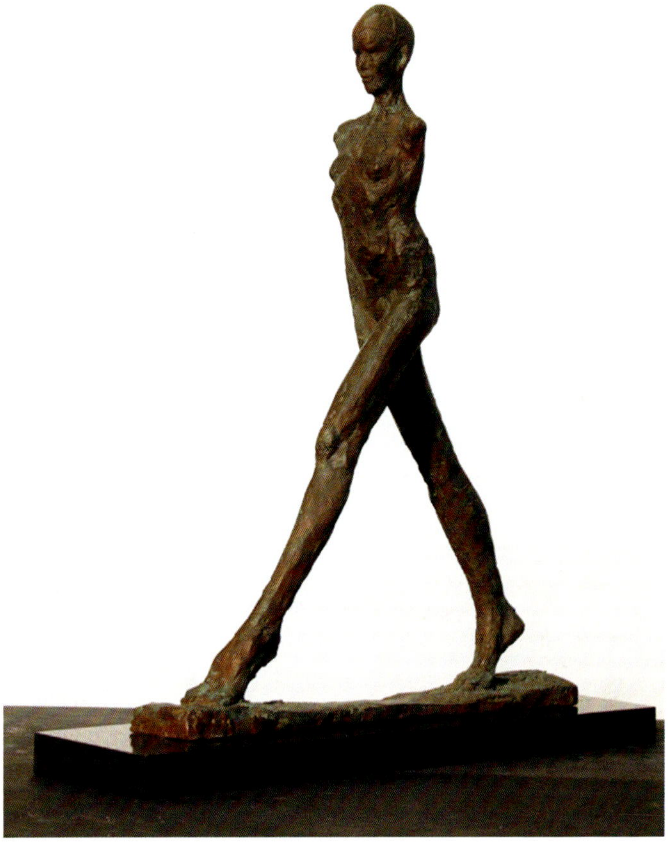

Arabella Brooke, *Her dream of perfect freedom.* Bronze, 70 x 17 x 7 cm (27½ x 6⅔ x 2¾ in.). *Photo: courtesy of the artist.*

This formed part of a series based on the concept of a tightrope walker. I liked the thought of the world falling away, until there was nothing apart from the wire, and the connection of the feet on the wire. Perfect freedom refers to the freedom that comes from not having time to think too hard about the next step.

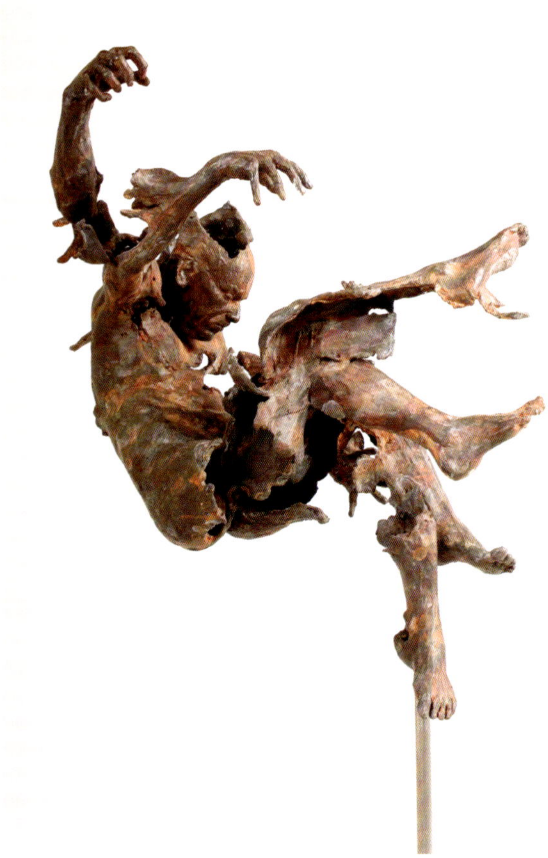

George Triggs, *Collision.* Bronze, 40 x 40 x 39 cm (16 x 16 x 15¼ in.). *Photo: courtesy of the artist.*

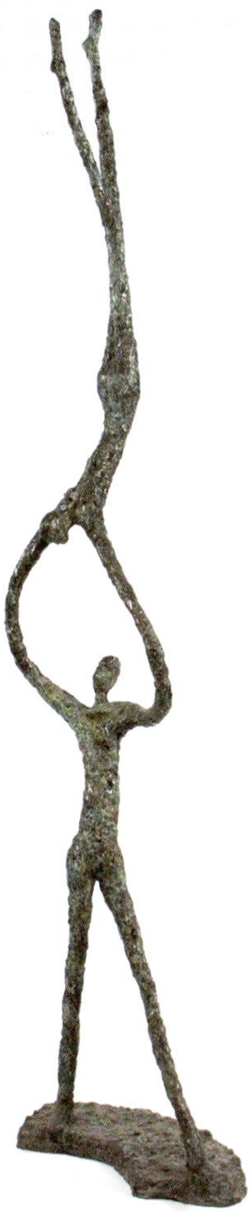

Michael Speller, *In Tune*. Bronze, 212 x 65 x 40 cm (83½ x 25½ x 33 in.). *Photo: courtesy of the artist.*

The sculpture is about balance in life and relationships. Nothing is perfect in the world, but natural rhythms between people can counterbalance to make the whole have a symmetry.

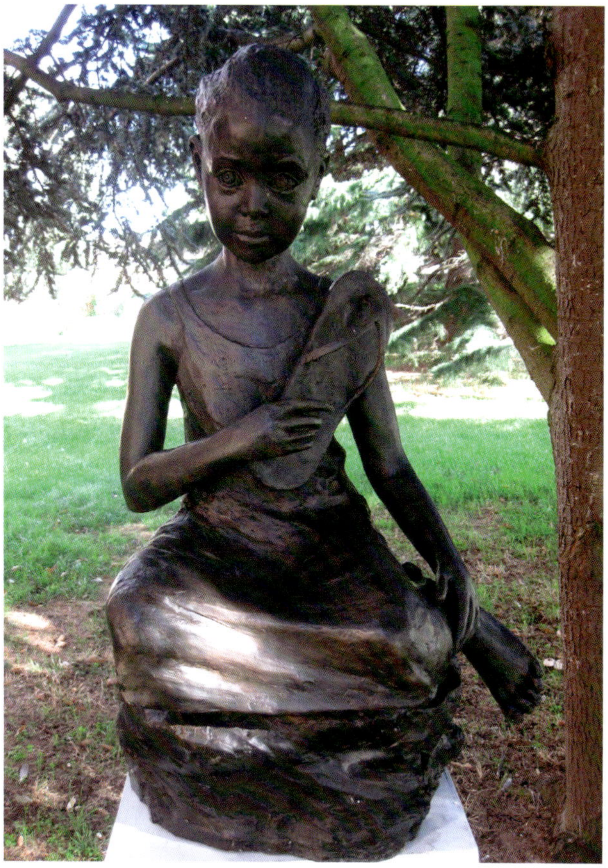

Tanya Russell, *Lost at War*. Cold cast bronze, 90 x 45 cm (35½ x 17¾ in.). *Photo: courtesy of the artist.*

This sculpture is for the people of Eritrea. There is a custom there that when the men go to war they leave their sandals for their children to remember them by.

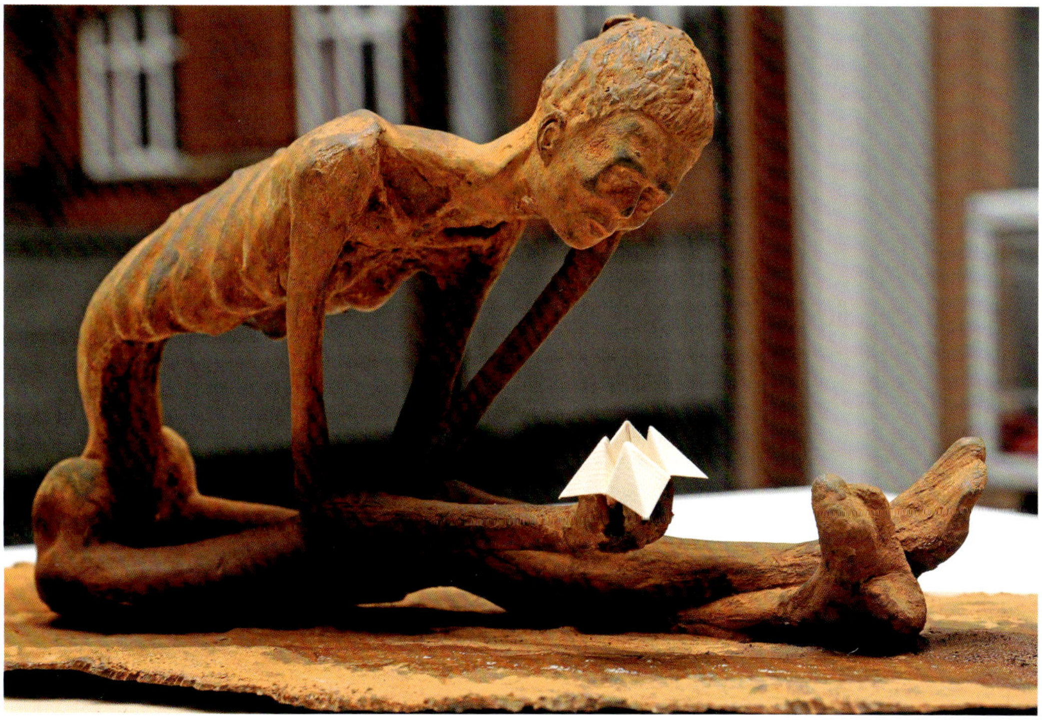

Joanne Weaver, *If only....* Cold cast iron, paper, 38 x 17 x 19 cm (15 x 6½ x 7½ in.). *Photo: courtesy of the artist.*

My aim was to express the anguish of anorexia; I wanted to express the physicality of anorexia alongside the mental torment the condition brings. This is a quiet, contemplative pose, yet the exaggerated skeletal frame expresses a history of suffering. The paper fortune-teller in her hand places the woman in a Western world – it is an innocent object from childhood yet in this context it becomes more potent. I chose to finish the sculpture in iron as it continues to rust and decay and as a material it seemed to exemplify anorexia.

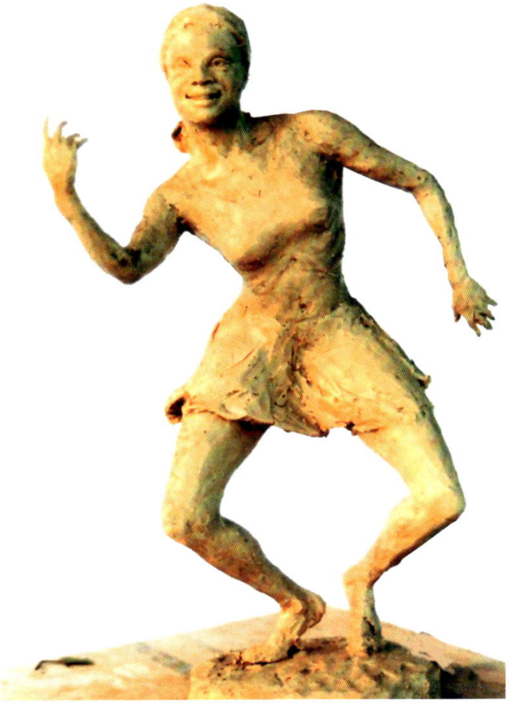

Tanya Russell, *African Dancer*. Plastiline, 25 x 18 cm (10 x 7 in.). *Photo: courtesy of the artist.*

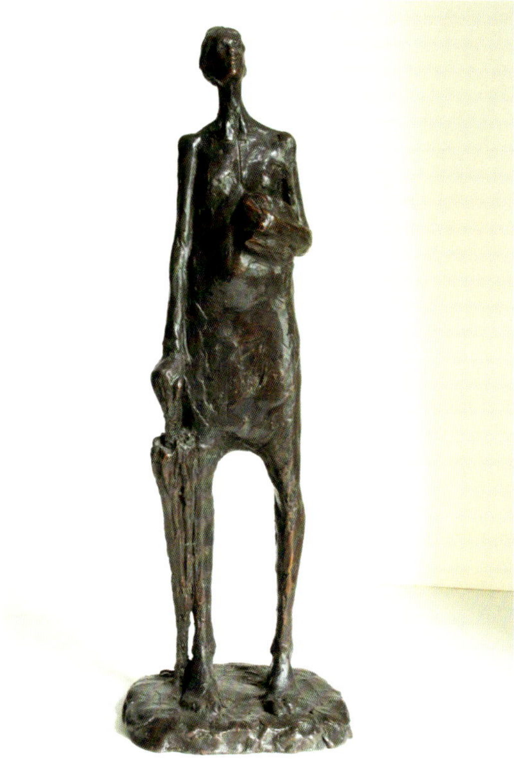

Arabella Brooke, *Rainy day woman*. Bronze, 40 x 20 x 14 cm (15¾ x 8 x 5½ in.). *Photo: courtesy of the artist.*

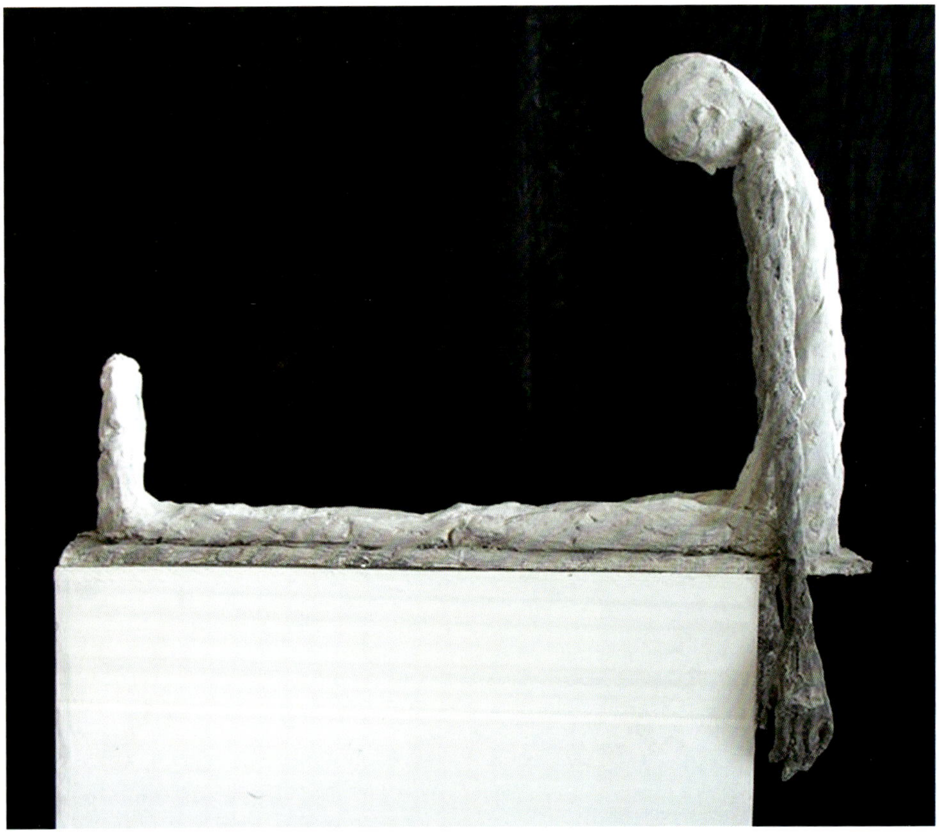

John O'Connor, *The darkest time of night*. Plaster/cold cast bronze, 40 x 80 cm (15¾ x 31½ in.). *Photo: courtesy of the artist.*

There is a point where we all have the opportunity to change. A moment before the night is over and the day is waiting to begin.

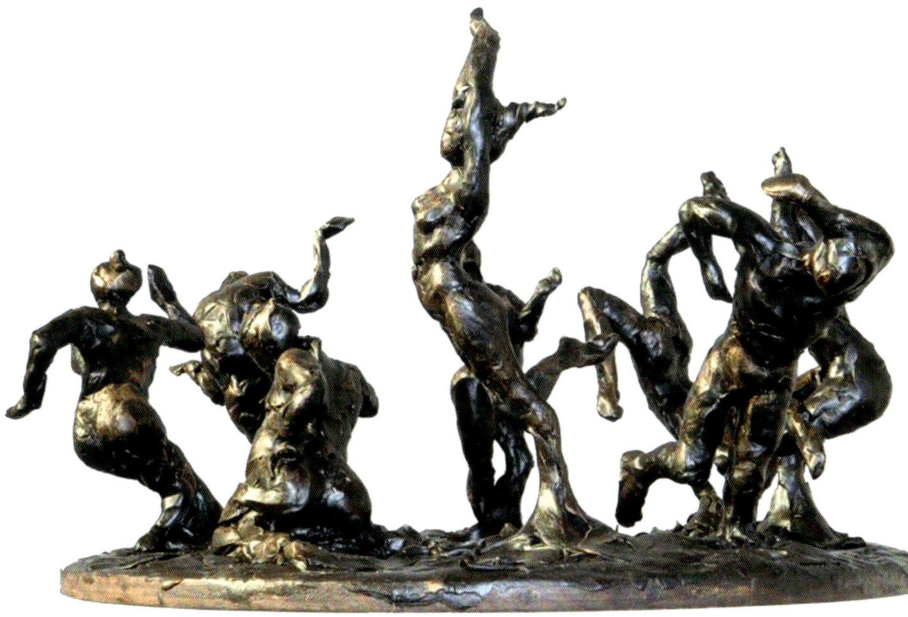

Hiromi Scintu, *Turtle island dance*. Wax, wire and wood, 18 x 38 cm (7 x 15 in.). *Photo: Wah Poon.*

This piece was conceived by listening to a piece of music then, in turn, it was used as inspiration for a composer to come up with a new piece of music. This was done at the Art Academy as part of a project working with young musicians from the South Bank Sinfonia.

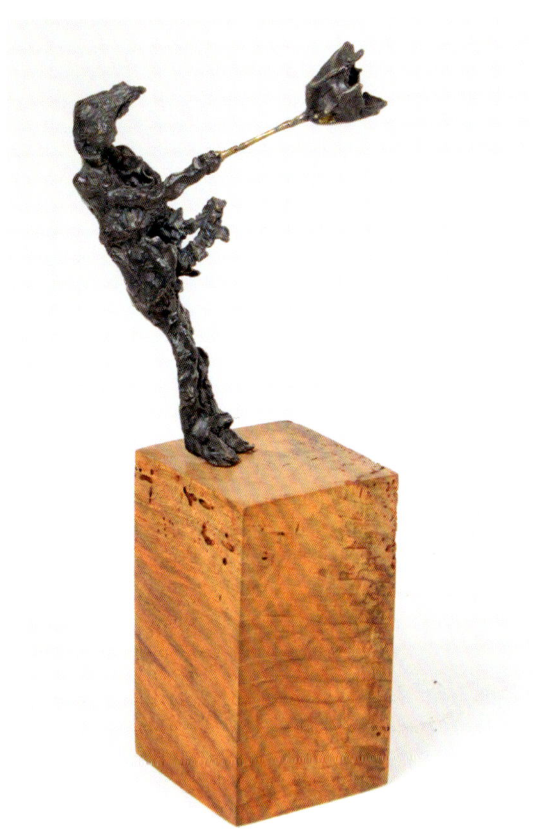

George Triggs, *The day the wind stopped*. Bronze figure, 17 x 14 x 6 cm (6¾ x 5½ x 2¼ in.). *Photo: courtesy of the artist.*

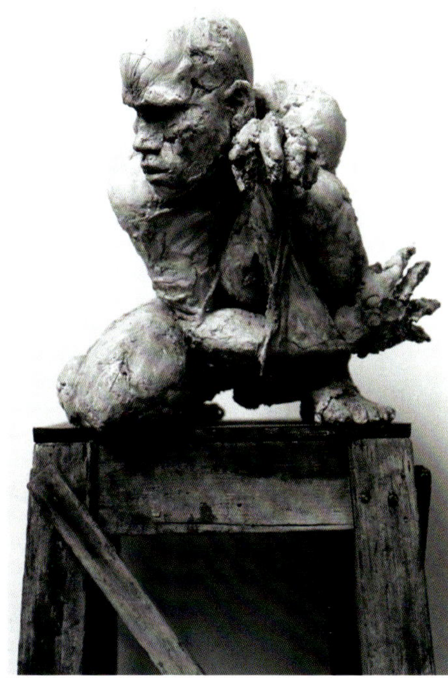

Damian Fennell, *Tyranny*. Plaster, 45 x 50 x 50 cm (17¾ x 19⅔ x 19⅔ in.). *Photo: courtesy of the artist.*

Tyranny *is about the inner state of the tyrant. It is bound and enslaved by the passions that rage within. Inspired by Socrates' description of the human condition that brings about tyranny, I also recognised the capacity for tyranny within myself.* Tyranny *was conceived and modelled in a sort of method-acting approach; I immersed myself in memory of the state every time I worked on the sculpture.*

Materials and Methods

We have talked about many materials and methods in the previous chapters, all of which can be used in sculpting the expressive figure, but keep experimenting with new ones as well as refining your methods.

Making Maquettes

Particularly for expressive sculpture, it can be useful to make a small maquette or sketch of what you intend to convey, or of what you have seen or experienced. This will help you when making the armature for your finished piece, and to resolve issues at a small scale to avoid incurring more serious problems in a big sculpture.

When making a maquette, we tend to be very free and uninhibited, not getting hung up on issues of creating a 'finished sculpture' or ensuring accuracy of anatomy; even if it is just a few blobs of wax, it captures everything we are trying to say. The problem then is that we like the maquette so much that we try to copy it while working on the finished sculpture, but because we are no longer working in the same free and natural way, the sculpture inevitably becomes boring and mechanical and is just a copy of the maquette. Ways to avoid this trap and use maquettes effectively is explained on pp. 114–5.

Making a modelled maquette is simple, but you must start with the sketch armature. Three examples – standing, seated and lying – are explained here.

Materials and Equipment for Sketch Armature

MATERIALS	EQUIPMENT
• Wooden board	• Pliers
• Copper wire (four gauges – 14, 16, 20 and 25)	• Wire snips
• Staples	• Hammer
	• Dividers

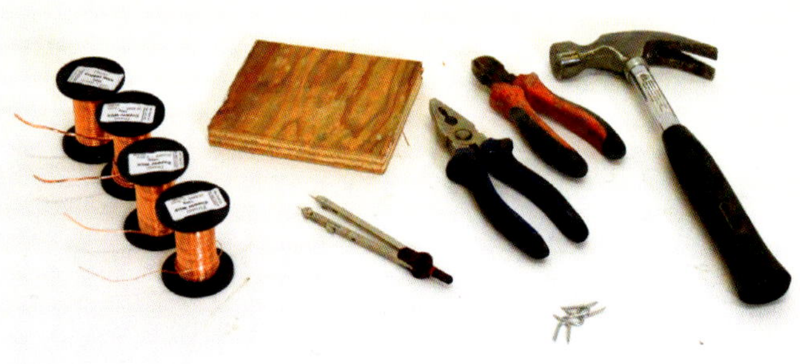

Materials and equipment needed to make a sketch armature.

Sketch Armature – Standing

It is best for sketch armatures to be no more than 15 cm (6 in.) high, ideally around 10 cm (4 in.). If they are too large you cannot get the material on quickly, and you want it small enough that you can just focus on what you are expressing.

Have a clear picture in your mind of what your sculpture will look like. Think about the base. Always leave room for at least a 2 cm (3/4 in.) base in your modelling material, even if you don't want one on the final piece, as this allows you to work up or down into the base if necessary. Also, if the piece is, for example, leaping or sitting on a rock, think about this and add extra length to the wire at the bottom.

Make sure to keep in mind your anatomical proportions and use the dividers to measure if you are at all unsure. The crotch point is generally about halfway down the body, but it is much better to have the legs too long than too short, as you can always build your base up a bit. As a guide, the arms come about halfway down the thighs but again it is better to make them too long as you can cut them off later.

Also ensure that you have taken into account any exaggeration or abstraction that you intend to try. It would be a great shame to compromise your idea because your armature is just made to standard proportions.

1. Take the 16-gauge copper wire for the supporting leg (use 14-gauge if it needs to carry a lot of weight). Put a coil on the end of the wire before cutting it and twist it upright.

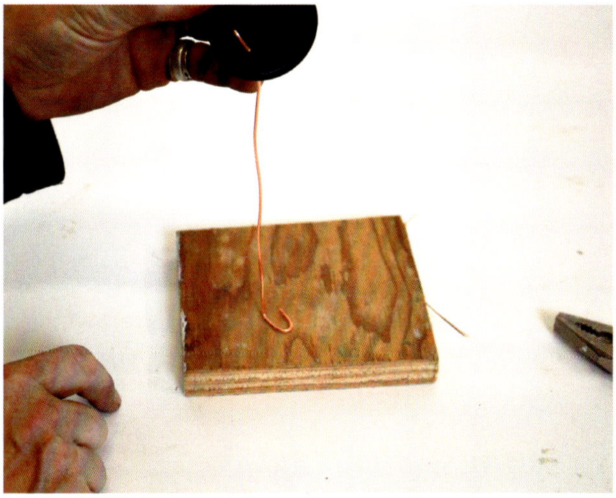

Put a coil on the end of the wire before cutting it and twist the wire upright.

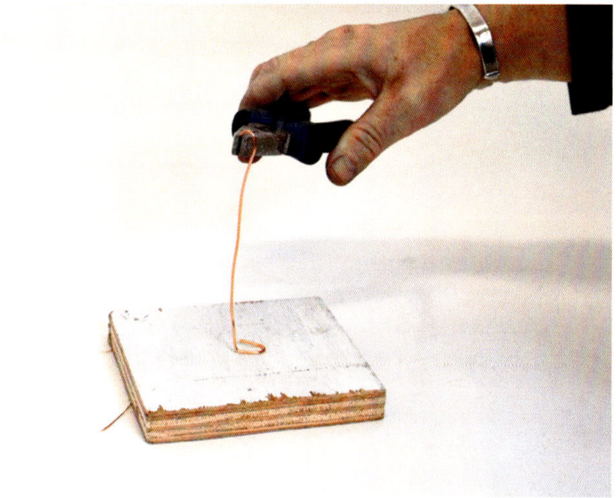

Cut the wire to the correct height and put a curl at the top for the head.

2. Put your hand on the base so that it holds the wire up – I use the thickness of my hand as a guide for the thickness of my standard base, so that I can accurately see the proportions of the final figure (see image below). During the rest of the construction of the armature you have to imagine that this thickness of base is there.

3. Cut the wire to the correct height and put a curl at the top for the head (see image top right).

4. Using the thinner 20-gauge copper wire, cut another length to act as the second leg and first arm (see image below). Again, choose the thickness that is right for the sketch. If there were, for example, going to be a bird flying off this arm, it would need to be a thicker piece of wire to support the weight. Always cut the wire too long, you can trim it once you have started modelling.

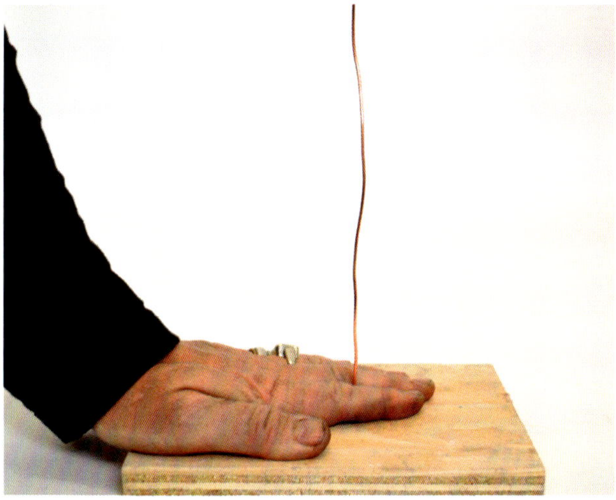

Use your hand as a guide for the thickness of the base.

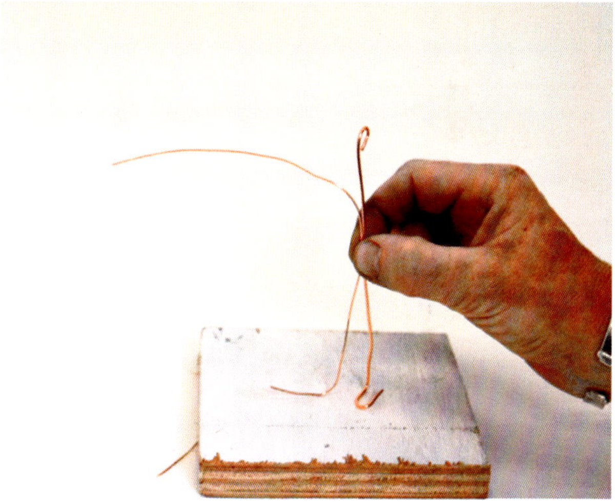

Cut a piece of 20-gauge wire for the second leg and arm.

5. Cut a third piece of 20-gauge wire for the second arm, making it much longer than it needs to be, as it needs to run down the central wire so that all the pieces can be tied together (see image below).

Always place two lengths of wire together and wrap another piece of wire round them like a bandage on a splint. Never try and tie wire any other way, e.g. just crossing the wires and trying to tie them.

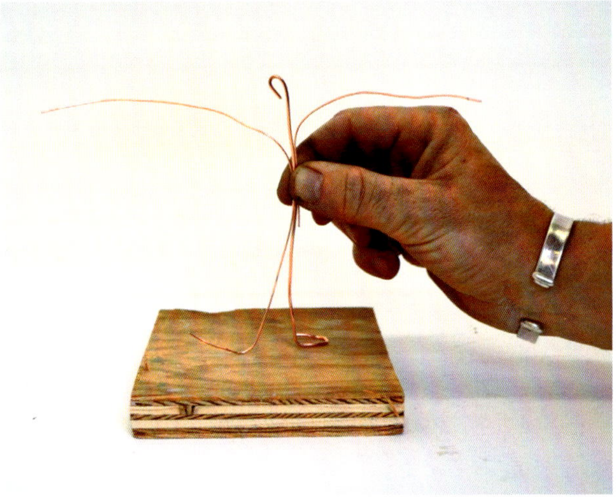

Cut a third piece of 20-gauge wire for the second arm.

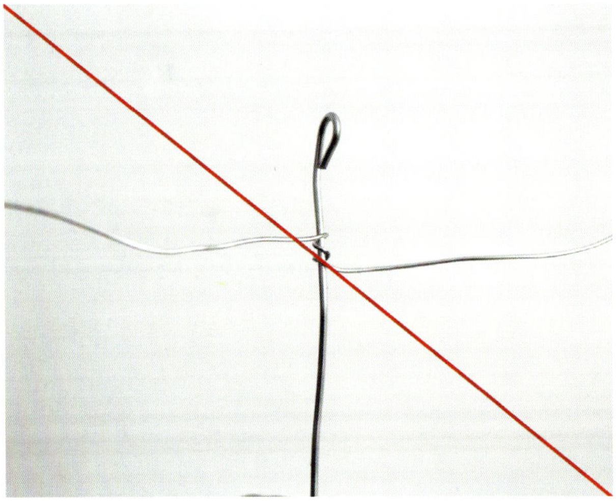

How **NOT** to attach wire sections of the armature together.

6. Tie the three pieces of wire together with the 25-gauge wire, pulling it tight at each turn with pliers. It is much better for it to be too tight and for the wire to break a few times than for it to be too loose – once tied each limb should move independently.

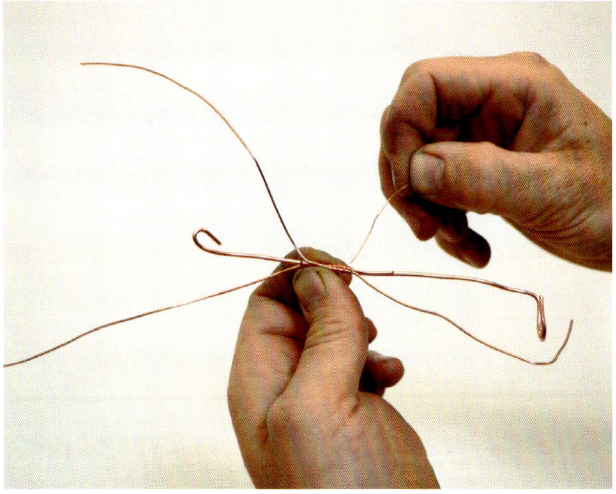

Tie the three pieces of wire together using another piece like a bandage.

7. Twist the 25-gauge wire around all the other limbs, as shown below – this creates a surface that your modelling material will stick to. Using small staples, staple the coil of wire in two places so that it is in the correct position on your board (the correct position obviously being determined by your pose).

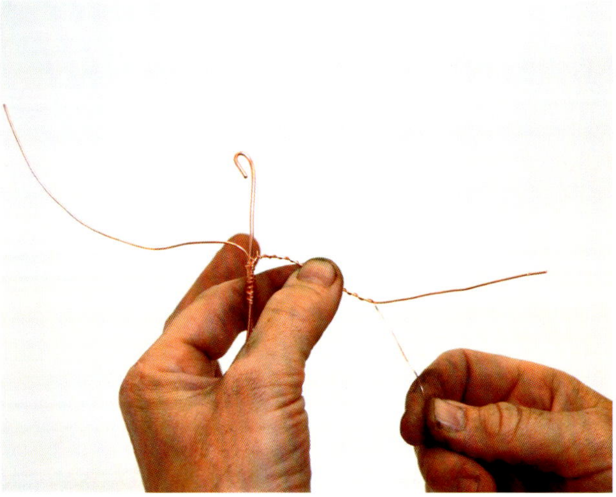

Twist the 25-gauge wire around all the other limbs.

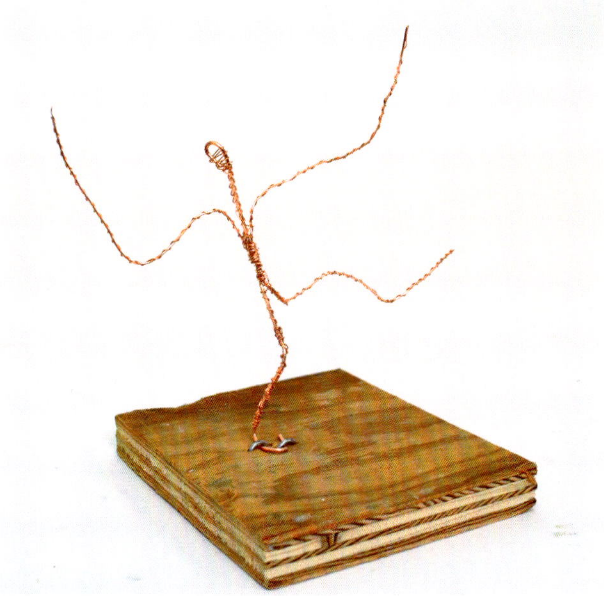

A sketch armature correctly stapled to the base.

The whole point of having the coil and stapling it twice in different places is so that the wire cannot spin. If you staple a length of wire without a coil, as soon as any pressure is applied, it will fall over.

You are now ready to start modelling on your sketch armature.

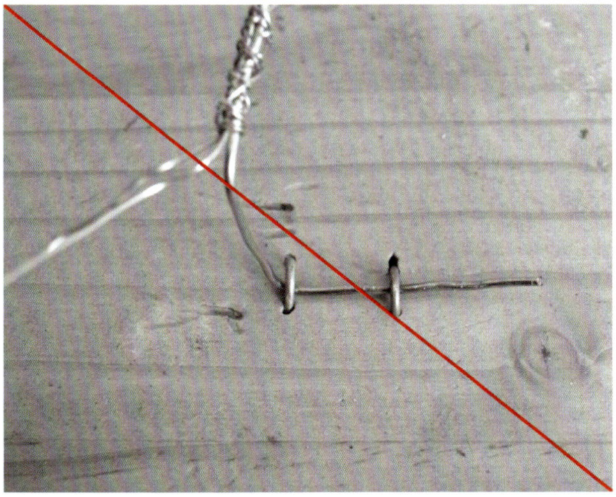

How **NOT** to attach wire to a base.

Sketch Armature – Seated

The process for making a seated armature is basically the same as for a standing one, except that the first piece of wire you use consists of the head and torso and then continues into the base – it is not one of the legs, as in the standing armature, but disappears into whatever the figure is seated on. The curl for this supporting piece of wire is stapled to the base. The length of this section of wire (below the buttocks of the figure) is determined by the thickness of the base on which it is sitting.

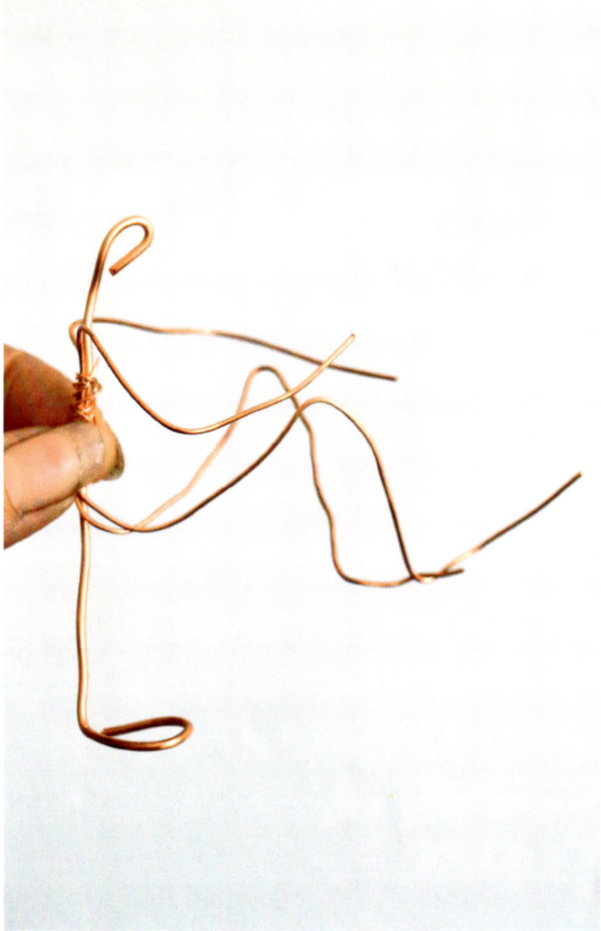

Seated figure sketch armature.

Sketch Armature – Lying

Make exactly the same armature as for the seated figure but twist the legs up so that they lie horizontally in relation to the torso and arms. The section of wire that you attach to the base comes out from the centre of the figure, and once again the length depends on the thickness of the base you choose.

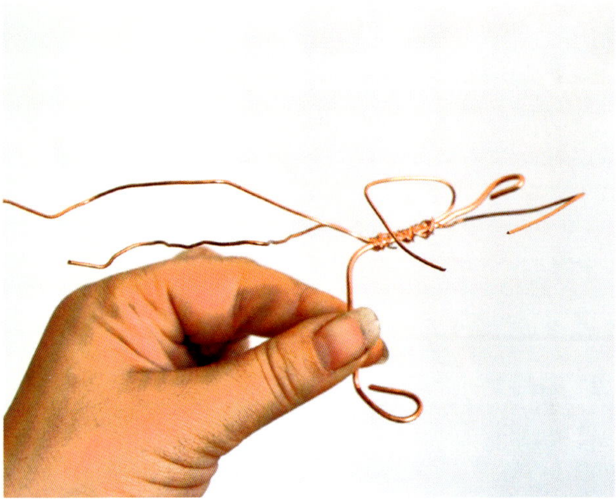

Lying figure sketch armature.

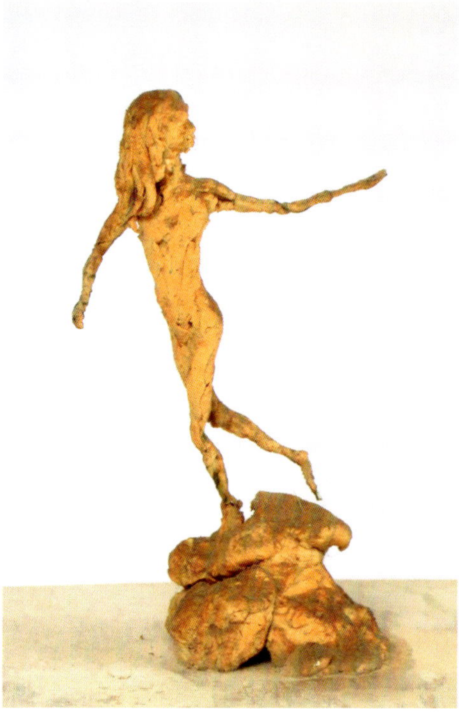

Tanya Russell, maquette for *Miranda*. Sculpted in Plastiline (soft grade – very good for quick sketches), 20 x 13 cm (8 x 5 in.). *Photo: courtesy of the artist.*

Modelling Materials for Maquettes

Pretty much anything can be used as a modelling material. The purpose of the maquette is to catch the pure essence of the piece, so think about what you are trying to say and choose the material that seems to express that best.

Some examples of different maquettes are illustrated here. Note that in all of them the base and support have been taken into consideration as part of the piece – this is very important for sculptors. These were all made quite quickly, although the time taken will depend somewhat on its purpose. For presentation to a client you would take more time and finish off the setting, as in Lorne McKean's *Canada Geese* (p. 112).

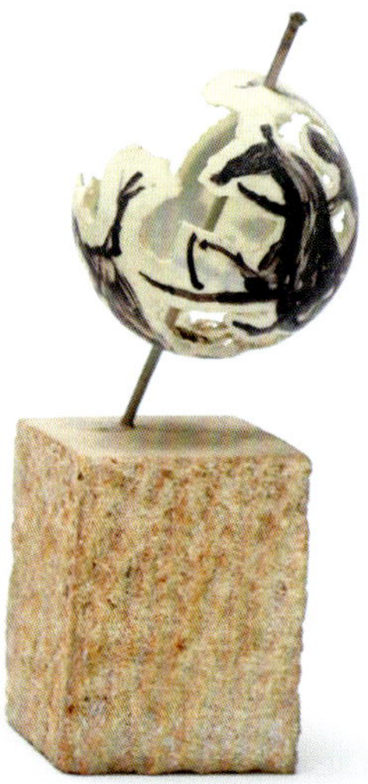

Edwin Russell, maquette for *St George and the Dragon*. Made from a cut-out ping-pong ball, 13 x 8 cm (5 x 3 in.). *Photo: courtesy of the artist.*

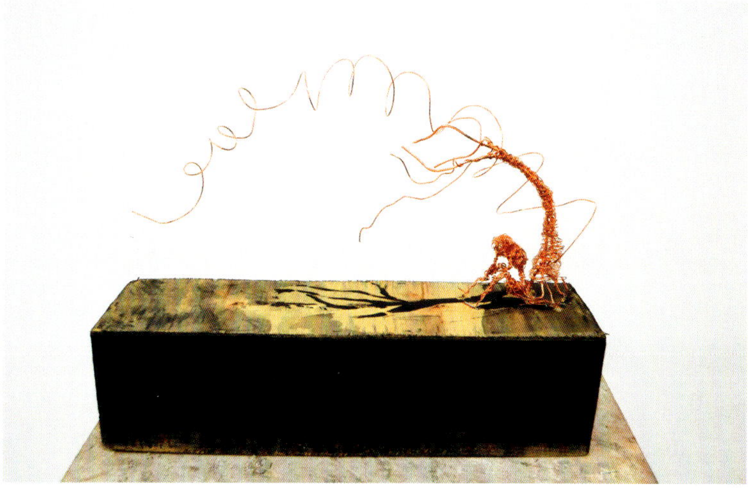

Saskia Gall, maquette. Made in wire, 30 x 25 cm (11¾ x 9¾ in.). *Photo: courtesy of the artist.*

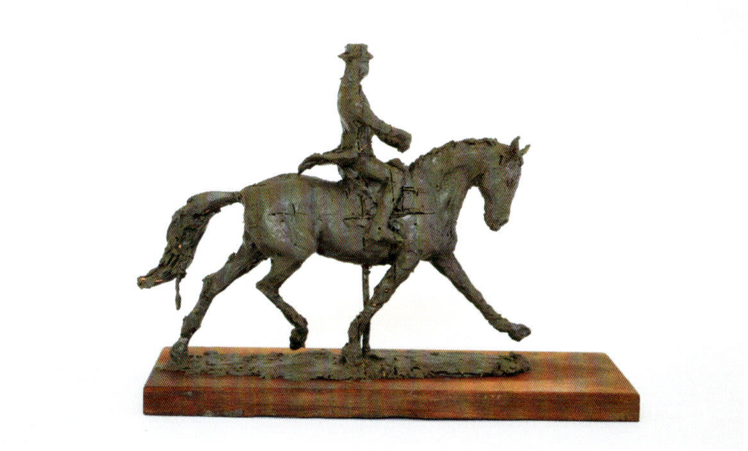

Lorne McKean, maquette for *Lee Pearson performing dressage.* Sculpted in hard Plastiline, which is good for sketches requiring more detail, or for use in warmer temperatures, 20 x 16 cm (8 x 6⅓ in.). *Photo: courtesy of the artist.*

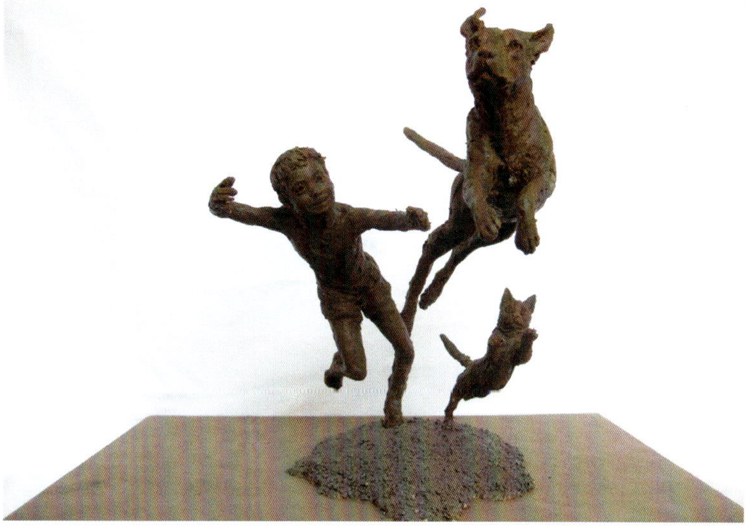

Tanya Russell, maquette for *Going home.* Commissioned for Battersea Dogs and Cats Home, sculpted in brown modelling wax, 30 x 23 cm (11 x 9 in.). *Photo: courtesy of the artist.*

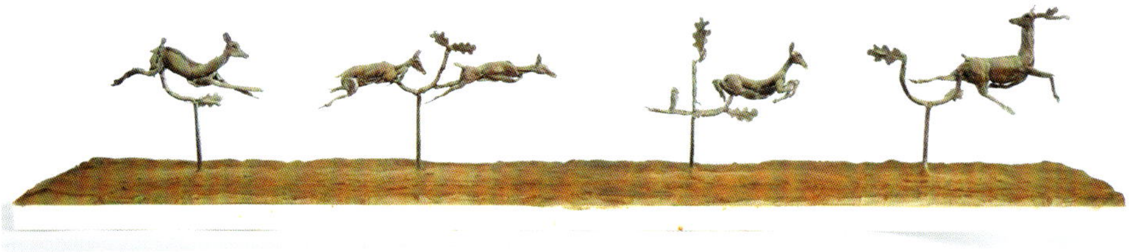

Edwin Russell, maquette for *Running deer*. Sculpted in Milliput, 65 x 7 cm (25⅔ x 2¾ in.). *Photo: courtesy of the artist.*

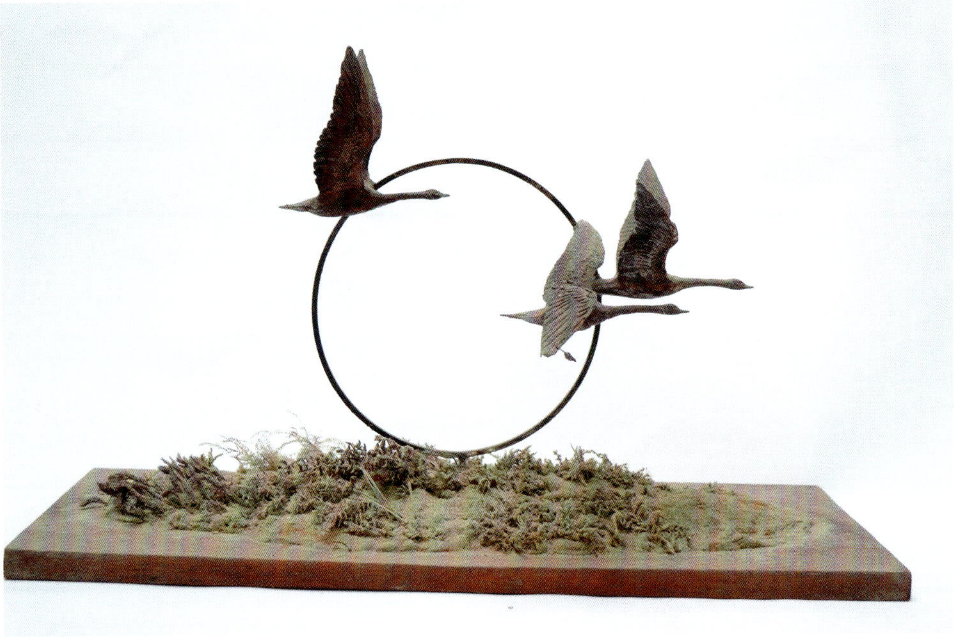

Lorne McKean, maquette for *Canada Geese*. Made from bronzed Milliput, copper ring and crumbled florist's Oasis with grasses for the base effect, 40 x 35 cm (15¾ x 13¾ in.). *Photo: courtesy of the artist.*

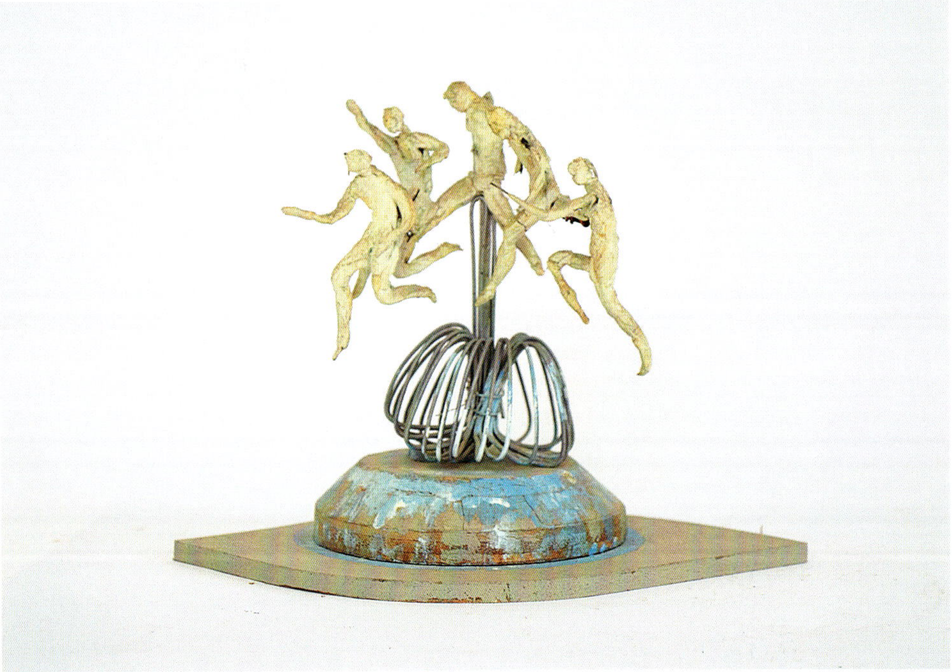

Edwin Russell, maquette for *Olympic runners*. Sculpted in Plastiline, wire and wood, 23 x18 cm (9 x 7 in.). *Photo: courtesy of the artist.*

Exercises for the Expressive Figure

As with the abstract figure, we will approach the expressive figure through a series of exercises, but ultimately it is important that you find your own expressive style. This should flow from your intention or inspiration, rather than from an imposed style or method.

These exercises are mainly about mark-making – the relevant information regarding form can be found in Chapter 5. They are valuable in exploring Stage 1 of the artist's process (Mastery of Skills) discussed in Chapter 1, p. 21.

EXERCISE 1

- Take a medium-size board and no tools at all. Ask the model to go into a simple lying pose. If no model is available, you can work from a series of photographs taken from different angles.
- With great care, taking your time and being constantly aware of the effect of each mark you make, apply pieces of clay one at a time. Once you have applied a piece you must not touch it again.
- You need to study the whole form carefully and consider which forms or parts of forms you are going to create with any given application of clay. This is a significant choice for an artist, as you can divide the component parts that make up the form of the model in many different ways.

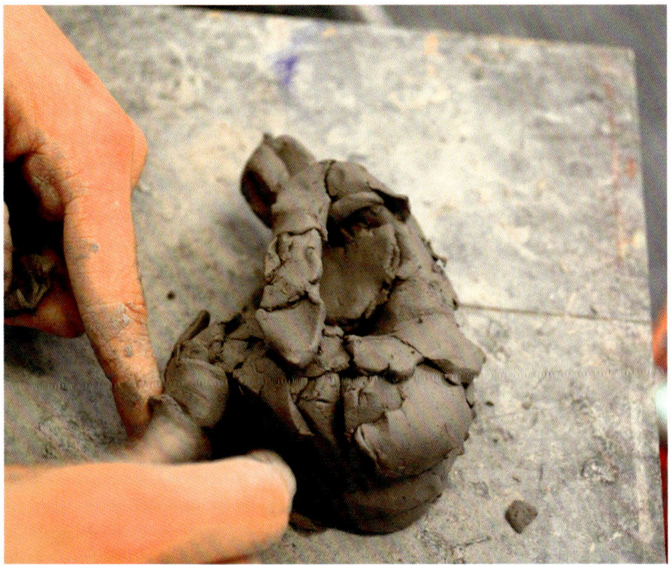

- See what interesting marks, depth of colour and contrast you get by applying clay in this way. You will discover marks that cannot be created with any tool.
- See how lively the sculpture looks. Clay has a memory and the more you work it the more dead and mechanical it becomes. It is important to learn to sculpt in such a way that the clay is manipulated as little as possible, but this takes, skill, practice and lots of conscious awareness.

  You will find that, when sculpting, it is better to cut away a whole section that needs remodelling and re-apply the clay than to try to manipulate the surface of the existing clay.

EXERCISE 2

- As in Exercise 1, take your materials and your model or photographs, but this time use a range of tools. This exercise is all about learning what marks and forms different tools can make.
- With each tool you apply to the clay, make different movements with your hands.
- Apply the clay in different ways.
- Apply different-sized pieces of clay.
- Use different pressure with each tool.
- Use each tool at a different angle.
- Watch really carefully what marks you have made.
- The biggest secret is actually noticing when you have made a great mark that expresses what you intended, and then having the courage to leave it. Many of us create great marks, then don't notice and model over them.

Very quickly but consciously apply pieces of clay and then don't touch them.

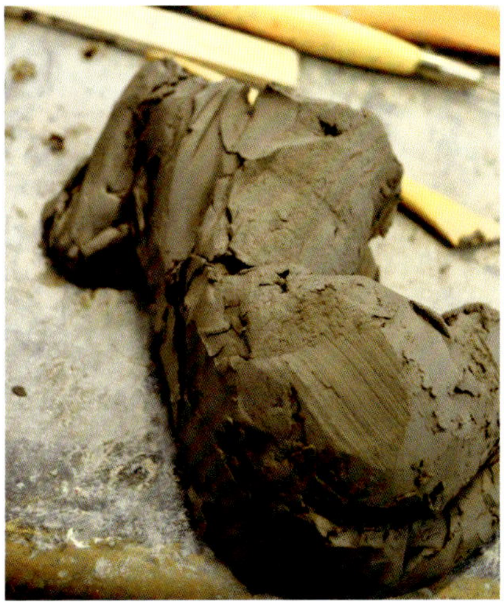

An example of a piece created quickly, experimenting with mark-making using just a short piece of lath.

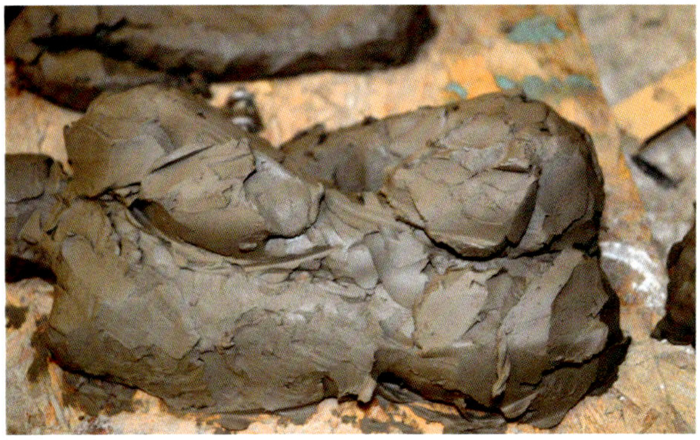

An example of a piece created quickly, experimenting with mark-making using different tools.

Creating the Sculpture

First Steps

1. Be very clear about your intention and inspiration, bearing in mind that your intention can be as simple as seeing where an idea or form takes you.
2. Write a list of qualities that you intend to express (this is very useful to refer back to if you go off track).
3. Go somewhere where you can relax and ensure that you are fully feeling what you are trying to express, like an actor getting into character in order to portray their role.
4. Make a number of maquettes that express your intention. Make them in different ways and in different mediums, but keep going back to your intention.
5. Find some people whose opinion you value, ask them to look at your maquettes, but do not tell them your intention. Ask them to tell you how they respond, what it makes them feel or think. If you are happy with the response, continue to the next step. If not, do some more maquettes. It is very important to be brave and honest with yourself at this stage. One of the main distinctions between a good sculptor and a great sculptor is this ability to be very objective and brave, being prepared to look at what you have done, see it is not working and adapt it or start again. Doing this does not imply that you have failed up to that point, it is just part of the process of making.
6. Once you are happy with your maquette, consider carefully the size, the material, the support and so on of your finished piece and then make your armature accordingly. Do not rush this process – if you do you will regret it later.

Sculpting the Figure Itself

While creating your finished sculpture, you are constantly juggling different aspects:

- Your inspiration – 'your moment', your feeling or your original intention; this is most important, so ensure that this is always in your mind and your being.
- Your maquette. Study this carefully, be clear about why it works, and use the aspects that do work in your finished sculpture.
- Your model and/or any photos or references. Not everything will work on your maquette, so you can use these as an additional source of information, but it is critically important to choose the forms, lines, planes and so on that are going to enhance your finished expression, not slavishly copy what is there.
- The incidental mark. Be brave enough to leave wonderful incidental marks that work just perfectly for what you are trying to say. Resist the temptation to sculpt over them, but have the courage to take out a mark that is wonderful of itself but not appropriate for this particular sculpture.

Your 'Language'

We have spoken a good deal about your basic tools for expression, but they are worth reiterating here.

Line

Follow all the principles set out in the earlier chapters on flow lines, good plumb line techniques and gridding. If using a maquette, study it according to these principles. You will always find a central line that balances and harmonises the maquette and other lines of importance. Ensure that your final sculpture follows these lines – they are so important for maintaining the quality of the work.

Modelling

Clay does not respond well to being carved. Each piece needs careful consideration as to where the form starts and ends, where the apex is, and so on.

When working on the expressive sculpture there are four things you are considering at any given time in relation to mark-making. Each is equally important.

- Is the mark expressing the quality that you are seeking to express?
- Is the mark expressive of the physical form you are creating (e.g. a shoulder or stomach) in so far as you need it to be?
- Is it an interesting mark in its own right, as a pure form?
- Is the mark working in the context of the whole form?

You can often distinguish an amateur artist from a professional because the former gets stuck in the detail and forgets the bigger picture, tending to put in unnecessary forms or marks that distract from the core intention of the piece. As soon as people get a model in front of them, they just focus on the lumps and bumps in isolation, and do not stand back and see how it all works together.

Apply your clay in such a way that it acknowledges the direction, flow and high points of the form you are creating. Only model convex forms – concave forms are created where these forms meet and if these points are left untouched and not modelled over, they create rich forms, textures and colouring over the whole sculpture.

At some point during the modelling process, it is best to stop looking at your maquette too much; you need to look at your sculpture properly rather than try slavishly to copy the maquette. The sculpture needs to take on a life of its own. On some occasions, if an artist has a very clear image in their mind for the finished piece, they may go straight on to the sculpture without making a maquette.

Tonal value

In painting, it is well understood that tonal values are important in that:

- they play a part in delineating forms;
- they create focal points and influence the way the eye moves around a picture;
- they contribute to the feeling and expression of the work.

Likewise in sculpture, during all stages of modelling, but particularly towards the end, you should look at the tonal values created by planes, mark-making and texture. Look carefully at the dark areas and the patterns they make. They should not be too uniform, as this makes the work look mechanical, nor too varied, as this makes the work look patchy or 'spotty'. Be bold and aim for just the right flow and balance of tonal values across the piece. Note that a flow line made up of dark areas is not necessarily composed of one line. It is subtly composed of a number of lines, shades, planes and textures.

Texture

Consider the texture that you want before you start, ensuring that it is in line with the qualities you are trying to convey. It is worth repeating that texture is not just on the surface of the piece – it starts from the very first piece of clay you apply and continues throughout.

Anatomy

Remember that, in terms of anatomy, you do not take every form or line that is there. Choose only the ones that work for your purpose and adapt them as necessary. For example, there may be an area on your maquette that is a bit 'fudged' and just looks wrong when sculpted in the same way on a bigger scale. Don't be afraid to adapt it so that it works for the full-size piece, but make sure to retain the qualities of the form on the maquette.

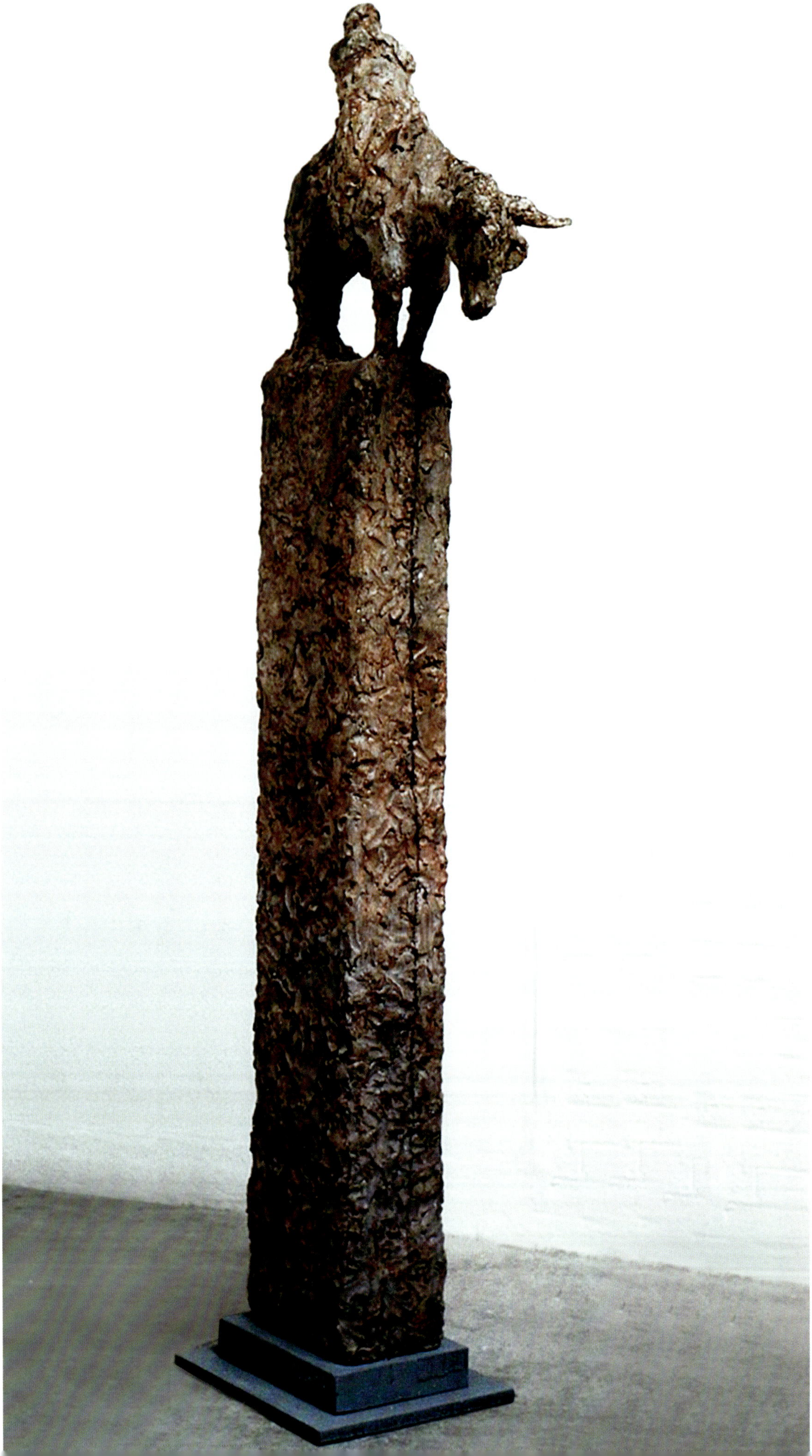

Damian Fennell, *Sancho Panza.* Ciment fondue, 230 x 18 cm (90⅔ x 7 in.). *Photo: courtesy of the artist.*

7

FINISHING

Finished Materials
Mounting
Presentation and Display
Animal Sculpture

Finished Materials

The modelling materials we have used so far in this book (clay, wax and Plastiline, etc.) are not finished materials – they will melt, break or squash. If you want to keep your sculpture, there are further steps to be taken to fire or cast it into a finished material.

Casting Your Finished Piece

Any sculpture in just about any material can be moulded and cast. Some are easier to cast than others and this is worth considering before you start a sculpture without letting it curb your creativity in any way. Bear in mind that wherever there is a large undercut or a hole in a sculpture, a separate section of mould would need to be made, so if you need the sculpture to be easy and relatively inexpensive to cast, then it is best to keep the form of the sculpture simple.

Bronze

Most people have heard of the lost wax process of bronze casting. It is the standard method that has been used since Greek antiquity and, amazingly, the techniques and materials have changed very little since then. The main difference is that, since the advent of rubber, moulds can be made in fewer pieces as a result of its flexibility. The basic lost wax process is shown in the following pages.

Bronze casting is still a very labour-intensive and expensive business, but bronze sculptures will always be popular and have an intrinsic value purely because of the material. In order to get your piece cast, you can take it to a bronze-casting foundry, where they will cast it for you.

Pieces can also be cast in other metals, such as aluminium, stainless steel, iron and lead. Because of its low melting point, pewter casting can be done in a domestic oven, but the technique remains the same, and professional technical training is needed for this to be done safely.

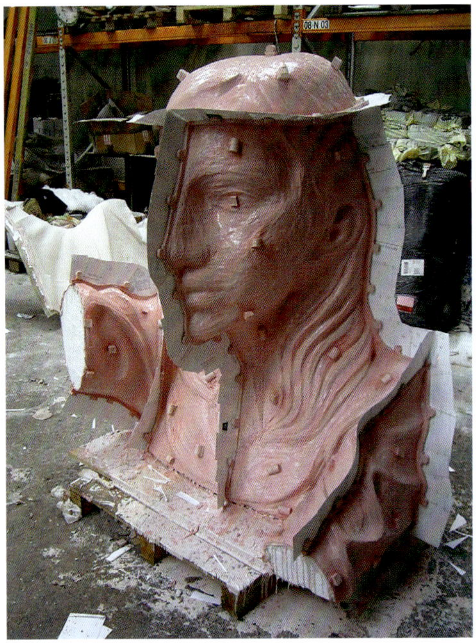

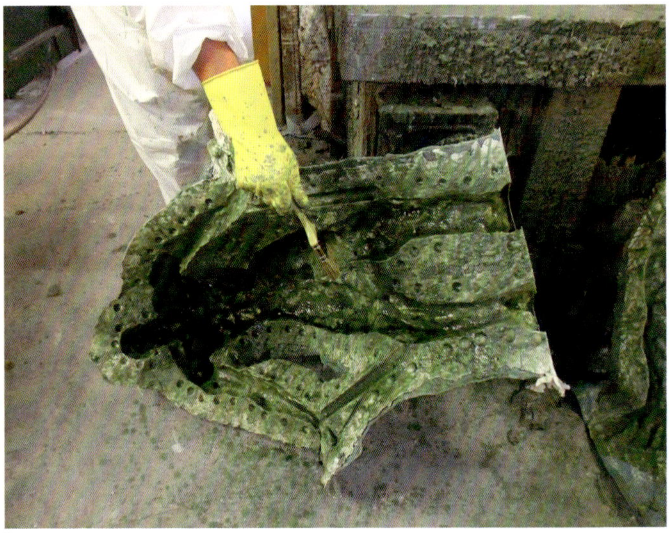

The mould is then pulled apart and the original sculpture discarded. Wax is painted into the mould at a thickness of around 3 mm ($^1/_{10}$ in.). *Photo: courtesy of Bronze Age Sculpture Casting Foundry, London.*

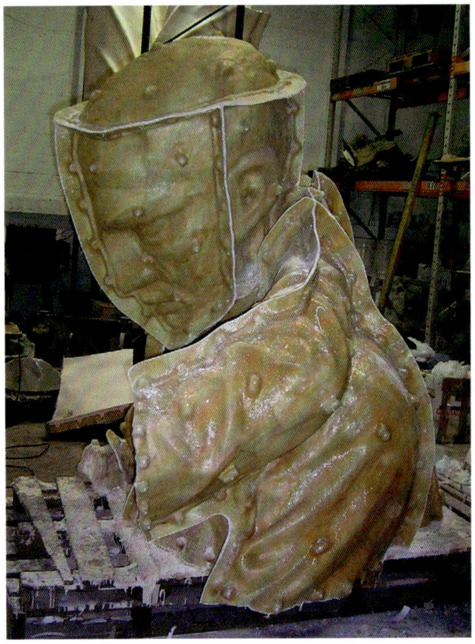

Two stages of the rubber mould-making process. Once the rubber has been applied and walls put in (top), a resin and fibreglass jacket is built up in sections to give stability to the rubber (above). *Photos: courtesy of Jim Guy.*

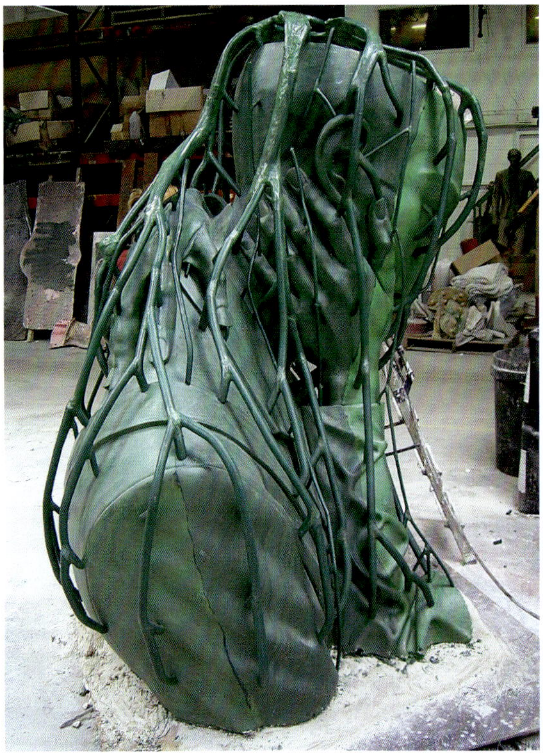

Once unmoulded, the wax copy is 'sprued' with a further structure of wax 'runners' that will provide paths for molten bronze to flow in and air to escape. *Photo: courtesy of Jim Guy.*

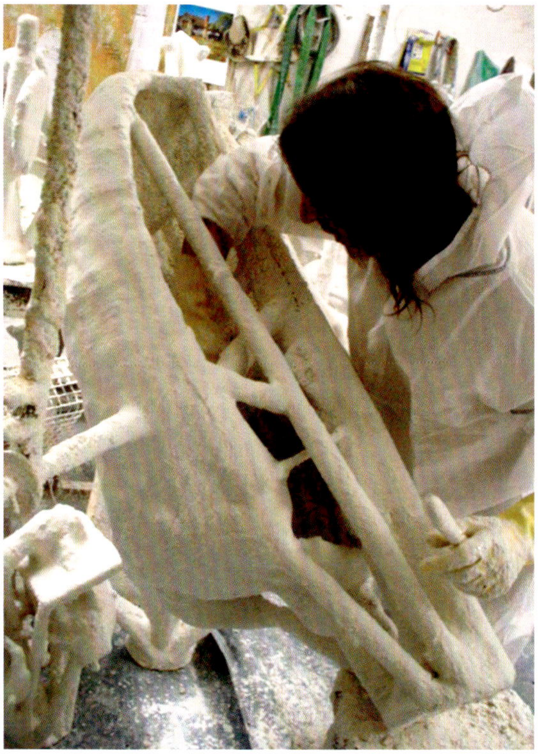

A ceramic shell coating is then created, covering the wax structure inside and out. *Photo: courtesy of Bronze Age Sculpture Casting Foundry, London.*

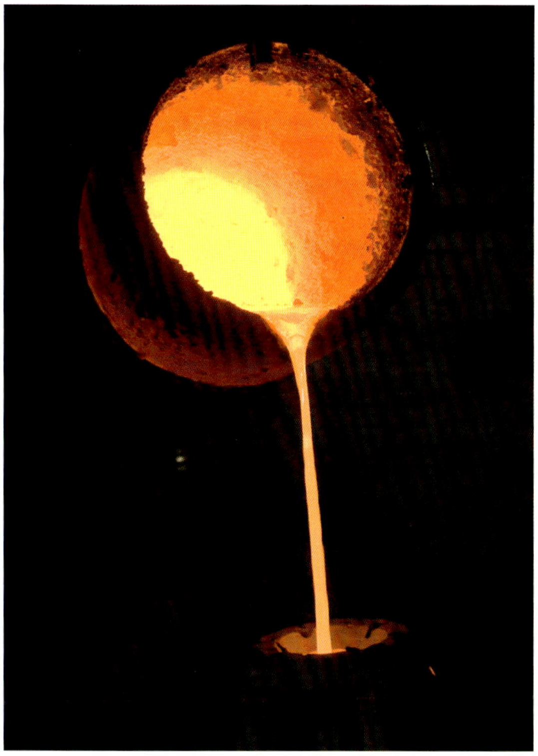

Having melted the wax out of the ceramic shell, molten bronze is poured through the runners into the cavity. The resulting bronze sculpture is then cleaned up and patinated. *Photo: courtesy of Bronze Age Sculpture Casting Foundry, London.*

Cold Casting

Cold casting is a cheaper alternative to bronze. In this process you are not using real molten metal but bronze powder mixed with resin on the surface, backed up on the inside with fibreglass and resin to give it strength. Cold cast bronze can be patinated (coloured with chemicals that react to the bronze powder) to look very similar to bronze.

Advantages of cold cast bronze over real bronze:

- The cost is about a quarter that of cast bronze.
- Once the method is learnt it can be done at home or in the studio without the need of a foundry environment (though many still choose to have someone else do it for them).
- If the piece breaks it can be mended far more easily than bronze.

Disadvantages of cold cast bronze over bronze:

- It does not have the intrinsic or perceived value of bronze.
- It is not as heavy.
- It is not as strong.
- Bronze can be guaranteed for hundreds of years, whereas cold cast can only be guaranteed for 20–40 years (though much depends on how well it has been cast and the environment in which it is kept, e.g. pieces kept in an outdoor setting, exposed to the elements, will degrade more quickly than those kept indoors.

Other cold casting materials and methods

It is not just bronze that can be cold cast; you can actually mix almost anything into a resin and put it on the surface – this is called the gel coat. You can use aluminium, stone, iron powders or more unusual things like glass beads, coal dust – even rice or beans!

Standard polyester resin has a chemical in it called styrene, and when the resin is mixed with its catalyst to make it set, it gives off toxic fumes. A good organic vapour mask and rubber gloves mitigate most of the problems in using this very effective casting medium. You can purchase an organic resin, which has no styrene and no smell, is more environmentally friendly, and hugely more expensive! Jesmonite is a very hard plaster made up of plaster powder mixed with a polymer rather than water, and it is more durable and waterproof than plaster. It is great with stone fillers but still not as strong or tough as normal resin. New products are coming out all the time, so hopefully soon there will be more alternatives to standard resin.

Plaster

Casting a piece in plaster is another option, but the result is much more fragile than resin or bronze and can look like a cheap alternative if you are not careful. It is important to use a very hard plaster like Crystacal or Alpha Plaster for casting. Pieces also generally need to be coloured once cast; this is hard to get right, as over-colouring risks making the piece look tacky.

Colouring on plaster is very much a process of individual experimentation, but the main materials that can be used are acrylic or oil paints, waxes, gold leaf, wood dyes, and tea and other stains. A light wash can be sufficient to emphasise the contrasts in the modelling.

Casting Considerations

Before starting a piece you do not always need to think about whether you are going to cast in bronze, cold cast bronze or a plaster material, but it is important to know the parameters of each. Some sculptures are structurally impossible to cast in cold cast or plaster. Any piece in which you have a very narrow joint supporting significant weight will not be structurally sound. Bronze and some other cast metals are the strongest, followed by cold cast resin, with plaster being the weakest.

Firing for a Ceramic Finish

If you model a self-supporting piece in clay without an armature, or a piece where the armature can be removed, you have the option of firing your finished work. This is done in a kiln at very high temperatures and you end up with a ceramic sculpture. If you wish to fire, you definitely need to think about this from the start, as you have to follow a different method of building your sculpture than if you were to cast it.

There are many excellent clays particularly suited to firing – crank, paper clay, porcelain, terracotta. Sculptures must be made with a maximum thickness of 15–20 mm (½–¾ in.) depending on the size of the piece. The thickness must be even throughout, and air bubbles or pieces of foreign matter may cause the piece to explode in the kiln.

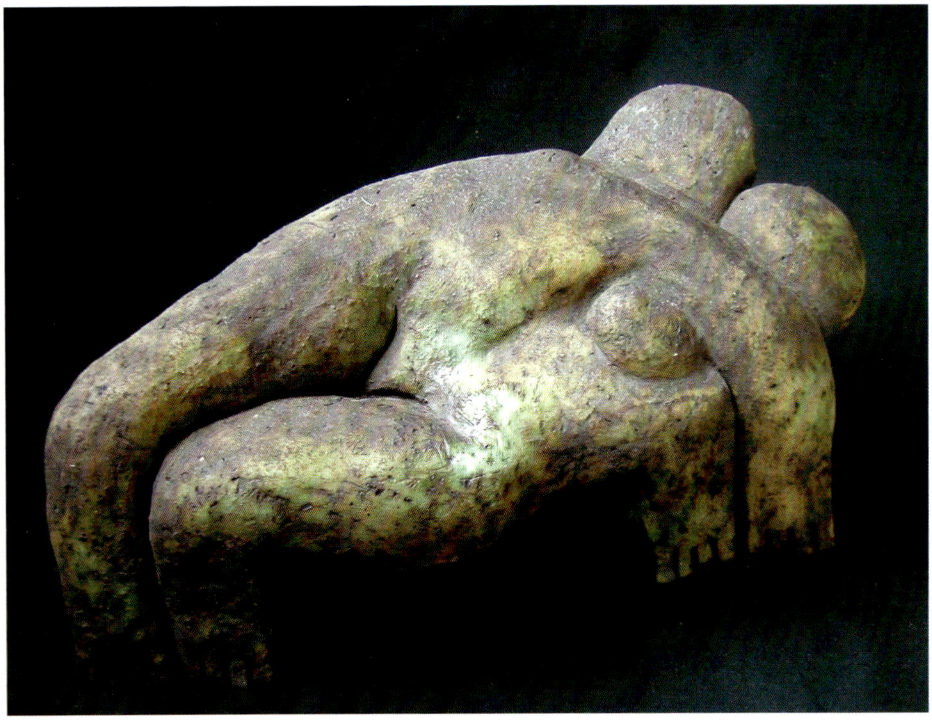

Paz Perlman, *Altar for Two*. Fired terracotta, 17 x 36 cm (6½ x 14¼ in.). *Photo: courtesy of the artist.*

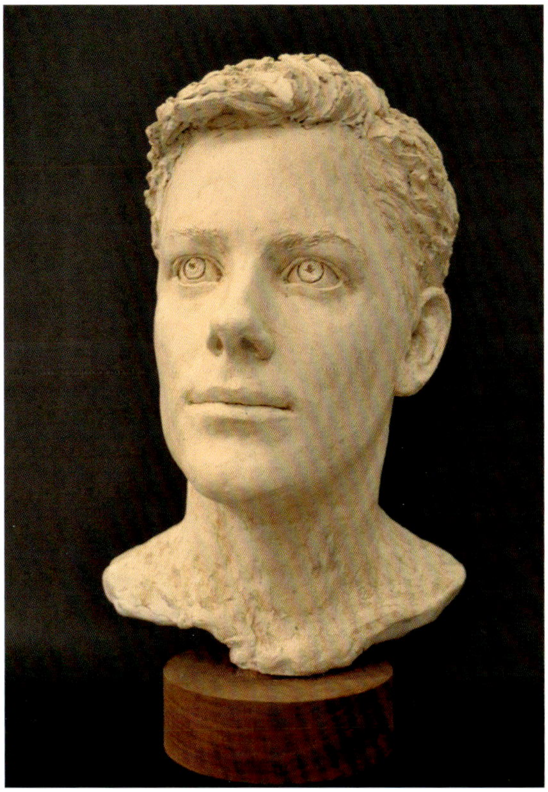

Tanya Russell, *William*. Life-size cast plaster, 38 x 25 cm (15 x 9¾ in.).
Photo: courtesy of the artist.

Mounting

Mounting is a very important aspect of sculpture and can make all the difference to the finished piece. You have to be just as creative and clear about your intentions for the base as you have been for the whole sculpture. The base should mirror the sculpture in feeling and work with it in form.

There are almost no limits to the materials that you can use for the base of a sculpture, nor any limit to the shape and size that you make it. On the other hand, when I have tried to experiment with bases by being quite adventurous or 'different', I have often realised that the base is actually distracting and detracting from the sculpture itself and have therefore reverted to the simplest possible solution!

Commonly Used Materials

- Wood (either a found piece, or one worked by a woodworker or turner)
- Stone (again, either found, or worked or cut by a stone carver)
- Perspex
- Glass
- Concrete (cast or modelled, with or without an underlying support, then stained or painted if required)
- Bronze or cold cast bronze (cast with the piece itself)

Have a look through all the images in the book and see how the sculptures are mounted and the materials used.

Selecting the Material, Size and Shape

I have gathered a selection of bases made from different materials in my studio so that I can test a sculpture on different options to see what will work best. It is very important to try things, as you can never really tell until you see it.

The best way to choose the size and shape for your base is with paper or thin card. You can construct the actual shape and size in paper and then you or someone else can hold the sculpture above it while you decide whether the exact shape and size works – keep tweaking it until you are happy. For large bases construct your experiments in strong cardboard.

Fixing

Fixing is usually done with mild or stainless steel rods – always use stainless steel for outdoor work. You have to be sure that there is enough material in the sculpture in the location that you need to drill. If not, then build it up. Also ensure that the base is strong enough and thick enough to take the weight of the sculpture.

Using plumb lines, carpenter's squares or your eye (and a helper if needed), drill holes at the correct angle in both the base and the sculpture, insert the cut rod and do a 'dry run' to ensure everything is sitting correctly. Then push epoxy glue into both holes, insert the rod and fix the sculpture and base together (epoxy glue is better in most cases than polyurethane, although polyurethane can be stronger for outdoor settings, so do your research with the suppliers). You can get epoxy glues in transparent or stone colours that go off in about ten minutes. You can mix different colours and dusts into the transparent epoxy, but do a test first to ensure the saturation is not so high that the glue won't go off. Clean off any excess glue when it starts going rubbery and tidy up at the end.

Sometimes, if the sculpture is very light and the base is large and flat, you can simply glue the two surfaces together without the need for pins.

If you want to be able to remove the base on a small sculpture, you can drill right through the base and countersink a nut into the bottom to screw onto the threaded rod and hold it all in place. If you choose this method you will usually need a small second pin between the sculpture and the base. This stops the base turning and the nut coming loose.

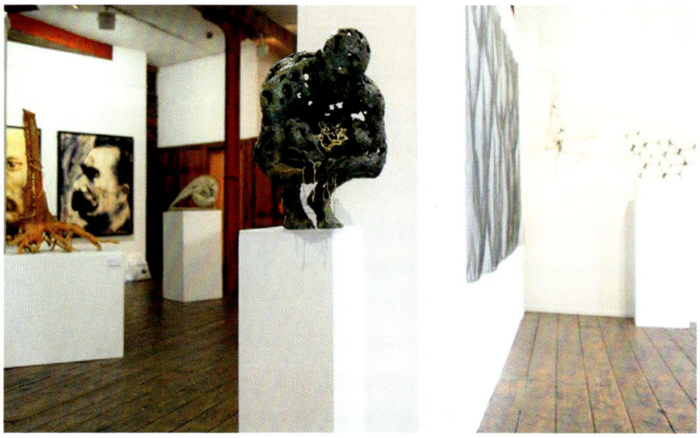

Art Academy exhibition *Create, Master, Inspire – 10 Years of the Art Academy*, July 2010, Menier Gallery, London. *Photo: courtesy of the Art Academy.*

Presentation and Display

As mentioned in Chapter 1, the presentation of sculpture is like the creation of an installation artwork. Consider the 'mood' that you want to create; consider the order in which you want people to see the work and very importantly what feeling or message you want them to walk away with. I think this is often the most telling part of an art show – how you are feeling and what you are thinking about when you leave, and how long this lasts.

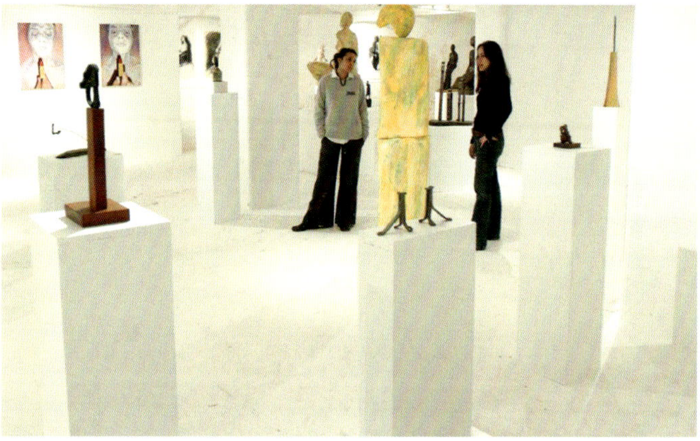

Art Academy Graduate Show. *Photo: courtesy of the Art Academy.*

Bearing this in mind, consider every aspect of the presentation: how many works you have, what height they are seen at, the lighting (natural and artificial), the labels for the work, the flow of people around the room and the work, the temperature and air flow, the colour of the plinths, the walls and the floors. I cannot overemphasise the difference this all makes. When an artist puts this much effort into their presentation and considers and responds to every detail, they enhance the power of their sculpture tenfold. It is so much easier for the viewer to see and respond to the work. Of course sculpture should 'stand in its own right', but it can so easily get lost and ignored. The more carefully you present it, the more likely it is to be properly seen.

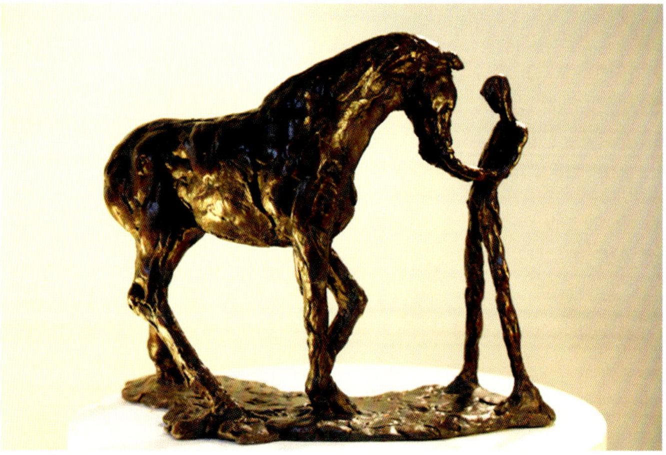

Arabella Brooke, *Man and Horse*. Bronze, 16 x 20 cm (6⅓ x 8 in.). *Photo: courtesy of the artist.*

Animal Sculpture

No figure sculpture book could be complete without reference to our animal cousins, as so many of the considerations, techniques and processes for sculpting them are exactly the same as described in this book. Indeed, many wonderful sculptures have been inspired by the interaction between animals and humans, and, in addition, mythology allows them to interact in extraordinary ways or even to come together in one form … but sometimes they are perfect on their own!

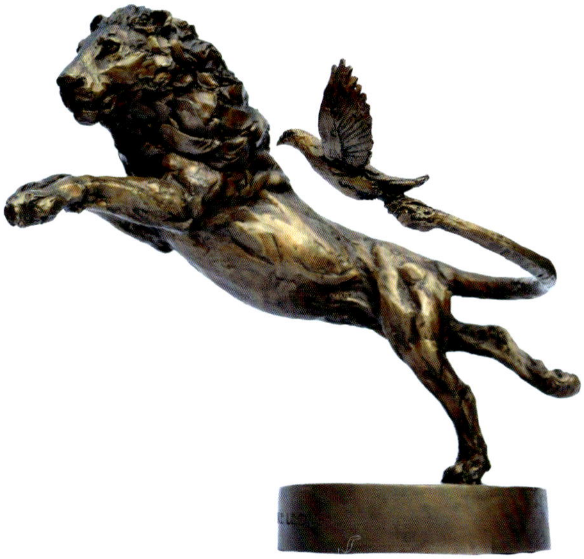

Tanya Russell, *The Lion and the Dove*. Bronze, 30 x 40 cm (12 x 15¾ in.). *Photo: courtesy of the artist.*

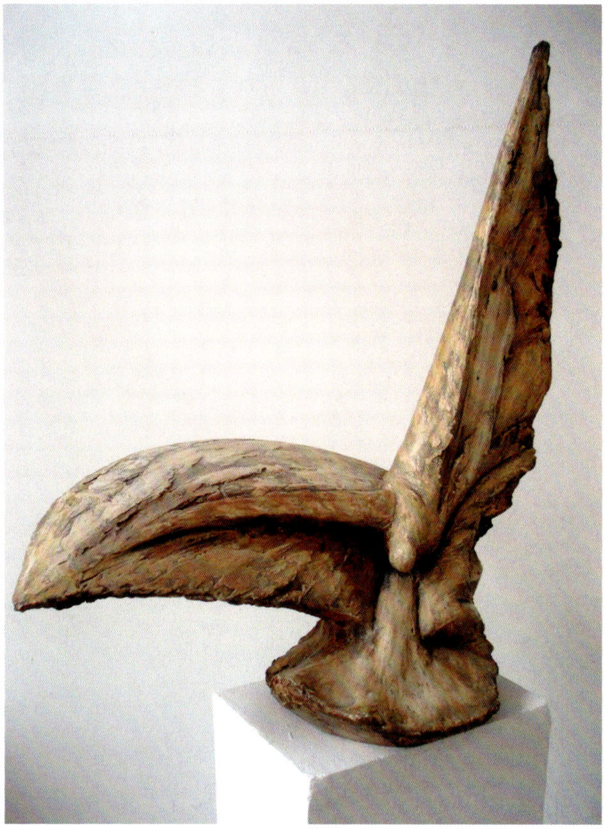

Chloe Leaper, *Psyche*. Plaster, 70 x 65 cm (27⅔ x 25⅔ in.). *Photo: courtesy of the artist.*

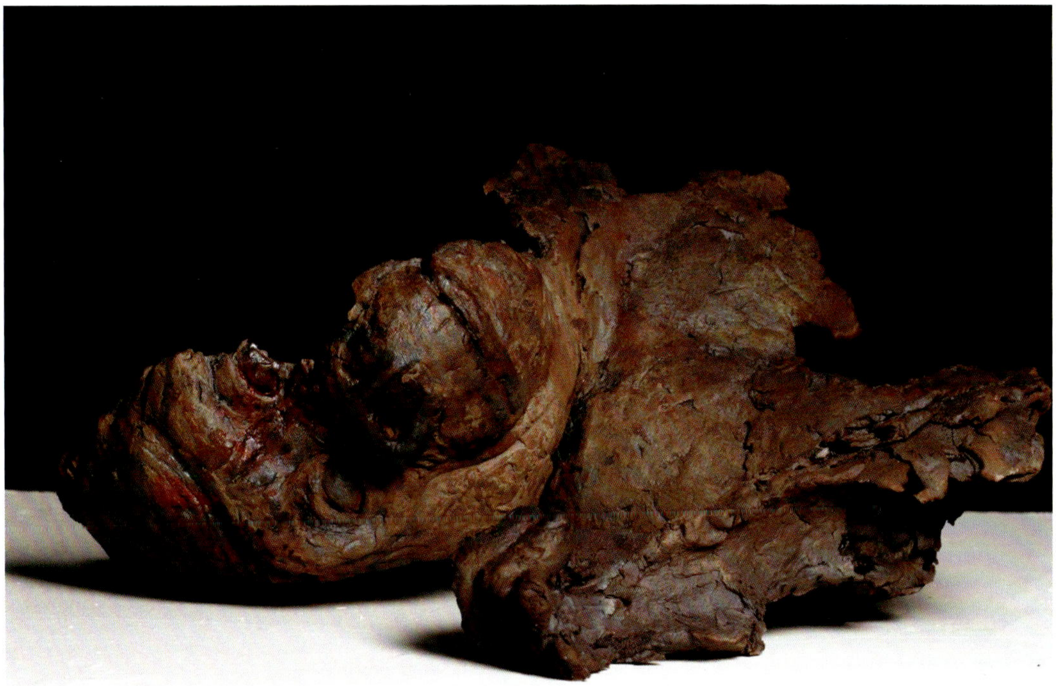

Kerr Gemmell, *Bananas*. Raku-fired clay, 20 x 45 x 30 cm (8 x 17¾ x 11¾ in.). *Photo: courtesy of the artist.*

Although 'protected', gorillas are still being shot by owners of banana plantations, which the gorillas enter to suppliment their diet. The owners cannot afford for gorillas to reduce their produce because of the low prices the consumers of the Western world demand for bananas. Would you be willing to pay more for a banana if you knew gorillas weren't being shot?

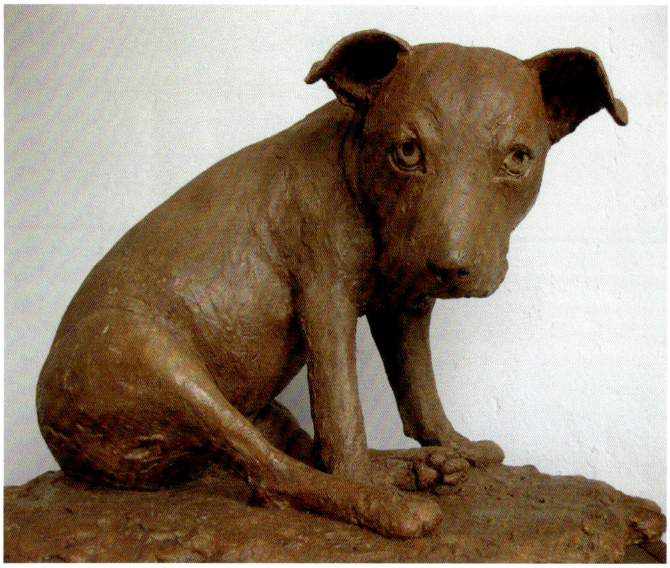

Tanya Russell, *Please take me home.* Cold cast sandstone, 35 x 51 cm (14 x 20 in.). *Photo: courtesy of the artist.*

My first and abiding memory of my beloved dog Asha, at Battersea Dogs and Cats Home.

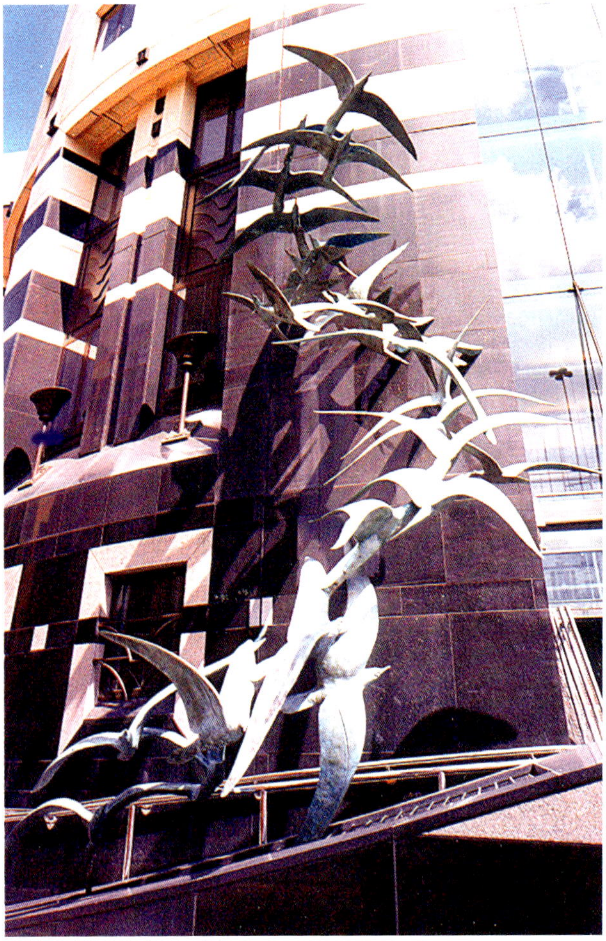

Lorne McKean, *Flight.* Bronze, commissioned by Norwich Union for 1 City Square, Leeds, Yorkshire, 850 x 450 cm (334½ x 177¼ in.). *Photo: Alan Marshall.*

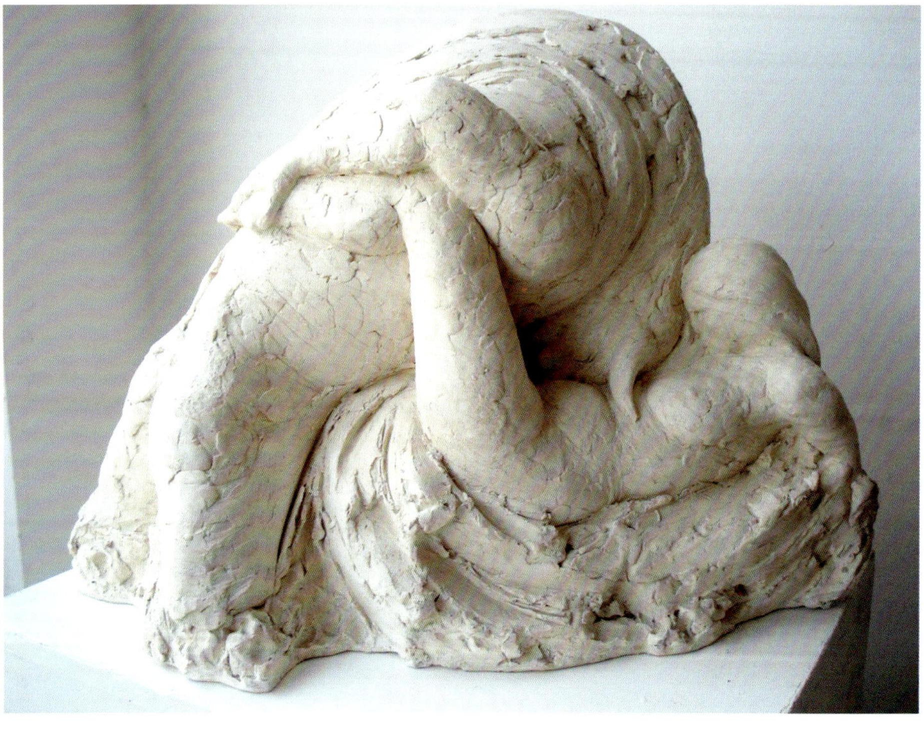

Chloe Leaper, *Creation 2.* Plaster, 49 x 62 cm (19⅓ x 24½ in.). *Photo: courtesy of the artist.*

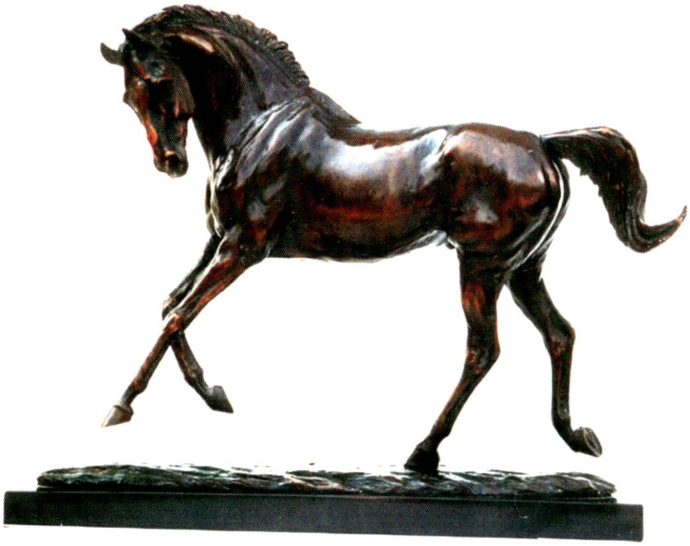

Tanya Russell, *Kensal*. Bronze, private commission, 30 x 27 cm (12 x 10⅔ in.). *Photo: courtesy of the artist.*

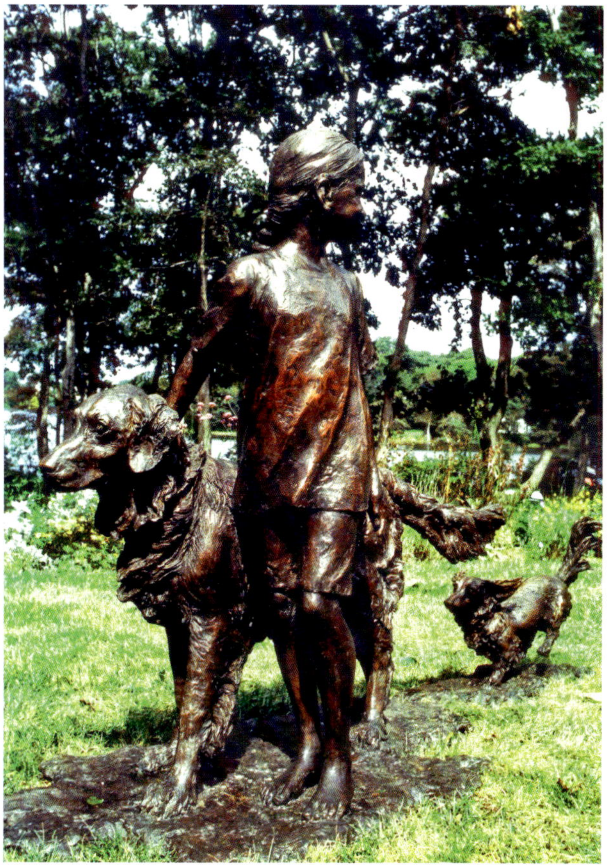

Lorne McKean, *Young girl with her dogs*. Commissioned for a riverside setting, Chiswick Mall, 150 x 600 cm (59 x 236¼ in.). *Photo: courtesy of the artist.*

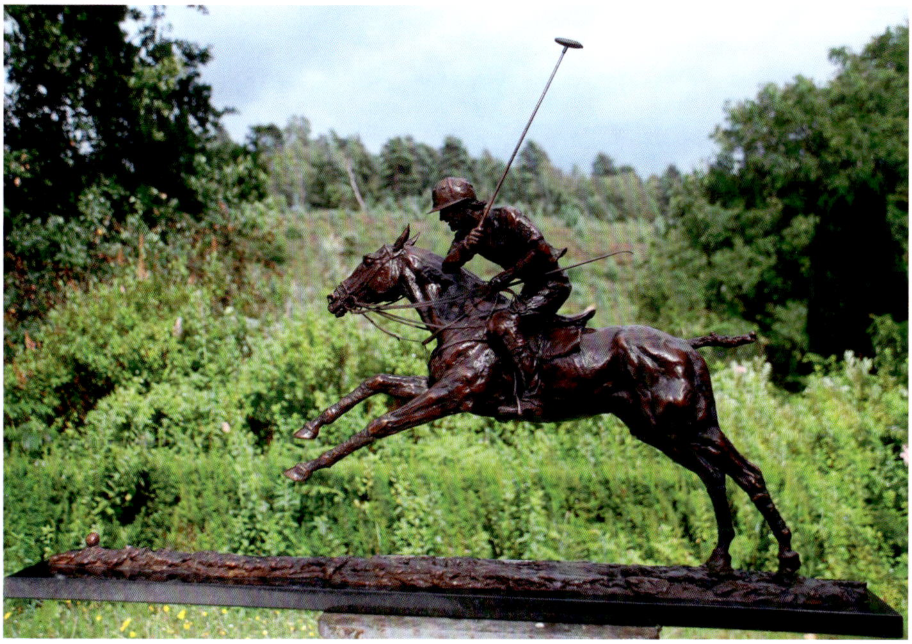

Lorne McKean, *Adolfo Cambiaso on Aiken Cura*. Bronze, 57 x 83 x 20 cm (22½ x 32½ x 8 in.). *Photo: courtesy of the artist.*

Further Reading

ANATOMY

Anatomy for artists is such a big subject that many books have and will be written about it. Some are excellent and I suggest that you buy at least three of them if you are going to pursue figure sculpture seriously.

Modelling the Figure in Clay: A Sculptor's Guide to Anatomy
Bruno Lucchesi (Watson-Guptill Publications, ISBN 978-0-8230-3096-5)

An Atlas of Anatomy for Artists
Fritz Schider (Dover Publications, ISBN 978-0-4862-0241-0)

Anatomy for the Artist
Sarah Simbet (Dorling Kindersley, ISBN 978-0-7513-3441-8)

SCULPTURE TECHNIQUES

Encylopedia of Sculpture Techniques
John Mills (Batsford Ltd, ISBN 978-0-7134-8930-9)

The Sculpting Techniques Bible: An Essential Illustrated Reference for Both Beginner and Experienced Sculptors
Claire Waite Brown (Chartwell Books, ISBN 978-0-7858-2142-7)

Modelling the Head in Clay
Bruno Lucchesi (Watson-Guptill Publications, ISBN 978-0-823030996)

The Sculptor's Bible: The All-media Reference to Surface Effects and How to Achieve Them
John Plowman (A&C Black Publishers Ltd, ISBN 978-0-7136-7132-2)

Coiled Pottery
Betty Blandino (A&C Black Publishers Ltd, ISBN 978-0-7136-6646-5)

The Complete Potter's Companion
Tony Birks (Conran Octopus Ltd, ISBN 978-1-8502-9917-2)

Titles in the Bloomsbury/A&C Black *New Ceramics* and *Ceramics Handbook* series
www.acblack.com/visualarts/Ceramics_Handbooks/books/list/227

The Mouldmaker's Handbook
J. P. Delpech and M. A. Figueres (A&C Black Publishers Ltd, ISBN 978-0-7136-6770-7)

ART THEORY

Ways of Seeing
John Berger (Penguin Classics, ISBN 978-0-1410-3579-6)

Concerning the Spiritual in Art
Wassily Kandinsky (Dover Publications Inc., ISBN 978-0-4862-3411-3)

Eye and Brain: The Psychology of Seeing
R.L Gregory (OUP Oxford, ISBN 978-0-1985-2412-0)

Language of Sculpture
William Tucker (Thames & Hudson, ISBN 978-0-5002-7104-9)

ART HISTORY

The Story of Art
E H Gombrich (Phaidon Press Ltd, ISBN 978-0-7148-3247-0)

Origins of Modern Sculpture: Pioneers and Premises
Albert E Elsen (George Braziller Inc., ISBN 978-0-8076-0737-4)

Sculpture Since 1945 (Oxford History of Art)
Andrew Causey (Oxford Paperbacks, ISBN 978-0-1928-4205-3)

Modern Sculpture: A Concise History (*World of Art* series)
Herbert Read (Thames & Hudson, ISBN 978-0-5002-0014-8)

INSPIRATION

500 Figures in Clay: Ceramic Artists Celebrate the Human Form
Veronika Alice Gunter (Lark Books, ISBN 978-1-5799-0547-7)

Naked Dance and Gymnastics
Ralf Mohr (Edition Reuss, ISBN 978-3-9340-2066-5)

Sculpture Inside and Out
Malvina Hoffman (W W Norton and Co, ASIN B0006AONRU)
This title is out of print, available second-hand.

Body in Sculpture (Everyman Art Library)
Tom Flynn (Weidenfield & Nicholson, ISBN 978-0-2978-2397-1)

Suppliers

UK

Abbey Dental Supplies – *moulding and casting materials*

23–27 Gladstone Road,
Croydon, Surrey CR0 2BQ
+44 (0)20 8683 4528

Alec Tiranti Ltd – *sculptors' tools, materials and studio equipment*

27 Warren Street
London W1T 5NB
+44 (0)20 7380 0808
3 Pipers Court, Berkshire Drive,
Thatcham, Berkshire RG19 4ER
+44 (0)845 123 2100
enquiries@tiranti.co.uk
www.tiranti.co.uk

British Wax Refining Company – *a wide range of wax-based products*

62 Holmethorpe Avenue, Holmethorpe
Industrial Estate, Redhill
Surrey RH1 2NL
+44 (0)1737 761242
wax@britishwax.com
www.britishwax.com

Canonbury Art Shop – *sculpture materials and equipment*

65 Halliford Street, Islington
London N1 3HF
+44 (0)20 7226 4652
sc@canonburyarts.co.uk
www.canonburyarts.co.uk

Notcutt Ltd – *mould-making/casting materials*

Homewood Farm, Newark Lane,
Ripley, Surrey GU23 6DJ
+44 (0)1483 223311
sales@notcutt.co.uk
www.notcutt.co.uk

South West Industrial Plasters – *a wide range of plasters, rigid and flexible mould-making, modelling and casting materials*

63 Netherstreet, Bromham,
Chippenham, Wiltshire SN15 2DP
+44 (0)1380 850616
info@industrialplasters.com
www.industrialplasters.com

Cold Casting

Jim Guy

Jguy13@tiscali.co.uk
+44 (0)7729 549466

Ridgeway Moulding and Casting

6 Wharf Row, Buckland Road,
Aston, Clinton, Aylesbury
Buckinghamshire HP22 5LJ
+44 (0)1296 620099
laura_robain@live.co.uk
www.ridgewaymouldingandcasting.co.uk

Bronze Casting

Art Bronze

1 and 3 Michael Road, Kings Road
London SW6 2ER
+44 (0)20 7736 7292
service@artbronze.co.uk
www.artbronze.co.uk

Atelier Fine Art Casting

Hulfords Lane, Hook
Hampshire RG27 8AG
+44 (0)1252 844388
amanda@atelierfoundry.com

Black Isle Bronze Ltd

4A Balmakeith Business Park
Nairn IV12 5QR
+44 (0)1667 455172
blackislebronze@btconnect.com
www.blackislebronze.co.uk

Bronze Age Sculpture Casting Foundry

Gallery Building, Basin Approach,
Limehouse, London E14 7JG
+44 (0)20 7538 1388
info@bronzeage.co.uk
www.bronzeage.co.uk

Castle Fine Arts Foundry Ltd

Tanat Foundry, Llanrhaeadr ym
Mochnant, Nr Oswestry
Powys SY10 0AA
+44 (0)1691 780261
info@bronzefoundry.co.uk
www.bronzefoundry.co.uk

Zahra Modern Art Foundries

9 Swinborne Drive, Springwood
Industrial Estate, Braintree
Essex CM7 2YP
+44 (0)1376 529797
info@zmaf.co.uk
www.zmaf.co.uk

USA

The Compleat Sculptor

90 Vandam Street, New York, 10013
+1 212 243 6074
TCS@SCULPT.com
www.sculpt.com

Pearl

www.pearlpaint.com

Dick Blick Art Materials

www.dickblick.com

Sculpture House Casting

155 W. 26th Street, New York,10001
888 374 8665
www.sculptshop.com

Douglas and Sturgess Inc

1023 Factory Street,
Richmond, CA 94801
+1 510 235 8411
730 Bryant Street,
San Francisco, CA 94107
+1 415 421 4456
sales@douglasandsturgess.com
www.douglasandsturgess.com

Index